Yugoslavia

Albanians living in the province of Kosovo. (Photo: Simon Palmour.)

Yugoslavia

Mountain Walks & Historical Sites

Piers Letcher

BRADT PUBLICATIONS, UK
HUNTER PUBLISHING, USA

IV

First published in 1989 by Bradt Publications, 41 Nortoft Road, Chalfont St Peter, Bucks, SL9 0LA, England. Distributed in the U.S.A. by Hunter Publishing Inc., Rariton Center Parkway, CN94, Edison NJ 08818.

British Library Cataloguing in Publication Data
Letcher, Piers
  Yugoslavia: Mountain Walks & Historical Sites.
  1.Yugoslavia – Visitors' guides
  I.Title
  914.97'0424

ISBN 0-946983-29-1

Maps by Hans van Well.
Photographs by the author, unless otherwise stated.
Cover photos. Front: the descent from Triglav, Slovenia; Sveti Jovan Kaneo, on the shores of Lake Ohrid in Macedonia. Back: Lake Bled, Slovenia.

Phototypeset from author's disk by Saxon Printing Ltd., Derby.
Printed and bound in Great Britain by
The Guernsey Press Co. Ltd, Guernsey, Channel Islands.

I dedicate this book to Martine Simon, and to the people of Yugoslavia.

The Author

Piers Letcher was born in 1960 and educated at independent schools where he still holds the local record for climbing giant redwoods. After four years in Cardiff studying computing, photography and journalism he went freelance in 1984. Since then he has published half a dozen books in the computing field and several hundred articles on the arts, travel and general interest. This is his second guidebook, following the Australian publication of his Eurail Guide. When not actively travelling he lives in southwestern France.

The author drinking home made Šlivovice with Parić in the remote village of Tomići near Paklenica. (Photo: Martine Simon.)

Acknowledgements

Special thanks to Neil Ambrose, Phil Hollins and Martine for making individual fortnights so wonderful, to Hilary Bradt for commissioning the book, to June and Lisa at Letcher and Son for countless faxes and photocopies, and to my parents for being the world's most reliable message and postal service. Digital Ferney Voltaire provided a better preparation than I could have asked for, Mme Jeanne Franco in Chamonix gave invaluable advance information on Slovenia and Croatia, and François Imbert and Sylvie Lissajoux helped with their mountaineering expertise. Keith and Dea Schofield were wonderful hosts on the way to and from Yugoslavia, and Brian Cross sent me useful climatic information.

In Yugoslavia I was made welcome and assisted by innumerable people and organisations. The following were invaluable: Danilo Sbrizaj of the Slovene Alpine Organisation; Irena Zdovc in Ljubljana; Jordan Plevneš, Vangel Naumovski, and Vladimir Tuntev and his wife in Ohrid; Mladen Berginc and Janez Bizjak of the Triglav National Park; Erisch and Helga Eiers; Inex at Biogradska Gora; Andrija Djurović of the Grand Hotel, Cetinje, for enabling us to reach Lovčen; Montenegrotourist in most of the republic but not in Žabljak; Atlas in Dubrovnik; Generalturist in Ohrid; the Yugoslav Tourist Board, especially Aleksandra in Zagreb, Mirjana Zečević in Belgrade, Huso Taslicak in Bosnia Hercegovinia, Grozdan Popov in Macedonia, Mirjana Darrer in Dubrovnik and last but not least Selim Selim in London.

PREFACE

Yugoslavia boasts some of the best walking in Europe: mountains over 2800m, deep gorges, unpolluted lakes, virgin forests, spectacular limestone scenery and the cleanest coastline on the Mediterranean. It is also one of the most culturally diverse countries on the continent, with seven nationalities speaking nine languages in two alphabets and practising three religions in six republics and two autonomous provinces.

Although statistically overtouristed (nearly nine million foreign and twelve million domestic tourists a year), most of Yugoslavia remains uncrowded – over 90% of the vistors never leave the coastal resorts and a handful of famous attractions.

Climbers and walkers of all standards will find something here, from the severest climbing near Triglav, to gentle hill walking amongst the monasteries of the Fruška Gora. Bears and wolves still populate the remoter forests, eagles and vultures can be found in the mountains and the interior is amongst the most unspoiled I've seen. Yugoslavia is its own best advertisement.

Most of the walks in this guide take from one to two days, and can be reached without your own transport. Several longer and shorter trails have also been included for the more and less adventurous, and pointers are provided to more inaccessible walking. While most of the major tourist attractions have been covered, you should consult one of the several widely available guidebooks for more conventional tourist information.

Note on prices and exchange rates: Prices in Yugoslavia are subject to massive inflation (over 200% in 1988), though travellers are compensated for this by frequent currency devaluations. For this reason prices throughout have been quoted in sterling and dollars – these should remain fairly constant. Accommodation prices are fixed annually in dollars and Deutsche Marks.

Updates

If you've got any comments, tips or ideas on how this guide could be improved, please write to us at:

41 Nortoft Road,
Chalfont St. Peter,
Bucks. SL9 0LA, England

I've tried to keep the information in this guide as up to date as possible, but obviously things will change – your comments will be greatly appreciated for the next edition.

Piers Letcher – 6th December 1988.

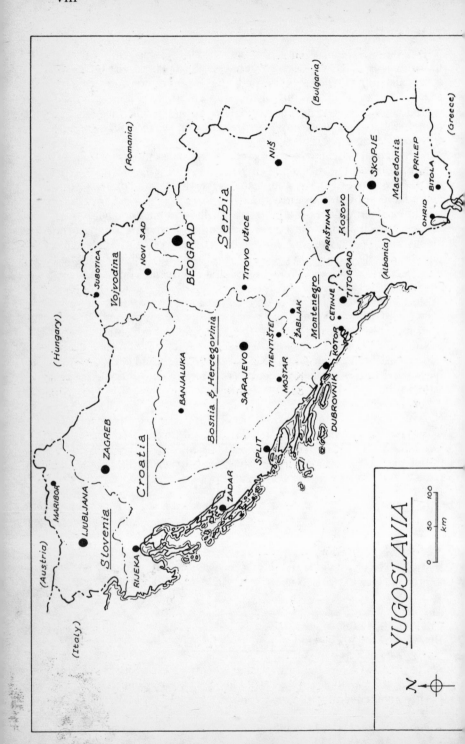

YUGOSLAVIA

Contents

Morača monastery, Montenegro. (Photo: Yugoslavia National Tourist Office.)

Introduction to Yugoslavia

BACKGROUND INFORMATION

A brief history

In a book this short it's impossible to give a detailed history of Yugoslavia – the following account is necessarily simplified, and only attempts to provide some background information.

Yugoslavia is still a young country: before 1918 it didn't exist, and its present borders weren't ratified internationally until 1945. The history of the country up to the First World War is unbelievably turbulent; fraught with foreign intervention, plagued by constant wars from the tenth century on and scarred by assassinations, intrigues and treachery.

A succession of empires invaded, occupied, enslaved, taxed and bled dry the country. Even now there are barren islands off the Dalmatian coast that were deforested by the Venetians and have never recovered. The Greeks, Romans, Venetians, Austrians, Hungarians, French, Turks, Bulgarians, Germans, Italians and Russians have all tried to grab parts of the country, and that it has resisted and remains independent is both commendable and extraordinary.

Recorded history of the area now called Yugosolavia starts with the Illyrians in the west and the Thracians in the east. Greeks moved up the coast in small numbers from the seventh century BC, and Alexander's Macedonian empire covered all of the southern Balkans by the end of the fourth century BC. The Romans were the first (and last until 1918) to unify the country, though it took them most of two centuries to do so against serious Illyrian resistance. From 9 AD for the next three centuries the Balkans provided essential troops and materials for the Romans, and Dalmatia gave them three emperors, including Diocletian, whose palace is now Split: its corridors are streets and its rooms houses.

In 295 Diocletian partitioned the Empire into the Western and Eastern parts. The frontier ran through Budva and Belgrade, with everything east of it becoming part of Byzantium and everything west part of Rome, leading to Orthodoxy and Catholicism. This division is still clearly marked by the use of alphabets – Cyrillic to the east and Latin to the west.

After the Roman empire collapsed in the fifth century the way was clear for invasions by Huns, Goths, Vlachs, Avars, Bulgars and Slavs. The Slavs finally settled the whole of the north of the country in the three distinct groups of Slovenes, Croats and Serbs.

By medieval times the pattern for today's republics had been established, with the creation of the independent kingdoms of Croatia, Bosnia, Hercegovinia, Macedonia and Serbia. Croatia and Slovenia were heavily subjugated by the Austro-Hungarian empire in all its various forms, as was the northern part of Serbia.

The Dalmatian coast, now part of Croatia, fell under Venetian influence from the 13th to the 18th centuries, and this shows in the coastal and island architecture. Ragusa was one of the most important – and independent – of the Venetian city states, and remains Yugoslavia's most fashionable tourist attraction … under its new name, Dubrovnik. Napoleon put an end to the Venetians, but after his downfall Dalmatia came under Austria's unbenign influence.

After two retrospectively gilded centuries of relative stability, Lazar, last of the independent Serbian rulers, fought and lost the decisive battle of Kosovo on 28th June 1389, heralding nearly five centuries of Turkish rule as part of the Ottoman empire.

From the middle of the fifteenth century Yugoslavia was partitioned between the Austro-Hungarian, Venetian and Ottoman empires. An impressive number of quashed uprisings, rebellions and revolutions testified to the unpopularity and harshness of the occupying regimes, but only the inaccessible and rebellious principality of Montenegro stayed independent – a feat it has managed to this day.

Various wars at the end of the last century finally saw off the Turks in all but Macedonia, though much of the country remained under unpopular Austro-Hungarian rule until the 525th anniversary of the Kosovo defeat, when Gavrilo Princip dealt with Franz-Ferdinand and his wife in Sarajevo, triggering off the First World War in the process.

Yugoslavia emerged from the First World War battered but unified for the first time since the Romans, and became a centralised kingdom, with most of the power (and the people wielding it) resting in Serbia. King Alexander was more or less forced to establish a dictatorship in 1929 after the disastrous failure of the young state's attempt at parliamentary democracy.

Alexander was assassinated in Marseille, in 1934, by an Italian sponsored Croatian conspiracy, leaving the ill-equipped Prince Peter (aged 10) and Prince Paul (his uncle) to mind the country. Neither could run such a diverse country effectively, and by the time the Second World War broke out Yugoslavia was badly divided internally. Croatian separatists, the Ustaše fascists, wanted complete independence. Macedonia was also trying to secede from Serbia. Only the Communist Party, which had been formed in 1920 and outlawed eight years later, had any kind of countrywide support.

Yugoslavia managed to remain neutral for the first eighteen months of the Second World War, but increasing axis pressure resulted in a pact being signed on 25th March 1941, aligning Yugoslavia with fascist Germany and Italy. Two days later a group of airforce officers, supported by both the communists and the Orthodox church, staged a *coup d'état* and placed Prince Peter on the throne. The pact was annulled and Yugoslavia reaffirmed its neutrality. Hitler responded by bombing Belgrade on 6th April. On the same day massive German and Italian armies entered the country, and Yugoslavia capitulated ten days later.

Resistance was organised almost immediately, but this was divided into two fiercely opposed groups, the Četniks and the Partisans. The pro-Serbian Četniks were aided at first by the allies, since they supported the government in exile in London, but they were regarded with distrust by most Yugoslavs. The Partisans, led by Josip Broz Tito, were the army of the communist party, and although only 42,000 strong at the outset, their effective resistance and daring attacks earned them wide support from communists and non-communists alike.

Tito's call for all out struggle eventually cost the partisans 300,000 dead and 430,000 wounded, but with the help of the British (aid was transferred from the Četniks to the Partisans in 1943) and the Red Army, Belgrade was liberated in 1944 and by 1945 a provisional government, in temporary accord with the government in exile, was in force.

The war had taken the lives of over 1,700,000 Yugoslavs (over a tenth of the population). Some had been killed in the Četnik – Partisan civil war, others were Croatian Ustaše fascists; most were civilian casualties.

Post war elections gave the communists 90% of the vote. The government set up a state on the lines adopted by Stalinist Russia, but in 1948 Tito broke with the Cominform, the economic groundbase for the countries aligned to the Soviet Union. This declaration of non-alignment was one of the greatest political acts of Tito's career, allowing Yugoslavia to develop its own distinctive brand of communism. It's also the reason why Yugoslavs are justifiably offended if you lump them in with the Eastern Bloc.

From the 1950s on Tito set about solving the nationalist problems by decentralising the state and giving each of the six republics complete control over its internal affairs. He also introduced the idea of workers' self-management. This means that all places of work – including schools, hospitals etc. – are controlled almost exclusively by those who work in them. Despite leading to sometimes excessive decentralisation, it has allowed competition within the framework of communism.

Tito died in 1980, and Yugoslavia is still suffering. Much of the country's success had come from his personal charisma and unifying strength, and since his death the old problems of nationalism, unfair distribution of wealth between the republics, and corruption in government, have resurfaced. The measure of having a new president chosen from a different republic each year doesn't seem stable enough, and I met very few people who even knew the name of the current leader.

Kosovo continues to be a problem area. Riots in 1968 and 1981 by the Albanians (a majority in the province) led to small reforms, but now the Serbian minority is complaining of discrimination, and in neighbouring Serbia there is wide support for their cause. Kosovo is too important historically for the Serbs to let go, but with a majority population of Albanians it will always be a problem area.

The world economic crisis has also hit Yugoslavia particularly hard. Unable to shelter under the Eastern Bloc umbrella and tied to huge debt repayments, the country has serious economic problems, with rampant inflation and increasing unemployment. Although this doesn't affect visitors much (tourist prices are tied to the west), it would be cheering to see an upturn in the country's fortunes.

Population

The Yugoslav population (22,400,000) classified itself as follows in the 1981 census:

Serbs	36.3%	(8,130,000)
Croats	19.8%	(4,430,000)
Moslems	8.9%	(1,990,000)
Slovenes	7.8%	(1,750,000)
Albanians	7.7%	(1,720,000)
Macedonians	6.0%	(1,340,000)
Yugoslavs (an option under the constitution)	5.4%	(1,210,000)
Montenegrins	2.6%	(580,000)
Hungarians	1.9%	(430,000)
Romanies, Turks, Slovaks, Romanians, Bulgarians, Vlachs, Ukranians, Italians, Czechs etc.	less than 1.0% each	

Each of these nationalities has its individual characteristics, based largely on historical and geographical factors. A Slovenian factory worker won't look or behave like a Montenegrin shepherd. And while I'm disinclined to generalisations about national characteristics (like saying all English people are snobs), it's fair to say that the Yugoslavs I've met have been, almost without exception, honest, friendly and generous. Along the coast people have been influenced, some might say hardened, by money from tourism, and this has provoked a certain amount of predictable greed and resentment – but as a nation the Yugoslavs remain more hospitable than most. This is particularly true in the remoter parts of Montenegro, Kosovo and Macedonia, where extreme poverty is still evident.

Culture

Twenty centuries of warfare and foreign occupation have meant that Yugoslavia has spent more time fighting off the enemy than building Sistine Chapels and Eiffel Towers. In terms of architecture only Split and Dubrovnik are internationally famous, and Yugoslavia has produced fewer 'name' artists than most other European countries. Few outsiders have heard of any artists other than the sculptor Meštrović and Nobel prizewinning author Ivo Andrić. Which is not to say that Yugoslavia lacks culture – simply that most of it hasn't been exported.

The country's best known and most valuable art is mostly religious, in the form of Serbo-Byzantine monasteries and churches, and the frescos and icons that adorn them. But modernism has flourished since the last war, with some particularly good naive and abstract painters recently being shown in commercial galleries, and theatre and literature are increasingly both good and well supported.

But much of the cultural development has rested with the folk tradition. While Yugoslavia has no major composers, most of the southern population sing well – and at every opportunity. Our mountain guide in Ohrid sang Macedonian revolutionary songs for the better part of two hours one afternoon, unaccompanied and unselfconscious. If an accordionist arrives at a bar everyone joins in. And any Orthodox church service will convince you that the clergy are born to chant so hauntingly.

Equally, many poems and legends are still unrecorded, but ready for recitation at the right moment. Yugoslavian art is a low-key, humanist affair, with a greater participation by the people than most of us are used to. This is largely the result of five centuries of keeping local culture underground, under the Turks, and a lack of the kind of patronage that dominates French and Italian art.

Very little Yugoslav literature is translated into English, exceptions being the epic metaphysical poetry of **Petar II Njegoš** (Prince Bishop of Montenegro, 1813-51), several works by Ivo Andrić (*Bridge on the Drina* and *Bosnian Story* being the best known), and a couple by Danilo Kiš (read his excellent *A Tomb for Boris Davidovitch*). Occasional pocket size paperbacks of Yugoslav works in translation can be found for well under £1 in the major cities – where you'll also see an excellent range of foreign authors, from Marguerite Duras and Henry Miller to Milan Kundera and Graham Greene ... in Serbo-Croat.

A great deal of sculpture, often in the form of liberation and Partisan war memorials, can be found in Yugoslavia and generally it's of a high standard. **Ivan Meštrović** (1883-1962) is easily the best known sculptor, and his works are on display everywhere. Influenced heavily by the Vienna Secession and meetings with Rodin in the early 1900s, Meštrović's work is distinctively different from either. Although flawed occasionally by delusions of grandeur, his sculpture still ranks among Europe's finest.

Yugoslavia's architecture was largely governed by its centuries of

Ivan Meštrović's statue of Njegoš at Lovčen, Montenegro.

foreign domination. In Slovenia and Croatia Austrian architecture is prevalent, while along the coast there are large stretches which could easily be mistaken for Italy. Some Bosnian towns are thoroughly Turkish in character, right down to the mosques, white minarets and ramshackle wooden houses. And in the south and east there are still hundreds of Byzantine monasteries, many with frescos in good repair.

Modern architecture here, as everywhere, has been influenced more by practicalities than aesthetics, resulting in tower blocks, concrete monsters and a few spectacular eyesores. Nonetheless these edifices have often been prizewinners, if only because of their resistance to earthquakes.

Language

Yugoslavia's main language is Serbo-Croat, and even where this isn't the first language it's almost always understood. Macedonian and Slovenian have equal rights and are widely spoken in their respective republics. Elsewhere a large variety of minority languages are also spoken, including Albanian, Hungarian, Turkish, Czech, Bulgarian and Italian.

If you're only in Yugoslavia for a short while then you probably won't have time to pick up much Serbo-Croat. Nonetheless you should learn a few phrases and a minimum vocabulary of numbers and greetings. Obviously it will increase your popularity enormously if you try their language before yours...

Although English is still spoken relatively little, German is widely known, especially along the coast and throughout the north. Older and well-educated people sometimes have a smattering of French. Italian is often understood in coastal resorts and on the islands.

Matters are complicated by the use of two alphabets. Cyrillic as opposed to Latin is used everywhere except in Slovenia and Croatia, though essential signs and place names are sometimes written in Latin too.

The Cyrillic alphabet was derived from the Glagolitic, invented by St. Cyril in the ninth century. This was done by St. Kliment, in Ohrid, and the alphabet's use spread rapidly with the Orthodox church throughout eastern Europe and Russia. Although initially intimidating, Cyrillic isn't difficult to learn, even if it means picking your way through signs a letter at a time until you discover that CAPAJEBO is the same as SARAJEVO and that a PECTOPAH is a place you eat at.

Cyrillic was designed so that each sound in the language could be represented by a single character. Unfortunately this system doesn't work for the Latin alphabet, where accents and occasional letter pairs are used in addition to the normal letters. The two alphabets and their pronunciations are given below:

Cyrillic	Latin	Pronunciation
А	A	as in party
Б	B	as in bed
В	V	as in vodka
Г	G	as in goat
Д	D	as in dote
Ђ	Dj	as in jive
Е	E	as in pet
Ж	Ž	as in treasure
З	Z	as in zoo
И	I	as in feet
Ј	J	as in yet
К	K	as in kept
Л	L	as in love
Љ	Lj	as in million
М	M	as in mother
Н	N	as in no
Њ	Nj	as in news
О	O	as in hot
П	P	as in pie
Р	R	as in run
С	S	as in sap
Т	T	as in too
Ч	Č	as in chew
У	U	as in hoot
Ф	F	as in free
Х	H	as in hat
Ц	C	as in fats
Ћ	Ć	as in chew
Џ	Dz	as in jam
Ш	Š	as in ship

It's a good idea to take a simple phrasebook or dictionary with you, if only for tricky situations. However I have yet to find a decent phrasebook: they all look wonderful in theory, but what matters is the time it takes to find what you're looking for. In many ways a dictionary is better, since simple words often communicate the feel of what you intend better than laboriously pronounced phrases. A two way dictionary also allows Yugoslavs to find the English for a word in Serbo-Croat. The *Langenscheidt Serbo-Croation Universal Dictionary* is excellent, pocket sized, and cheap (£2).

The following is a list of some of the more useful words you'll need:

| thank you / please | *hvala / molim vas* |
| yes / no | *da / ne (nema = none, emphatic no)* |

hello / bye (informal)	*zdravo*
cheers!	*živeli!*
good morning	*dobro jutro*
good day	*dobar dan*
good evening	*dobro veće*
good night	*laku noć (on leaving)*
yesterday	*jučer*
today	*danas*
tomorrow	*sutra*
entrance / exit	*ulaz / izlaz*
men / women	*muški / zenski*
toilet	*toalet*
police	*milicija*
one	*jedan*
two	*dva*
three	*tri*
four	*četri*
five	*pet*
six	*šest*
seven	*sedam*
eight	*osam*
nine	*devet*
ten	*deset*
twenty	*dvadeset*
thirty	*trideset*
one hundred	*što*
one thousand	*hiljada*
left / right	*levo / desno*
ahead / behind	*naprijed / iza*
straight on	*pravo*
over there	*tamo*
up / down	*gore / dolje*
under / over	*ispod / preko*
metre / kilometre	*metar / kilometar*
minute / hour / hourly	*minuta / sat / svaki sat*
north / south	*sjever / jug*
east / west	*istok / zapad*
footpath / track	*pješačka staza / trag*
corner / road	*ćošak / cesta*
hill / mountain	*brežuljak / planina*
can you tell me the way to ...	*da li možete da mi pokažete put do ...*
how do I get to ...	*kako da stignem na ...*
is this the right way to ...	*da li je u ovom pravcu ...*
is it far to walk?	*da li je deleko hodom?*

is this the turning for ...	*da li se ovde skreće za ...*
can you show me on the map?	*da li možete da mi pakažete na mapi?*

Natural History

Yugoslavia's flora and fauna is as diverse as everything else about the country. Since large areas are virtually uninhabitable (because of the mountains and the frequent lack of water), there is still a good deal of wildlife here that is now rarely found in the rest of Europe. An impressive 90 species of mammal and 508 (of Europe's 660) species of bird live in Yugoslavia.

The lynx, which is all but extinct in western Europe, is found in Slovenia and Macedonia, while in the remoter forests and mountains there are still a considerable number of bears. You're extremely unlikely to see either animal – they're both very cautious. The mountain guide I met in Ohrid had only seen one bear in forty years of walking and climbing in the area, though near the Plitvice Lakes in Croatia a man trying to snare a cub was killed by its justifiably upset mother only a week before I was there. The Koprivnica reserve in Bosnia, originally created so that Tito could hunt, now has over 1,500 of Yugoslavia's 4,000 bears – compare this with the resident population in France of just thirteen. Sadly, the only bear I saw was attached by a chain to a gipsy caravan near Split.

Wolves are apparently still common too, especially in the inland mountains, though they are hardly ever seen except in winter, when they come down to raid villages for scraps and small animals.

Wild boar frequent the northern forests, while red, fallow and roe deer are found throughout the country. Chamois and mouflon can be seen in the mountains, and all game birds are found across the country. Far too many of these animals and birds are being killed by well-heeled hunters though, and even bears aren't exempt – 180 are killed annually.

Snakes are fairly common, but there are very few poisonous ones. The old saying is worth remembering – they're much more frightened of you than you are of them. Snakes will avoid regularly walked paths or roads, but if you're going across country it's as well to make sure you have sensible shoes or boots on. I saw perhaps two dozen snakes of four or five varieties without coming across anything dangerous. Please resist the temptation that many have to kill them out of ignorant fear.

You'll also see several species of lizards while out walking and these charming animals, with their foolish antics, can make even the sternest people smile. Near water you'll often hear vociferous frogs, and several varieties of toad live in the woods on limestone mountains. Also look out for martens, wild cats and red squirrels.

Everywhere in Yugoslavia in early summer there are abundant butterflies, often of species rarely seen in England –swallowtails are commonplace in Montenegro, and white admirals are by no means rare on the islands.

When in the mountains keep an eye out for eagles, hawks and vultures. These are more common in Macedonia than elsewhere, but it's not impossible to find them even amongst relatively populous mountains like the Slovenian Alps.

One of the most attractive features of Yugoslavia is its flora. In many places this is unusually unspoilt, and in two there are still areas of virgin forest – which you won't find anywhere else in Europe except in Poland. Most varieties of trees and forests can be found across the country, with beech and pine being the most prominent in the areas in which you'll be walking.

Above the tree line there is frequently beautiful summer grazing, and the open expanses here are home to flowers and herbs which smell wonderful as you walk across them. In southern Macedonia and in the Fruška Gora there are dozens of herbal plants which aren't found anywhere else: some of these are used to make delicious teas and infusions – others are used locally for everything from curing warts to staunching cuts.

In the lower meadows there is a huge range of wild flowers and it is perhaps these that attract such large numbers of butterflies in spring and early summer. As the summer wears on the colours fade and everything dries out, leaving an arid impression across the whole country which doesn't really wear off until the leaves change to their superb autumn colours.

Climate

Yugoslavia has three distinct climatic patterns – Slovenia is temperate central European, the coast is Mediterranean and the interior is continental. What this means very roughly is that Slovenia has cold winters and cool summers, the coast has mild winters and warm summers, and the interior has cold winters and hot summers.

Slovenia is temperate central European, the coast is Mediterranean and the interior is continental. What this means very roughly is that Slovenia has cold winters and cool summers, the coast has mild winters and warm summers, and the interior has cold winters and hot summers.

Apart from the coast, which is climatically stable (Dubrovnik boasts about its 250 days of sunshine), the climate varies a great deal regionally, and depends on local factors such as altitude, lakes, prevailing winds and topology. For example Ohrid's altitude (695m), lake and sheltered position give it a mild maritime rather than continental climate.

Average temperatures inland are 0°C in winter and 22°C in summer, but vary greatly over the day, with temperatures as low as -30°C and as high as 39°C being recorded. Last time I was in Belgrade – in early July – it was 34°C at 11am. Along the Adriatic the averages are slightly higher (6°C in winter, 24°C in summer), but the range is much smaller (rarely below 0°C or above 30°C). In the mountains above 2000m, especially inland, average temperatures stay below zero from November to April.

Rainfall is heavier than you might expect, but mostly falls in winter and early spring; the average for the whole country is a little over 1000mm. (For comparison, the London average is 610mm, and Skye, the wettest place in the UK, receives 1805mm.) The slopes of Mt. Crkvice in Montenegro have the highest rainfall in Europe (over 5000mm – and 660mm in December alone), while lowland Macedonia has virtually none in summer (Skopje: annual 443mm, July 19mm). May and June can be rainy months, particularly in the mountains, but fortunately it tends to fall in short, heavy showers.

Weather is unpredictable in the mountains all year round and you should be equipped accordingly. Snow can fall in every month of the year above 1700m, and I was once caught in a hailstorm at 1200m, near the coast, in June. Equally the temperature inversion in the north can mean that instead of cooling by about 1°C for every 200m you climb up, it increases instead.

Further reading

Guides:
The Rough Guide to Yugoslavia – Martin Dunford and Jack Holland (RKP, £4.50). This is an excellent general guide, full of useful information for rough and/or budget traveller using public transport. The authors are currently giving it a much needed update.

Fodor's Yugoslavia, annually (Fodor, £10.50). Aimed at the better off traveller with own transport, good on culture and monuments.

The Companion Guide to Jugoslavia – J.A.Cuddon (Collins, £9.95). An idiosyncratic personal tour in 500 pages by someone who indisputably knows the country, but fails to hold my attention despite choice morsels scattered throughout.

Nagel's Yugoslavia (Nagel, around £16) – Excellent ancient history, but not a modern guide.

Le Guide du Routard, Europe du Nord et du centre (Hachette, FF58). A well written fifty page section (in French) on Yugoslavia. Also includes a good guide to Scandinavia.

General:
Handbook on Yugoslavia (Federal Secretariat for Information Belgrade, £8). All the facts, from how many students graduated in natural sciences and maths in 1945 (8) to Relations with Its Neighbours ('Cooperation is successfully going ahead with Romania and Hungary, but this is not quite the case with Bulgaria'). Good accounts of the

resistance and current political state of the country.

Black Lamb and Grey Falcon – Rebecca West (Papermac, £8.95). Certainly the most comprehensive (1200pp) and best written account of Yugoslavia up to the last war. Rebecca West visited the country in 1937 and spent seven years researching and writing the book, which is one of the best I've read – on any subject. Fatally flawed in places (the Macedonian politics are unclear and inaccurate, considering that under Alexander's dictatorship Macedonians had no rights whatsoever. And the conclusions are naive), it is nonetheless by turns funny, passionate and tragic, and always brilliant. Parts of it are reproduced in the *Essential Rebecca West* (Penguin, £4.95), but buy the original.

Yugoslav Story – John Phillips (Jugoslovenska Revija, £2). A hardback coffee table book of excellent black and white photographs available in some tourist offices in Yugoslavia. The text is a highly subjective look at the country by an American photographer who befriended Tito in 1944.

Eastern Approaches – Fitzroy Maclean (Papermac £5.95). An autobiographical account by the man who switched aid from the Četniks to the Partisans. Action packed and eloquently written. *Tito – A pictorial biography* is illuminating, and *Disputed Barricades*, the detailed biography, is first class. Both books are out of print.

Tito – Phyllis Auty (Longman, 1970, out of print). An objective, readable account.

Tito – The Story from Inside – Milovan Djilas (Weidenfeld and Nicolson, 1981, out of print). Djilas was one of Tito's closest allies and friends during the war but fell out later and was imprisoned as a dissident. His account of the not so perfect Tito makes engaging reading and contains plenty of hard fact, but it shouldn't be taken as entirely objective.

The Mountains of Serbia – Anne Kindersley (John Murray, 1971, out of print). The best advantage was taken of her husband's three year posting to Yugoslavia, and this rambling account of travels and encounters provides a unique insight to the people and country.

Voyage en Orient – Alphonse de Lamartine (Paris, 1875). An excellent account of his travels by opinionated but well-informed French poet.

A Short History of the Yugoslav Peoples – Fred Singleton (CUP, £7.50). Clearly written and recently published history.

Finally, although most of the books listed by Rebecca West in her bibliography are now long out of print, a number turn up in second hand bookshops and they almost invariably make for interesting background reading.

Natural History Books
The Natural History of the Mediterranean – Tegwyn Harris (Penguin, 1982, £7.95).

The Natural History Book Service publishes an extensive catalogue and supplies books on mail order from 2 Wills road, Totnes, Devon TQ9 5XN (Tel. 0803 865913).

PLANNING AND PREPARATIONS

'The good traveller doesn't know where he's going. The great traveller doesn't know where he's been.' – Chuang Tžu, quoted by Martha Gellhorn in 'Travels with myself and another' (Eland, London)

Health, safety and insurance

Health

A reciprocal health agreement between the United Kingdom and Yugoslavia means that UK passport holders will be treated free while visiting the country. Even if you do have to pay for treatment this is very cheap by European – and especially American – standards.

Before you go: Yugoslavia is, on the whole, a healthy place. All publicly supplied water is drinkable, if often heavily chlorinated, and there's no need for vaccinations – though it won't do you any harm to be up to date on tetanus.

If you need to use needles for any reason you should take a doctor's note explaining why, and if you wear glasses or contact lenses then take a spare pair – it's not impossible to get replacements, but it is time-consuming. It also does no harm to go and see your doctor and dentist before leaving, just for a check-up – much easier at home than abroad. Women should bring sanitary towels and tampons with them – for some reason they're hard to find outside the big cities. And if you need contraceptives, bring those too.

Fitness: If you're planning a walking or hiking holiday then obviously it's a good idea to get fit before you go. The best exercises are cycling and hill-walking – preferable to running and jogging. If you're surrounded by an absence of hills, then stairs make for easily the best mountain training.

Common problems: Don't forget that you're less resistant to diseases during your first weeks abroad, so you should make sure your food contains enough vitamins, and take extra if you're not sure. Use mineral or sterilised water if you're unsure of the source. In the mountains melted snow is usually safe, but water from streams and rivers often isn't. Take iodine-based water purification tablets.

It's worth carrying both a mild laxative and something for diarrhoea, though both problems can usually be cured by a change of diet – soft fruit for the first problem and dry skinned fruits for the second (I find bananas and apricots particularly effective). It's essential to replace lost body fluids when you have diarrhoea, and sweet drinks are recommended.

I used to be badly prone to attacks by mosquitoes, but have recently found that a course of tablets containing Vitamins B1, B6 and B12 will make them dislike you nearly as much as you dislike them. I discovered this in the mosquito infested north of Sweden, where I was also warned that the active ingredient, Vitamin B12, is dangerous if taken on its own.

Take along small quantities of sticking plaster (Band-Aids), anti-septic cream and aspirin – or paracetamol if you've got a sensitive stomach.

Finally, don't hesitate to see a doctor or pharmacist if you're unsure of the diagnosis or cure. But be careful about blood transfusions – although Aids is still extremely uncommon in Yugoslavia you can't be too careful.

Mountain health problems
The best protection is prevention, so all walkers and backpackers should be conversant in first aid – or carry a suitable booklet. It's especially important to know how to deal with injuries and hypo-thermia.

Hypothermia: This is responsible for the deaths of more hikers than any other cause. It occurs when the body loses heat faster than it can be generated, and the commonest cause is a combination of wet or inadequate clothing, and cold wind. It is easily avoided by making sure that you always have a waterproof, a sweater and a survival bag with you – even if you're hiking with a day pack.

If one of your party is showing signs of hypothermia – uncontrollable shivering, followed by drowsiness and confusion –it's essential that s/he is warmed up immediately. Exercise is not the way to do this. Wrap the victim in warm clothing, or even better a sleeping bag, and then increase the blood sugar levels with food and hot sweet drinks.

Injury: Again, prevention is better than cure. Try and avoid climbing or walking beyond your limit. If scrambling or bouldering avoid using your knees or elbows, and keep at least three points of contact with the rock (two hands and a foot or vice versa). In the event of being injured use surgical tape for cuts that would normally be stitched, and then bind the wound laterally with zinc oxide tape. If you're going a long way off the trail then take an inflatable splint.

Altitude sickness: This doesn't have any serious effect under 2400m, and so isn't a problem in most of Yugoslavia. However, walking from sea-level up to altitudes of over 1500m, or from below 1000m to above 2200m can cause mild dizziness, a racing heart and confusion, to those unused to altitude. This isn't dangerous in the first instance, but can impair decision making – a short break is normally a sufficient cure. Return to a lower altitude if this doesn't work. Finally, remember that altitude sickness is impartial; youth and fitness don't help.

Sunburn: Altitude and wind combined tend to make you forget that the sun is burning you. Take high protection suncream (factor 10-15) and use a hat and sunglasses until you've got a protective tan. Above 2200m, and on snow, be careful of the sides of your eyes, and your lips, nose and ears. If you get badly burnt apply an after sun lotion and use a total block cream until the skin has recovered.

Snakes: In the extremely unlikely event of being bitten, take the plastic part of a syringe and use it to suck out the poison immediately. Apparently, if you do this within a minute or two of the bite, it will save you from the majority of poisonous snakes. I haven't had occasion, fortunately, to test this.

Insurance

A good idea – it's reassuring to know that you can be flown home if you need to be. Read the fine print and make sure that it covers walking in the mountains. A general policy, which covers health, theft and third party insurance, is generally cheaper and less trouble than several different policies. The major banks and travel agents (Thomas Cook, American Express etc.) all supply policies. Arrange your insurance to cover your journey to and from Yugoslavia, and keep the policy safe with your other travel documents.

Safety

Although you're unlikely to be confronted by them, it's worth knowing that both the police and the army have fearsome powers. Don't provoke them, and remember that freedom of dissension isn't automatically guaranteed. Telephone 92 throughout the country for emergencies.

Police: If you do find yourself involved with the police stay courteous, even (especially) when it's difficult to do so. Stand rather than sit (it puts you on an equal footing), and establish eye contact – if you can without being brazen or offensive about it. Some people recommend shaking hands with officialdom, but it does depend very much on the circumstances. Wait until an interpreter arrives (or anyone who understands you clearly) rather than be misunderstood.

Although the police have a high and armed profile, they are almost invariably friendly and helpful, and most tourists only brush with them when being fined for minor traffic offences. But you must carry your passport with you at all times, and very occasionally your visa (or entry stamp) will be checked.

Army: In some parts of the country you'll find a very heavy army presence, although it's mostly young national servicemen, off duty. Where you see this there's invariably a military base nearby, and if you find soldiers on duty you should be wary. Don't even have a camera on show, let alone take pictures: it's expressly forbidden to photograph strategic or military installations. Usually, but not always, you'll see pictures of antiquated cameras crossed out. Take these seriously.

Armed patrols along some borders (notably Albania and Bulgaria) have orders to shoot to kill in suspicious circumstances, and apparently they're bored and trigger happy in some areas. I haven't had this confirmed first hand, but it's not a theory you'll want to test.

Yugoslavia's heavily defensive attitude is at times intimidating, but nonetheless understandable. The country is only in its second generation of hard won freedom in a thousand years, and is guarding it carefully.

Theft: Your biggest danger of theft comes not from Yugoslavs, who are among the most honest people I've met, but from fellow tourists. The majority of robberies – and there are very few – occur in youth hostels or on international trains on their way through to Greece. The crime rate within Yugoslavia is unusually low, and the normal minimum precautions of watchfulness and keeping your valuables on or very near your person are more than adequate. On aeroplanes, buses and trains I keep my cameras and documents in a separate day pack, so that even if most of my luggage is lost I still have the essentials. If you're the victim of a robbery, report it to the local police (*milicija*) straight away.

Consulates: As a British passport holder you can be repatriated if you really insist, but you will eventually have to pay through the nose for it. You will never, in any circumstances, be lent or given money by the consulate.

Sexual harrassment: Women on their own may be subject to minor hassles, from Moslem-frustrated inquisitiveness to attempted coastal pickups. Behaving sensibly, dressing unprovocatively inland and speaking firmly (in any language) should make your intentions clear.

THE GLOBETROTTERS CLUB

An international club which aims to share information on adventurous budget travel through monthly meetings and *Globe* magazine. Published every two months, *Globe* offers a wealth of information, from reports of members' latest adventures to recent travel bargains and tips, plus the invaluable 'Mutual Aid' column where members can swap a house, sell a camper, find a travel companion, or offer information on unusual places or hospitality to visiting members.

Enquiries to: The secretary, Globetrotters Club, BMC/Roving, London WC1N 3XX.

Visas and red tape

If you hold a full passport from the UK or any other EEC country then you don't need a visa for stays of up to three months. For longer stays your best bet is to leave the country and return for a fresh stamp – extensions are difficult to arrange.

Australian, Canadian and U.S.A passport holders need a visa, but this is issued free, on the spot, at any Yugoslav consulate:

7 Lexham Gardens, London W8 5JU, England (Tel. 01 370 6105).

2410 Calif. St., N.W. Washington D.C. 20008, USA.
17th floor, 767 Third Ave., New York, N.Y. 10017, USA.
Suite 1600, 307 North Michigan Avenue, Chicago, 60601 Illinois, USA.
Suite 1605, 625 Stanwix St., Pittsburgh, Pa. 15222, USA.
Suite 406, 1375 Sutter St., San Francisco, Ca. 94709, USA.
Suite 4 R, Park Centre, 1700 E, 13th St., Cleveland, Ohio 44114, USA.

17 Blackburn Ave., Ottawa, Ontario, KIN 8A2, Canada.
377 Spadine Road, Toronto, Ontario, N5P 2V7, Canada.

PO Box 161, 11 Nuyts St., Manuka, A.C.T. 2603, Canberra, Australia.
PO Box 147, 58 Lisson Grove, Hawthorn, Melbourne, Victoria 3122, Australia.
PO Box 505, 24 Colin St., West Perth, 6000 Western Australia.

New Zealanders and holders of British Visitors passports have to pay £4.50, and South Africans are not admitted, period.

Visas can be obtained on the border but it's discouraged, and time-consuming as a result. If you arrive by train you may have to surrender your passport. Don't panic – it will be returned to you later, duly stamped.

Accommodation coupons: the law is that every night you stay in Yugoslavia must be registered by accommodation coupons. In theory these can be checked at any time, and nights unaccounted for constitute a finable offence. In practice many hotels and most private rooms and campsites won't issue these, and I've yet to hear of anyone having their coupons checked or being retrospectively punished. A high up tourist board official in Macedonia described the coupon system as 'unnecessary, a waste of time, bureaucratic nonsense'. Freelance camping, or sleeping on the beach, will, however, earn you an on the spot fine (but only if you're caught). Overnight bus and train journeys are exempt from the system.

Getting there

There are five main ways of travelling to Yugoslavia: plane, train, bus, car or boat.

Plane: If you're using public transport then flying to Yugoslavia is the best and cheapest way of travelling there. Official fares start at around £250 return from London, but you shouldn't have to pay more than £130 if you look for a charter or a partial package. Ring the Air Travel Advisory Bureau in London (01-636-5000) for the agents handling the cheapest flights at any time. In season charters and scheduled flights are available to most parts of Yugoslavia from several UK airports. Another option, if you can't find a reasonable flight, is to take one of the very cheap charters to northeast Italy and take the train from there – it's dirt cheap, and only five hours from Trieste to Ljubljana.

Train: If you're under 26 then taking the train is a viable option. Either buy a one month Interrail pass for £120 or a Transalpino ticket to Belgrade for around the same price. You won't get much use out of your Interrail pass in Yugoslavia, since the trains are both cheap and slow, but it gives you the option of travelling to and from the country by a more interesting route, perhaps making several stopovers on the way. If you're over 26 then the full price return fare is about £180. It's almost always better to fly, particularly when you take into account the 48 hour train journey from London to Belgrade.

Bus: Although theoretically the cheapest way of arriving in Yugoslavia (London to Belgrade is around £45 single) the bus has several disadvantages, not least of which is the 48 hour journey. Most of the buses are run by long distance Greek operators who aren't really meant to stop in Yugoslavia. The chances are that you'll be dumped several miles outside a city and left to fend for yourself. Other disadvantages include the very real prospect of losing your baggage on the way, and the cost of meals and breaks along the way. It adds up to the same cost for a great deal more hassle than a charter flight.

Car: Easily the nicest way of getting to Yugoslavia, if you have the means, is in your own car. If there are two or more of you then it needn't be more expensive than the plane, and the freedom of movement you'll have once you're there is easily worth the long drive down. If you're going to the south a more expensive, but undeniably attractive way of getting to Yugoslavia is to drive down through Italy and then take a ferry – these run from Rimini, Ancona and Bari to Split, Dubrovnik and Bar.

A few words of warning about driving: Make sure that your car is in good repair and insured against fatal breakdown – repairs are often lengthy and expensive, and spare parts are in very short supply; don't let drunks or children under 12 travel in the front seats – it's illegal; keep to the speed limits – fines are steep; and remember that you are legally obliged to stop and offer assistance if you see an accident or breakdown.

Boat: Ferries regularly ply the whole coast from Rijeka to Bar. There are also costly but spectacular international routes from Patras and Igoumenitsa in Greece and Bari and Rimini in Italy to Split, Dubrovnik and Bar. It costs around £30 single with no accommodation; considerably more if you want to bring a car and have a cabin.

More idiosyncratic ways of arriving are **on foot**, by **bicycle** or by **hitching**. Hitching is only recommended for the impecunious and ambitious – it's hard to get to Yugoslavia and even harder once you're there. Cycling is a wonderful way of seeing the country, and the ones you cross to reach it, but you need a lot of time and energy. A better option is to take bikes to Yugoslavia on the plane or by train, and then cycle thereafter. I met two Canadians (at 1450m in Montenegro) who had cycled from Paris. Walking requires even more time. Patrick Leigh Fermor strolled from the Hook of Holland to Constantinople in 1933 and 1934 with a budget of a pound a week, but it did take eighteen months. Fifty years later Simon Palmour walked across Europe in just seven months – see p. 190 for his account of the Yugoslavian traverse.

When to go

The best months for walking in Yugoslavia are September and June, closely followed by October and May. There are a number of disadvantages with July and August; you'll be subject to the 30% high season surcharge, many accommodations will be full and public transport gets crowded. And for walkers the weather can be uncomfortably hot and stormy.

By September there are fewer tourists, the weather is usually fine, the sea is at its warmest and the prices are down from the summer. In October the weather is cooler, but still dry, and in the first fortnight there is the added advantage of the wonderful autumn colours. November heralds the first snows in the mountains and the weather is generally much gloomier.

May and June are excellent. Despite variable weather, the colours are spring fresh and bright, the tourist industry is still welcoming (it becomes somewhat jaded by the end of the season) and even the resorts are not too busy. Finding rooms and space on public transport is easy, and the only disadvantage is that on the bigger mountains there's still a considerable amount of snow. Patches are found from 1600m upwards on north facing slopes in the interior, and in some places are still there until the first half of July. Some of the harder walks require the use of ice-axes until then.

Yugoslavia's weather is damp and miserable in the winter, except where it's freezing and miserable. Unless you're going specifically for the winter sports (which are only really for beginners) you should avoid it from November until March.

What to bring

The best way of packing for Yugoslavia is to set out all the things you think you'll need and then take about a third of it. When walking with a full pack I don't like to carry more than 14kg, but invariably end up with 17kg, because of cameras and notebooks. If you decide not to camp (see below, and p. 29) then this can be reduced to an easy 12kg.

Clothes

Trousers: Long trousers – I use Rohan bags, which are comfortable, light and windproof, and they dry in half an hour. Their two disadvantages are price (£35) and durability (they won't stand hard rock climbing or bad abrasions), but they always look good and have excellent large, deep, zipped pockets. (I've never held with jeans, which are, quite simply, dangerous if you're caught in the cold and wet and they're your only trousers.); cotton shorts (nearly knee length, but can be rolled up); Three pairs of cotton underwear.

Tops: Long-sleeved cotton shirt (dark colour to avoid unnecessary washing, and always looks good for that important dinner); short-sleeved cotton shirt (primarily for travelling and evenings); medium thick close weave woollen sweater; Gortex waterproof top (expensive but worth it); Two T-shirts (light cotton, one sleeveless).

Footwear: One pair of long, thick woollen socks; one pair of short, thick woollen socks; two pairs of thin cotton socks; one pair of boating shoes; walking boots (essential that they are light, waterproof, support the ankles, and Vibram or similar sole – Raichlie boots, made in Switzerland, are superb, as they should be at around £100).

Sundries: Large cotton square (which can be used as shawl, scarf, pillow, tablecloth etc. Mine's an arab headdress.); swimming costume; small towel.

Equipment

Rucksack: Comfort is essential. All new ones are designed with an internal metal frame and these are infinitely more comfortable than having an external frame. Make sure that it has well padded straps and a wide supporting belt (on the hips). I prefer ones that are high rather than wide, partly for mountaineering, partly because it makes walking through doors much easier. My rucksack is a Lafuma mountaineering model (French, and expensive – about £100), which I can also use for carrying skis, crampons etc. in winter. In the UK Berghaus and Karrimor are the best. Label your bag clearly inside and out.

Day pack: A small rucksack, which should be able to take all you need for a one day walk, or for city tourism. This allows you to leave heavy equipment behind if you have a base, or in left luggage in a town.

Walking equipment: Compass; altimeter (not essential, but I have always found it useful); water bottles (1 x 1 litre, 2 x 0.6 litre); a double survival bag (also serves as a bivouac); whistle; syringe (for snake-bites); torch and spare batteries; penknife; sunglasses.

Camping equipment: Two person tent (I recently upgraded to an Ultimate Peapod, which although slightly heavier than my last is easier to pitch and more spacious. Also take tent sealant and repair material); sleeping bag (down filled if you can afford it – more compact when rolled up, warmer in use); sleeping mat (Karrimats are cheaper but less effective than Thermarests); stove and fuel (Camping Gaz is cleanest and easiest, but the fuel is unavailable in Yugoslavia – and you're not supposed to take it on aircraft. Spirit and petrol stoves are always problematical, but the MSR and Whisperlite stoves are better than most); aluminium pans; knife/fork/spoon; lighter and waxed matches; camping candles; water purifiers; emergency food (nut bars, mintcake); trail snacks.

Note: Official camping in Yugoslavia is rendered less attractive than you'd expect by high prices and poor locations. I intended to camp wherever possible and ended up under canvas on only three nights on my first trip of eight weeks. Even with a car I mostly stayed in private rooms. See p. 29 for more details.

Even if you're bent on camping you might consider not taking the cooking materials and implements. Most places are within a few hours of a bar or café where you can at least get an omelette or a *burek*, and some hot drinks, and café food is cheap. Picnic food is easy to come by, and in the summer you don't need much hot food, especially if you're not camping every night.

Photography: I took a Nikon FE2 with Nikkor 35-200mm lens, an Olympus XA and lots of Ilford (black and white) and Agfa (transparency) film. Everyone will have their own preferences. Remember that cameras are heavy. Most people won't need more than a compact, though a long focus lens is the only way of taking pictures of mountains. A good zoom lens is a great, if expensive, idea – what little quality you lose is easily made up for by convenience. Film is very expensive and sometimes unreliable within Yugoslavia. Technically you're only allowed to bring in five rolls, but I haven't heard of anyone challenged on this. Take your films home to be developed.

Documents: Money belt or pouch; passport; tickets; Eurocheques and card; travellers cheques; some cash in US$ and sterling; Access and Visa credit cards; medical insurance; driving licence; IYHF card (membership of the International Youth Hostels Federation will gain you access to hostels throughout the world – contact a local branch of the Youth Hostels Association (YHA) for more details); four recent photographs; small, medium and large notebooks; two books (one light, one heavy); diary; list of addresses; dictionary; phrasebook;

guidebook; maps; postcards of home; pictures of family (these last two are the best known ice-breakers when language is a barrier). And take a student card if you have one.

Miscellaneous: Spare glasses; pocket calculator; pens; pencil; travel alarm; comb; toilet paper (often not provided); metal mirror; toothbrush and toothpaste; soap in container; tube of travel detergent; nail scissors; plastic bags (several sizes); nylon string; needle and thread; safety pins; suncream; lipsalve; earplugs.

Obviously you can take more than this; I find life difficult with much less.

Good boots and a comfortable rucksack are essential. Kamniške Alps, Slovenia.

Money

The Yugoslavian currency is the dinar. When I first went to Yugoslavia in 1985 the exchange rate was less than din 170 = £1. By May 1988 it was din 2,600 = £1, and in December 1988 the rate went over 10,000 dinars to the pound. High inflation means that prices are relatively stable when measured in sterling or dollars.

Take money in a combination of travellers cheques and cash. Cash is easier to change, but travellers cheques are more secure. American Express remain the best, both for fast refunds and universal recognition. You'll need small denomination notes or cheques (US$20 is perfect) as the exchange rate may be changing daily in your favour. Money can be changed at a single countrywide rate with no commission at travel agencies, tourist hotels and some tourist offices. The only thing to check is that you are being offered today's rate. Banks also change money, but it seems to be an incredibly time-consuming business, with papers being filled out in triplicate and queues for two or even three counters before you finally see your dinars.

For emergencies, credit cards are useful if you have them, and are widely accepted. Small denomination dollar bills or deutschmarks work in minor emergencies in even the remotest areas, but remember that you're not supposed to pay for anything in Yugoslavia in anything other than dinars – the only exception is in Duty Free shops, which sell pricey goods unavailable to Yugoslavs. You should only change money in official offices – in any case the black market is one of the most inefficient I've encountered, with frequent offers of less than the official rate. It's not worth the trouble, even when advantageous.

Finally, do take a reasonable amount of money and/or resources with you – having money sent out from home is a hassle.

Budget

Your budget depends primarily on how much comfort you want. A camping holiday using public transport can be had for around £9 (US$16) per person per day; taking your car and staying in A or B class hotels (average US$20 per person per night) costs a good deal more.

An eight week trip in May and June (medium season) of 1988 cost me just under £13 (US$24) a day, plus the cost of travelling to and from Ljubljana by train from southwest France (£90, US$160). This included: all transport (three domestic flights, eight train rides, 29 long distance buses and all city public transport); accommodation (three campsites, eight B, C and D class hotels and the rest in private rooms); food (restaurants or cafés at least once a day); drink; maps; guides; and souvenirs. I'd recommend counting on a little more, especially if you're only going for a short trip – say £15 (US$27)a day. If you're travelling alone (mostly I wasn't) you need to allow about 30% extra for accommodation. The same applies to travelling in high season. In September, with a car, a three week trip worked out at £15 (US$27) per day per person (for two), with the transport costs to and from Yugoslavia adding £300 (US$540) for the 2500 mile journey.

IN YUGOSLAVIA
Transport

You can get round Yugoslavia by plane, train, bus, car, bicycle and hitch-hiking, and up and down the coast by ferry. Public transport is regular, effective and cheap; but often slow, dirty and crowded too.

Plane: JAT's domestic flights are, at the time of writing, ludicrously cheap – between £10 and £15 anywhere in the country. This makes it a very real option, especially if you've already seen the scenery one way by bus. I flew back to Dubrovnik from Ohrid in 40 minutes, having taken 21 hours to do the trip down. Buy tickets at JAT offices or travel agents, and confirm your flight a couple of days beforehand. I've never had any delays or luggage hassles, but apparently in high season overcrowding causes problems. Be warned that JAT's standard international flights are, by comparison, extravagant (£240 Belgrade-Paris, for example).

Train: The railway network is fairly limited and often both slow and crowded. Prices are similar to those on buses. Any routes which cross mountains – and all of those leading to the coast – boast superb views and are major engineering feats. The Yugoslavs are justifiably proud of the Belgrade-Bar line, completed in the mid seventies, which sports literally hundreds of tunnels, bridges and cuttings. It's a wonderful journey, but be warned that in summer it's very very crowded. The trip from Sarajevo to the coast (Kardeljevo) also crosses some splendid mountains and includes a fine zigzag which brings the train down about 200m.

Local trains (those not marked in red on timetables) are only a little slower than expresses. On these you can usually find a seat. Although trains are slow (count on an hourly rate of 35km) they are generally punctual.

Bus: The bus network is comprehensive, reliable, cheap and regular. Buses are run by a whole group of companies more or less in competition with one another, and offer the best way of seeing local people as well as travelling. They are the best option for distances up to 300km, averaging 45km an hour and costing about £1 per 100km, though prices and speeds vary, with a downward trend in both as you go inland.

If a bus originates at the town you're leaving from, then you can buy tickets and make reservations at the bus station – and you should do this at least a day ahead if you can. Otherwise you must wait for the bus to arrive and fight for a seat. In this case, or when you're catching a bus from a wayside stop, you pay on board. If you can't get a reservation don't buy a ticket either – since several companies often ply each route your ticket may only be valid on one bus a day.

Luggage is invariably stowed in the holds under the bus and you have to pay anything from 10p to £1 for this privilege. The tariff appears to be completely arbitrary, and gives you an insurance of about £3 – this may seem paltry, but is much more than the company can afford to lose, so your bag will be guarded safely.

If your bus breaks down the chances are that it will be taken away and repaired enough for your journey to be completed. Your luggage won't be returned to you until repairs are complete, so keep out anything you may want in the next few hours, even on short journeys.

Buses stop regularly for a *pausa* and the conductor shouts the duration of this above the din: *pet, deset, petnaest* and *dvadeset minuta* are the commonest break lengths (5, 10, 15, 20 min). These invariably occur where you can grab a drink / snack / meal. Watch the driver and you won't go far wrong, but be warned that the bus will go without you if you've made a mistake. Buses sometimes change drivers at these stops – this would have caught me out several times, were it not for the vigilance of fellow passengers.

It's sometimes difficult, particularly away from the coast, to obtain reliable information on bus departures. Sometimes this is out of helpful ignorance, sometimes from a willingness to please – if it's known that you want a bus at 11am you may be told there is one, just to make you feel better. Ask several sources and you may find that they're not all contradictory. Another problem is that information is very localised. If you have to change buses to reach your destination your chances of finding out the timings for the second part of the journey are very slim. Often all you can do about this is go to the next stop and see what the situation is on arrival.

Car: The most comfortable and often the quickest way of travelling is by private car, and sometimes it's the only way to reach remote areas. Road quality is improving fast but is still poor in many places. Yugoslav drivers are ambitious, to the extent that minor obstacles like oncoming traffic and blind corners don't stop them overtaking, and this is your biggest hazard. Speed limits are strictly enforced. In the event of an accident or breakdown, help is available by phoning 987.

Bicycle: The main problem with cycling in Yugoslavia is that on the main roads there's very little courtesy extended to two-wheelers. It remains one of the best possible ways of coming into contact with a country, but it takes a lot of enthusiasm and stamina.

Hitch-hiking: This is not a recommended option. Lifts are few and most people are only travelling short distances. Buses are so cheap that if you can't afford them in Yugoslavia it's hard to see how you could afford to reach the country in the first place.

Boat: One of the pleasanter ways of travelling along the coast – and the only way of reaching the islands – is by boat. They are cheap, well organised, regular and fairly crowded. Buy tickets along the quays from which the boats leave. Local ferries tend to be slightly cheaper than the main coastal service.

Accommodation

Official accommodation in Yugoslavia falls into three categories: hotels, private rooms and campsites. The law (see p. 19) prohibits you from staying with friends or camping out in the wilds, but except for instances of being caught red-handed (and this usually implies an indiscretion) I have yet to hear of the rulings being enforced.

All prices are fixed annually in dollars or Deutsche Marks, but you shouldn't take these too literally. Lists of all of the hotels and campsites, with prices, can be obtained from the Yugoslav Tourist Board, 143 Regent Street, London W1. Be warned that in July and August it can be difficult to find any kind of accommodation – even the campsites are full in places. Arriving early or booking ahead are two ways of avoiding the problem.

Hotels (prices for double rooms with bath): These fall into five categories, *Luxury*, followed by *A, B, C* and *D*. There are hardly any D class hotels left after recent upgrades, but B and C class are fairly plentiful. Luxury and A class hotels are comparable with the same in England or France, and cost accordingly (L, Intercontinental, Belgrade, US$140; A, Palace, Dubrovnik, US$115). B, C and D class prices are more reasonable, but standards are lower, especially in the interior – occasional cracks in the plaster, intermittent hot water, etc. (B, Palas, Titovo Užice, US$55; C, Astoria, Belgrade, US$53; D, Central, Sarajevo, US$35, w/o bath).

Prices vary enormously from area to area, and this isn't necessarily dependent on the tourist trade. Usually you don't need to use the hotel system, which is overpriced. Instead try and keep to private rooms and campsites, which offer much better value for money.

Private rooms: Easily your best accommodation option. Anywhere that has some kind of tourist trade has a system of private rooms available. They are the equivalent of breakfastless B&Bs in the UK, and are generally clean, comfortable and friendly. You'll always have access to a bathroom, sometimes shared with the family, and although rumours persist about a lack of hot water, I've yet to find anywhere that didn't have plentiful supplies.

The biggest advantage private rooms have over other forms of accommodation is that it offers you the chance to meet local people, although in the most popular areas families are beginning to insulate themselves from their lodgers.

The local tourist office (or travel agency where there isn't one) handles private rooms, but you can often save money by stopping and asking where you see signs saying any of *sobe / zimmer / chambre / camare / rooms / privat*. At the more touristed bus stations gaggles of old women will offer you rooms. Check price and location carefully, but normally these are a good bargain – especially if you're staying for less than four nights. In theory if you stay three nights or less you're subject to a 30% surcharge – and if you go through the tourist office you have a better chance of paying it.

Rooms are classified into three categories, which range down in price from about £18 for a class I double room in a resort in high season to £7 for a class III double in a small town inland and out of season. I never paid less than £5 for a double room (Cetinje, class III, in June) or more than £14 (Plitvice lakes, class I, in May). On average it was £7-8, compared to the hotel range (of the cheapest I could find) of £12-30. For a single private room you'll have to pay at least 70% of the cost of a double.

At any time other than in July and August (when most rooms are full) you can bargain the price down a little. In tourist offices start by trying to negotiate away the surcharge – it's in everyone's interest that the available rooms should be filled. At bus stations you should be able to knock the price down by 20% or so, but be aware of what the official prices are locally before you start.

Youth Hostels and student dormitories: Student dormitories are found in the larger towns, and Youth Hostels are spread across the country. *Studentski Doms* are only open in July and August and cost around £3 a head; Youth Hostels are open all year and range up to £4 a head. Bear these in mind, but private rooms are usually a better option.

Camping: In a country with fine weather and beautiful countryside, camping ought to be the ideal option. It ought to be, but camping is unreasonably expensive, and sites are often crowded and far from where you want to be. Freelance camping is not allowed – and you will be fined immediately and fairly heavily if you're caught. In practice, however, there are so many places that you can camp, away from roads and tracks, that if you're discreet you're not likely to be spotted. If you choose to do this please, please, don't let it be you that starts off the forest fire. Many areas of the country, especially in the mountains, have no free water supply and fires are a serious hazard – so much so that in some areas even smoking is forbidden.

Campsites are generally clean and well-equipped, with many having hot showers, fresh water, a shop, some kind of café or restaurant, toilets and electricity supplies. Prices (for two people and a tent) range from £2-7 per night and average around £5. Add around £1 for a car, £2 for a caravan and £1 for electricity. For an extra £2 a night, two people can stay in private rooms. My decision not to camp was influenced by a profound dislike of vast campsites (from 100 to 9,000 people, averaging over 1,000), their inconvenient location, and an unusually wet May and June.

Mountain huts and refuges: In most of the mountain parks there are mountain huts and refuges, though these aren't always open and sometimes you must arrange to collect the key from the mountain centre in the nearest town. When available, they're cheap (around £1-3 a head). In the Julian Alps a network of regularly spaced refuges allows for more conventional long-distance hiking.

Food and drink

Food

Eating in Yugoslavia is cheap unless you're trying something either really special or really touristy. Unfortunately most of the fish along the coast falls into this category – it's easy to pay £12 for two for the fish alone. Compare this with normal meals which cost £2-4 a head (two courses, wine, coffee, liqueur).

The food reflects the past: dishes in the south and east have a markedly Turkish flavour; along the coast the Italian pasta, pizza and rice influence is strong; in Slovenia the food is as filling as in Austria; and the stews and spices of Vojvodina and northern Croatia are close to those of neighbouring Hungary.

Snacks are popular and cheap throughout the country, with the traditional standby being the *burek*, a greasy Turkish pastry filled with cheese (*sa sirom*) or meat (*sa mesom*). In Bosnia you'll find the best of the lot, filled with spinach (*spinat*). Burek is sold from kiosks and cafes in the morning and often washed down with sheep's milk yoghourt (*jogurt*). *Hamburger* and *sendvić* are also increasingly popular.

Even the smallest towns have a *bife* (bar, rather than buffet) or *rostilj* (grill bar) and these often sell *ćevapčići* (spiced meatballs – or small sausages – in groups of ten, which come with spring onions and lethal green peppers), *pljeskavica* (a wad of minced meat served in pitta bread) and *ražnjići* (kebab).

Hotel breakfasts are generally poor, consisting of undrinkable tea or coffee, a couple of slices of stale bread and some jam or cheese. If it's an optional extra don't bother – you're far better off in a café or snack bar.

Yugoslavs eat almost as much ice cream (*sladoled*) as the Italians, and the country is littered with confectioners (*slastičarna*) supplying it, along with wonderful cakes and pastries (*kolać*) similar to those of Greece and the Middle East.

Restaurant eating is generally good value, though there may be a tourist premium on fish or grilled meat. The following list should give you a good idea of what's on offer or what you could ask for.

Essentials:

Voda – water
Pivo – beer
Vino – wine
  Bijelo – white
  Crno – red
  Domaće – house wine
Rakija – spirits

Doručak – breakfast
Ručak – lunch
Večera – dinner

Hladno – cold
Vruće – hot
Hleb – bread
Dzem – jam
Kava – coffee
  Turska kava – Turkish coffee
Čaj – tea
  Sa limunom – with lemon
Sir – cheese
Juha – soup
  Čorba – thick soup

Jaje – eggs
Šunka – ham
Pršut – smoked ham
Riba – fish
Pomfrit – chips
Meso – meat
Povrće – vegetables
Voće – fruit

Domaće – home-made
Sa rostilja – grilled
Pečeno – baked
Przeno – fried
Kuvano – boiled
Punjeno – stuffed

Fish:
Pastrmka – trout
Letnica – salmon trout
Skuša – mackerel
Grgeč, smudj – perch
Luben – bass
Cipalj – grey mullet
Barbun – red mullet
Zubatac – bream

Sardina, srdjela – sardines
Tunj – tuna
Lignje – squid
Dagnje, skoljka – mussels
Skampi – scampi
Rak – crab
Jastog – lobster

Look out for *crna rizoto*, literally black risotto. It's made with squid's ink and a mixture of shellfish. It's pungent, distinctive and I think it's wonderful, though many find it too 'exotic'.

Meat:
Govedjina – beef
Svinjetina – pork
Divlja svinja – wild boar
Jagnjetina – lamb
Ovčetina – mutton
Teletina – veal
Piletina – chicken
Sarma – cabbage or vine leaves stuffed with rice and minced meat
Gulaš – goulash
Musaka – moussaka
Saturas – meat stewed with peppers and tomatoes
Ćulbastija – grilled meat with onions
Djuveč – meat stewed with rice and tomatoes
Pasticada – beef with dumplings

Vegetables:
Krompir – potatoes
Riza – rice
Paprike – green peppers
Luk – onion
Beli luk – garlic (young garlic, which doesn't *look* significantly different from spring onion, is sometimes served raw!)

Salads:
Krastavac – cucumber
Kupus – cabbage
Paradajz – tomato
Zelena – lettuce
Mešana – mixed
Srpska – mixed, with chilli peppers

Fruit:
Narandza – oranges
Limun – lemon
Šljive – plums
Dinja – melon
Kruške – pears
Breskve – peaches

Regional pride means that many of these dishes may have different names locally – the names given here should nonetheless be understood.

Menus may look extensive, but usually only those dishes with prices against them are available. Menus are translated amusingly in tourist resorts (typical desserts: Home-made cheep cheese, Chose in oil, Pancaces or Organges) and not translated at all elsewhere. Sometimes your choice is impossible – Macedonian (in cyrillic) or Dutch, for example.

Finally, vegetarians aren't going to find life easy here. Meat is the staple and fish is often expensive. Many dishes that purport to be vegetable contain meat, and most food is cooked in meat broth or lard. Life is complicated by the general acceptance that chicken isn't meat. Almost any place will rustle up a cheese omelette (*omlet sa sirom*) for you, but remember it will be cooked in lard. I tend to compromise and eat what's on the menu – if you're scrupulous you'll have to stick to insubstantial salads and shelled nuts (cheap, and available in shops and markets).

Drink

Alcoholic drinks are ridiculously cheap in Yugoslavia. **Beer** is sold by the half litre and costs from 20p-£1 depending on the establishment and the area it's in. You may be charged more for export or foreign beers. Local brands are fine.

Wine is invariably drinkable and on occasion good – especially in wine growing areas. In restaurants the house wine is rarely over £1.50 a litre, and even by the bottle it's easy to find wines under £2.50. *Rizling* is Yugoslavia's most famous wine, but I prefer *Babić* (red wine from the coast, and much better than the more common *Plavac*), *Zilvaka* (Mostar's sometimes excellent white wine) and *Zupska* (Serbian red wines). Beware of *Prošek*, sold as wine but not dissimilar to sweet port, and popular all along the coast. *Spricer* (pronounced spritzer), fifty fifty white wine and soda, is an excellent refreshment in hot weather. Buy it by the glass.

Spirits (*rakija*) are common, dangerous and dirt cheap. In supermarkets there are a worrying number of bottles with unreplaceable caps which go for under £1 a litre. The better brands (with screw tops) sell for £2-3. The quality of all spirits varies enormously and can't be determined from the label – price is probably your best indication.

One of the most widely drunk is *Šlivovica*, a dry spirit made from plums. Regional variations are remarkable, with Serbian brands being some of the best. *Maraskino* and *Kruškevac* are sweet liqueurs made from cherries and pears respectively. A Macedonian friend described them as 'drinks for Dutch women' – which they may be, but they're both deceptively strong.

Vinjak is the general name for all of the domestic brandies. It's easier to drink than Šlivovica, but the less good brands give you a really terrible hangover. *Mastika* is the local anis drink, not dissimilar to Turkish Raki or Greek Ouzo. It's most popular in Macedonia. Strongest of all the commercially available spirits is *Lozova*, a plain, addictive drink that comes in 45%, 50% and 55% brands. The locals drink it down in one at breakfast time. Local vodka isn't a patch on anything Russian or Polish.

Friendships, business deals and meetings are all cemented with *rakija*, and it's surprising how often you'll find yourself downing lethal spirits. Be warned that many Yugoslavs distil their own, the strongest and most dangerous of all drinks.

Soft drinks, by comparison, are really limited. Coca Cola is mind-numbingly popular, as are bottles of sweet fizzy orange drinks sometimes served deceptively from non-functioning freezers. In Bosnia you can drink wonderful home made lemonade with your *burek*; in most other places yoghourt is the standard. Fairly pungent mineral water comes in heavy glass bottles which are worth more than the contents – decant them into your water bottles in the shop.

Coffee is widely drunk and is Turkish throughout the country except in Slovenia and along the coast, where Italian espresso is more common. Tea comes in dubious looking bags, but is refreshing with a slice of lemon thrown in.

Communications

Post: Post offices are marked PTT and called *Pošta*. They're open Monday to Saturday 9am to 5pm, with longer hours in cities and for telephones. Staff often speak some French or English and tend towards the helpful. Mail out of Yugoslavia takes anything from three days to three months, but it does arrive in the end. Letters can be even slower than postcards. Parcels are reasonably priced but very very slow. Don't seal them until you've given the cashier time to check you're not posting bombs or contraband. If you send back anything valuable then you may have to pay duty on it when you get home.

If you want mail sent to you have it addressed to Poste Restante, Pošta, town name. It will be delivered to the main post office if there's more than one. If your surname is in capitals or underlined then the letter is more likely to be filed correctly. If there's nothing for you then ask them to look under your Christian name. Incoming post seems to arrive in a week, but I haven't had enough to be sure that this wasn't just a lucky break.

Telephones: Almost all post offices have metered cabins. Insist on dialling direct or you'll be faced with an indefinite wait – and it doesn't take you as long to find out if the phones are functioning. Dial 99 to get out of Yugoslavia and 44 to get into the UK. If you have an engaged tone at this point, start again. If you haven't got through after ten attempts you're advised to come back at another time. In Montenegro it once took me two days to make a call to France; calls to England at the same time were no problem.

Internal calls are more difficult. Last time I was in Dubrovnik it took a tourist office over half an hour to reach their head office in Belgrade. This is apparently worse than average, but don't be surprised if you have to keep trying for ten or fifteen minutes.

Phone boxes are fairly plentiful, but useless for all but local calls – they took 10 and 50 dinar pieces in 1988, at a time when a one minute call to England cost 2,000 dinars (actually very cheap, at 40p). You can call international from your hotel, but this is much more expensive.

Post offices are also the places to go if you need to send a **telegram**, but a quick phone call is often cheaper and more efficient.

Maps and information

The Yugoslav tourist office in London (143 Regent Street, W1, Tel. 01 734 5243) can furnish you with a certain amount of countrywide information including a map, lists of hotels and campsites, and a whole heap of publicity on the various regions. If you allow plenty of time (and a little luck) then more detailed information can be had from the following organisations within Yugoslavia:

Tourist Association of the SFRY, Moše Pijade 8, 11000, BEOGRAD. Tel. (011) 339780

Tourist Association of SR Bosnia and Hercegovinia, Maršala Tita 80, 71000, SARAJEVO. Tel. (071) 533955

Tourist Association of SR Croatia, Amruševa 8, 41000, ZAGREB. Tel. (041) 432612

Tourist Association of SR Macedonia, Maršala Tita 39, 91000, SKOPJE. Tel. (091) 234442

Tourist Association of SR Montenegro, Bulevar Lenjina 2, 81000, TITOGRAD. Tel. (081) 41591

Tourist Association of SR Serbia, Dobrinjska 11, 11000, BEOGRAD. Tel. (011) 645166

Tourist Association of SAP Kosovo, Maršala Tita 25a, 38000, PRIŠTINA. Tel. (038) 22375

Tourist Association of SAP Vojvodina, Maršala Tita 6/VII, 21000, NOVI SAD. Tel. (021) 51663

Tourist Association of SR Slovenia, Miklošićeva cesta 38, 61000, LJUBLJANA. (061) 312087

These offices are the formal headquarters of the tourist associations. Once in the country you are more likely to be using normal information offices which go under a variety of aliases, though all contain the word *Informacije* or *Turistički*.

Travel agents are also a good (and sometimes the only) source of information. The bigger ones are all in competition with one another and are usually helpful. Generalturist, Atlas, Putnik, Kompass and Montenegroturist are the biggest and best known.

For walkers the biggest problem is the paucity of maps. Michelin provide a clear road map (1:1,000,000) and Freytag and Berndt an even better one (1:600,000, with six coastal inserts of 1:275,000), but neither is remotely sufficient for walking.

Some of the national parks are excellently mapped in either 1:25,000 or 1:50,000, but others have either no map or 1:100,000 sketches which are dangerously inaccurate. See individual chapters for more details. Detailed maps are available outside the country for much of Slovenia, but for the most part you'll have to wait until you arrive. This is a pity, because in the 1940s the U.S. army charted the whole country and published a complete series of wonderful 1:25,000 contour maps. I've seen these in Germany, and theoretically they're commercially available, if expensive. Don't even consider buying them – they're strictly illegal in Yugoslavia. I saw a photocopy of one section in a travel agent's office in Macedonia, but it was made clear that even this represented a serious transgression. National security in Yugoslavia is a highly sensitive issue and it's not a good idea to provoke suspicion.

Handicrafts and what to buy

When Rebecca West travelled round Yugoslavia in 1937 she spent a good part of her trip buying antique peasant costumes, while noting that fewer and fewer people were wearing them. This trend has continued unabated to the present, so that traditional clothes are now only worn in the remotest parts of Macedonia, Montenegro and Serbia – and then only by the elderly. Some traditional costumes are also kept on display by the troupes of dancers and folk musicians who tour the luxury hotels, and the shop assistants in the better class department stores.

The young favour denim fanatically, fashions drift along ten years behind Paris and the beautifully hand-embroidered waistcoats and skirts are about as popular as flared trousers back home. Old women still make the original costumes, but the real thing is virtually impossible to find. What's on sale in most resorts is mass produced to fill a tourist need.

The same applies, sadly, to carpets. Under the influence of the Turks, the Bosnians and Serbs became great carpet makers and testimony to their skill can be seen in some of the bigger mosques. Nowadays quality carpets are hard to find, and not significantly cheaper than at home. *Kilims* (patchwork carpets) are increasingly popular, as they are in Turkey, because at £25-100 they fit better into the average tourist's budget. If you know your subject this is one area in which you can still pick up bargains, but you need to know your wool and dyes, which aren't all as natural as you'll be told.

In mountainous areas you'll sometimes see beautiful hand made sweaters for sale. These are of excellent quality, and you shouldn't have to pay more than £10-15 apiece. I'm still kicking myself for not having bought a handful in Montenegro which were under £10.

In Moslem areas there is still a strong emphasis on the hand-crafted, and in street markets and bazaars you can see things being made and then buy them. Most shoes and a disappointing amount of the metalwork can be left in Yugoslavia – the quality simply isn't as good as you'll find elsewhere, or even at home. Some of the brass, beaten copper, silver and gold is, however, very good. Look out for Turkish coffee sets, trays and jewellery. In Sarajevo I recently bought a Turkish coffee maker, a tray, four cup holders and a sugar bowl in brass, and the small china cups to go with it – all for a little under £4.

Some of the best souvenirs are cassettes of Yugoslavian music, a bargain at around £1 a go. Avoiding the really dreadful imitations of the worst of western rock music, you can easily pick up good indigenous pop (the sort of thing you hear on buses), Macedonian folk, Bosnian chants, Serbian dances and Montenegrin *gusla* improvisations. Go into any shop which sells cassettes and get them to play you a selection of local music. It's an odd fact, but the more tacky the cover the better the music tends to be inside.

Behaviour

Minimum impact: All tourists have an effect not just on a country but on its people too. There are unlimited arguments for and against this which don't need to be enumerated here – suffice to say that as someone interested in walking you should consider both the environmental and sociological effects of your visit.

Yugoslavia's environment is in surprisingly good condition. The country boasts with some justification about having the cleanest waters of the Mediterranean, Europe's clearest freshwater lake (Ohrid), some tracts of virgin forest and many rare species of animals and birds. It's in everyone's interests that these should be preserved.

The single biggest danger in Yugoslavia is that of fire. If a forest fire starts in one of the drier areas there's nothing that can be done.

Recently, part of the virgin Peručica forest in Bosnia-Hercegovinia was damaged irreparably by a fire which was probably caused by a cigarette butt. Don't start fires, and even avoid naked flames in areas which don't have supplies of water close to hand.

Litter, by comparison, is a simple question of ugliness. Paper tissues take months to deteriorate, orange peel positively glows, and tin cans always look horrible. Take your litter home with you, and if you also collect any you find along the way then you can feel suitably saintly. If you can't find a toilet on your route then do at least bury your excrement and the paper. There are few sights – or sensations – that are more unpleasant than finding someone else's doings.

Yugoslavia has been affected hugely by tourism, which has brought wealth and an undreamed of standard of living to thousands if not millions of people. However, when you're walking you're more likely to meet one of the majority who haven't directly profited from tourism. There are hundreds of opportunities you have for fostering good relations between foreigners and local people, from showing people what your life is like back home (remember the photographs and postcards) to sharing in a drink or a smoke with chance acquaintances.

On many occasions I've been invited into the homes of people who have virtually nothing, only to be offered the little that they do have. Bring pictures and locally available sweets for the children, and western cigarettes for the adults – I haven't yet met a Yugoslav who doesn't smoke. There's a good argument against giving sweets away to kids in the street, or fostering beggars (both encourage dependence) but in people's homes there's very little else that you can do to return what is an extraordinary level of hospitality.

Photography: Most people in Yugoslavia are used to camera-clicking tourists, but you will still find people in less visited areas who are intimidated by photography. Respect their feelings by asking if they mind before taking a picture. In the majority of cases people are delighted and flattered, but there are exceptions, and market stallholders have been known to take offence – with reason – at being treated like exhibits.

If you're using a long focus or zoom lens then it won't be so obvious that you're taking pictures. Use your discretion. Equally snapshots taken with compact cameras are unlikely to cause offence.

Drugs and Sex: Illegal drugs should be avoided while you're in Yugoslavia. They're available, but the penalties are stiff, and harsher still for smuggling – don't be tempted to carry anything across borders. I was asked to carry a small package out of Ljubljana on the grounds that my bag wouldn't be searched. I declined.

Dress isn't strict, to the extent that Yugoslavia has more official nudism than any other country in Europe, but you will not be allowed to enter churches or active mosques if your knees or upper arms are on show. As you would anywhere, follow the example of local people and you won't go far wrong. Nudity isn't a good idea except on beaches and in places designated for that purpose (marked FKK).

Reading matter isn't usually a problem, but steer clear of material that's pornographic or sensitive to the military (or could be construed as such). I had trouble a few years ago with Germaine Greer's *Female Eunuch*, and failed to persuade the authorities of my good intentions.

Suggested Itineraries

Scenic interest: The Julian Alps (with the bonuses of Lakes Bled and Bohinj, and Yugoslavia's highest mountain, Triglav) lie in Slovenia, the most accessible part of the country. There is enough here alone to occupy you for several months.

For wild karst scenery right on the seashore there's nothing to match the pair of splendid gorges of the Paklenica National Park, which has well marked trails for all grades of walking. Less rugged scenery punctuated by falling water can be found around the Krka falls and the Plitvice lakes, which both outshine the crowds.

Offshore, the islands of Mljet and Lokrum are of exceptional beauty, one with its seawater lake and the other uninhabited and charmingly wooded. Neither would keep you busy for a week, but they're both easily combined with other attractions.

There's little in Europe to compete with the ancient beauty of the Biogradska Gora and Peručica virgin forests, both of which merit a calm week's exploration. Older still are the ancient lakes of Skadar and Ohrid. Skadar remains mysterious and deserted, while Ohrid has the added attractions of superb hillwalking and peerless icons and frescoes. Steeper mountains are spread across the country from Pelister in the south, through Durmitor and the Zelengora up to the Alps in the north.

Monasteries: Yugoslavia's monasteries are spread across the eastern side of the country. The most interesting are in the hills of the Fruška Gora in the north and those hidden away in the wilds of Macedonia, but there are hundreds more to be found throughout Serbia. They are mostly hard to reach by public transport so having a car is a considerable advantage. A trip through Macedonia will allow you to see a representative selection, along with some of the best frescoes.

Wildlife and botany: The Julian Alps offer the best naturalist's view of the country, if only because it's the best maintained and best documented area. Botanists will want to head for the virgin forest of Biogradska Gora, certainly the best example in Europe and one of the most accessible in the world. Rare and interesting plants (numbering a whole range of medicinal herbs) can be found in the hills of the Fruška Gora and on the mountains of southern Macedonia.

Although the country has abundant bears, wolves, wild boar and lynxes these animals shy away from attention and you're unlikely to see them, even when nearby. Bears however can be seen (and, unfortunately, shot at) in Bosnia in the Koprivnica reserve, near Bugojno – apply to the regional tourist board well in advance. Bird life is especially varied on Lakes Prespa and Skadar, and all of the mountain ranges have their share of eagles and hawks.

Transport dependent: All of the walking described in this book can be reached by public transport, but if you have a car then the Kamniške Alps (Slovenia), the Durmitor National Park (Montenegro) and Pelister (Macedonia) are much easier to reach. The easiest places to reach by bus are the Julian Alps, Ohrid, the Paklenica National Park (on the coast) and the Fruška Gora.

My top ten

This list isn't in any special order – I couldn't rate them in order of preference – but represents the ten places I was most impressed with in Yugoslavia.

Ohrid: Monasteries, mountains, the best trout I've ever eaten, frescoes, icons, a brilliant lake and hospitality unlimited.

Triglav: Not just the mountain, but the National Park, the people who befriended me, the preservation of nature, and Lake Bohinj.

Biogradska Gora: The virgin forest.

Lovćen: A mountain with a stunning mausoleum on top, a fitting place to encounter Njegoš, Montenegro's finest poet, warrior and prince bishop.

The Paklenica National Park: A pair of karst gorges running down to the sea, backed by the Velebit massif.

Lokrum: Just off Dubrovnik, a small, uninhabited island nature reserve, complete with butterflies and a ruined monastery.

Sarajevo: Mosques, bazaars and a seedy downtown, all overshadowed by mountains and an assassination.

Durmitor and the Tara Canyon: River deep, mountain high; Partisan memorials, summer pastures and breathtaking views.

Lake Skadar: Mirages across the mudflats.

The Filopivski altar screens: A pair of carved walnut iconostases by the Macedonian brothers – 18 years in the making. See one in Skopje, the other in Sv. Jovan Bigorski, near Debar.

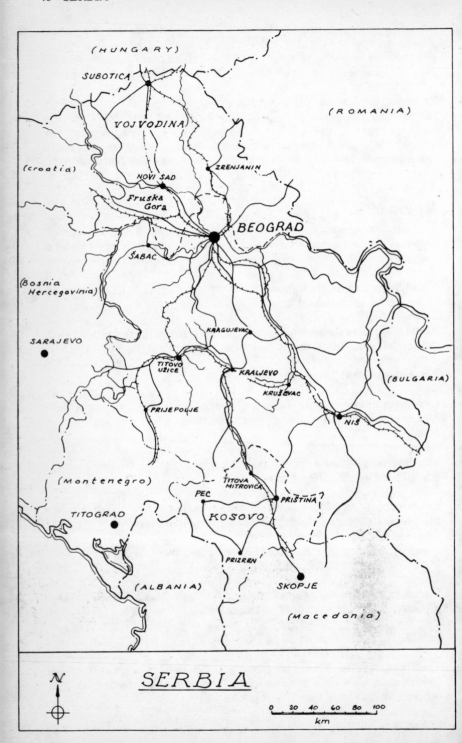

SERBIA

Serbia

Serbia is the largest of Yugoslavia's republics, containing over a third of the population and much of the country's richest agricultural land. Neither as rich as Slovenia nor as poor as Macedonia and Montenegro, it provides a fairly accurate barometer of Yugoslavia's fortunes, and even after decentralisation remains the home of most of the political power. Despite having monasteries by the dozen and some of the most interesting stretches of the Danube and Sava, Serbia remains the least visited republic – most of the tourists I saw were the crowds stranded at Belgrade station trying to catch a train down to Greece or back home.

Brief History: Serbia has always been the key to the Balkans, a kind of frontier between East and West, and the lands were much fought over before being wholly subjugated to the Ottoman Empire from the 14th to the 19th century. After the First World War Serbia provided the inspiration for the first efforts at a united state, and even though these weren't entirely successful (to the extent that King Alexander got assassinated by Croatian separatists) they helped lay the foundations for post war Yugoslavia, under Tito.

What to see One of the republic's most obvious claims to fame is the Danube, which comes through from Hungary and Vojvodina, passing through Belgrade before running along the Romanian border. The last section is the long Djerdap gorge with cliffs up to 300m high, and the river is forced here to a width of just 150m – upstream it's nearly two kilometres wide. It used to rush along, providing one of Europe's most treacherous navigable stretches of water, culminating in a narrow corridor known as the Iron Gates, and it made one of the most spectacular sights in Europe. It has since been dammed, in a joint project with Romania, and its impressiveness now stems as much from the engineering project as the natural wonder of the Iron Gates.

Serbia's second river is the Sava, best seen from the window of an aircraft going to Split or Zagreb. It meanders hugely across a masssive flood plain, and has left large muddy islands where the corners have been cut, shortening the river by kilometres at a time. At ground level it's considerably more prosaic, running across immense dusty wheatfields with almost flat horizons. And the climate here is truly continental; I found the still heat oppressive – and that was in June.

Serbia's biggest attraction is its liberal sprinkling of ancient monasteries set in gentle, often forested, agricultural land. The towns are, for the most part, drab and uninspiring, though Belgrade is home to an excellent fresco museum, and Niš is a must for the macabre.

Serbia has three **national parks**. The first of these, Djerdap, is the stretch of the Danube running up to the Iron Gates. Contact tourist information in London or Belgrade for more information. Both of the other national parks are in the more mountainous regions to the south.

The Kopaonik National Park is an interesting sub-alpine region, based around a high plateau at 1700m. It's situated about 30km northeast of Novi Pazar, near the town of Raška, which is where you'll find the park's information office. The area is in the process of being developed as an important ski station, and it may soon be a popular resort. For the moment it's still unspoiled.

The other mountainous national park is the Tara (not to be confused with the Tara canyon in Montenegro). This park is based around Mt. Tara, and contains an attractive portion of the Drina river gorge just north of Višegrad in Bosnia Hercegovinia. The best way of seeing the park is probably on one of the boats running downstream from Višegrad, but there are also some points in the fairly dense forests that can be reached on foot. The park management office (in Bajina Bašta, 25km northwest of Titovo Užice) will provide you with further information.

Unfortunately neither park is easily accessible on public transport, though services are said to run in July and August. Otherwise you'll have to rely on your own transport.

BELGRADE (BEOGRAD)

Strategically situated on the high ground above the impressive confluence of the Sava and the Danube, Belgrade must nonetheless be one of Europe's greyest and least attractive capitals. From 441, when it was looted and burned down by the Huns, until 1941, when the Germans bombed the city to destruction, its history has been one invasion, demolition and rebuilding after another. It has had over thirty changes of proprietor, but today there is almost nothing left standing in this rapidly expanding city that predates the 19th century. Nonetheless, Belgrade has its attractions, and if you're on your way to Greece, Bulgaria, Romania or Hungary then the chances are that you'll be stopping off here at some time.

The best place from which to see Belgrade is the Kalemegdan fortress, now a large, airy park above the confluence of the city's rivers. Since pre-Roman times this was the strategic point which held control of the Balkans, though these days the only remains are from an Austrian fortress.

The park is a refreshing break from the heat and dust of the city, and is home to a number of interesting statues, including the one you'll see on all the brochures, the Monument to the Victor, by Ivan Meštrović. This provocative nude was originally to have been placed downtown, but local prudery had him put up here, facing modestly away from the onlookers. You can still see the other two symbols – the falcon representing liberty, and the sword, Yugoslavia's intention to defend itself.

Also look out for Meštrović's fairly excessive Monument of Gratitude to France – though personally I prefer a small fountain nearby, with a man dramatically strangling a serpent. At the top of the park there's a large military museum, which is especially interesting for its exhibits on the Partisans, including some really chilling black and white photographs of defiant young men just minutes before their deaths.

In town, quite close to the park, there's a first class fresco museum. This contains excellent reproductions from all of the major monasteries in Yugoslavia, with the added advantage that you can see them here in close-up. It's best to see this before going to the monasteries, since it provides a clear perspective on the development of the art, and also provides the incentive to go and see them *in situ* – an incentive you'll need as the monasteries are sometimes difficult to reach, even with your own transport.

The other essential visit if you've time to spare in Belgrade is to the National Museum. This provides a complete history of this part of the Balkans, and though it's not the world class collection that's claimed, there are nonetheless enough top quality artefacts for even the most demanding. These include some beautiful gold jewellery and a splendidly patrician head of the Roman Emperor Constantine. Upstairs there's a very mixed collection of art ranging from minor Flemish masters to a handful of fine Impressionists and a couple of interesting works by Utrillo and Picasso.

Midway between Kalemegdan and the thriving commercial centre is the old quarter of Skadarlija, latterly the centre of cultural and artistic life, and with a reputation for being the Belgrade equivalent of Montmartre. This is true, at least to the extent that, as in Montmartre, you'll now find that most of the 'atmosphere' is being generated artificially for the benefit of tourists. But it's still worth a visit, if only because it's arguably the most animated part of the capital.

Practical Information: The chances are that you'll arrive near the train station – it's the most convenient of the three stops the airport bus makes, and the bus station is also just down the road. One of the train station counters acts as an impermanent looking tourist information office (it's been this way for at least five years) and will provide you with a map and point out where things are – should you go to the trouble of asking. The window next door will change cash as well as booking couchettes. Note that banks in Belgrade are incredibly slow at cashing cheques or changing money: use travel agencies instead.

The Kalemegdan fortress is only about fifteen minutes from here on foot; the town centre's even closer, up the hill in front of the station. If you want to dispose of your luggage, don't be tempted to use the office in the train station – you may be able to leave it there easily enough, but I once missed a train while waiting to recover a bag. Across the road from the station there's a Putnik left luggage office which is problem free, though they do take random half hour breaks.

Accommodation in Belgrade is something of a hassle. The cheapest and perhaps simplest option is to camp at the Koštunjak site (Kneza Višeslava 17, bus 53 then five minute walk; open all year round), though apparently the restaurant there plays music loud and late into the night. Over in Novi Beograd the Nacional campsite (Bežanijska Kosa 1a, bus 601; open May to September) is even further away.

Some private rooms are handled by the Lasta Travel office (Trg Bratstva i jedinstva 1a) across from the station. They're open from 7am to 8pm daily (not Sunday), and if you can face their outright rudeness they'll find you a room for upwards of £14. In theory you may be offered a private room if you look hopeful at the station, but after four fruitless visits I'm beginning to doubt it.

Hotels in Belgrade are either expensive or very expensive. The five C class hotels are usually full, and even in these you should expect to pay at least £25 for a double with no bath; £17 for a single. The Hotel Astoria, right across the square from the station (Milovana Milovanovića 1, Tel (011) 645422), is certainly the best located, but understandably enough it's usually full.

Food, as a pleasant contrast, is available in literally hundreds of small and reasonably priced restaurants and snack bars. Menus tend towards the spiced and the Turkish, but you can find most other Balkan cuisines here too. In many of the cheaper places you have to pay and then take the ticket to the person serving – this means finding out how much the dish that you want costs and then explaining this to the cashier, sometimes a stimulating challenge. Note that most of the restaurants in Skadarlija are as overpriced as you'd expect.

Belgrade is very evidently the shopping capital of Yugoslavia, and you can find some things here, such as English newspapers, that are virtually unavailable in the rest of the country. Try the Prosveta bookshop and the kiosk outside the Hotel Moskva.

Public transport is a comprehensive (if crowded) mixture of trams and buses, which run more or less regularly from 5am to midnight. A whole system of underpasses and subterranean shopping centres testify to an ambitious scheme for a Metro, but it doesn't look as if it's going to be ready imminently. Taxis queue up in droves outside the station, where you'll also find a JAT bus stop – they leave every half hour or so for the airport, half an hour away.

However you're planning to leave Belgrade, you should think about it ahead. Buy bus tickets and make reservations at least two days ahead if you can, and don't lose the *jeton* which lets you into the area the buses leave from. Train tickets can be bought from travel agencies and this saves a long wait at the station.

Finally, Belgrade trains, in my experience, invariably leave on time and arrive late. This means that if you allow say three hours to change trains here then the chances are you'll miss your connection. This has happened to me three times – I wish you better luck.

Serbian Monasteries

The Serbian Orthodox movement in the Middle Ages led to the building of many monasteries and monastic churches, and their architecture and decoration is quite distinct from the other branches of the Orthodox church, let alone the rest of Christianity. Many of these monasteries and their frescoes have survived (against the odds – four centuries of Turkish domination didn't do much to protect them), and though they are almost universally difficult to reach without your own transport, the effort is well worth it.

The best preparation for the churches is a visit to the Fresco Gallery in Belgrade, which contains excellent copies of frescoes from all of the best known monasteries. As well as putting the movement into perspective, this distinguishes between the different schools, and also allows you to choose which churches to visit.

The surviving Serbian Orthodox monastic churches considerably outreach today's Serbian borders, and extend into Macedonia, Montenegro and parts of Bosnia. They were built from the 12th to the 14th centuries, usually with the patronage of a local king or noble, and there are nearly three hundred left.

Architecturally they are different from Western churches, having no nave and choir but instead a central plan, often domed. An altar screen (iconostasis) separates the clergy from the congregation, creating an air of mystery as to what's going on behind. This is enhanced by the absence of seats. Until the Middle Ages they were decorated with mosaics of formalised classical scenes.

The techniques of fresco painting made mosaics redundant – frescoes were quicker, cheaper, and nearly as durable. After plastering the walls several times a sketch would be drawn on the penultimate layer. The final layer was then added in small patches, with liquid pigments being brushed onto the wet plaster, causing a fusion of the picture with the fabric of the wall. The pigments had to be applied quickly and definitively – once dry there was no way the artist could make alterations without adding a further layer of plaster. Just occasionally you can see where this has been done, most notably in the apse of the Cathedral of St. Sophia in Ohrid.

The Serbian Orthodox churches fall into three distinct categories, the Raška, Central Serbian (or Macedonian) and Morava schools. The Raška school is clearly dated from the foundation of the Serbian state in 1190, in opposition to expanding Byzantium. Of the three the style is the most independent, owing as much to Romanesque architecture as to Constantinople. The frescoes are rigidly formal, with traditional compositions and still rather than moving compositions. Some of the better known examples (completion dates in brackets) include Studenica (1209), Mileševa (1237), Morača (1252), Peć (1263) and Sopočani (1265).

The Central Serbian school monasteries were built from the end of the 13th century until the middle of the 14th. The style is markedly more Eastern, with the traditional cruciform shape being abandoned for a cross inside a rectangle. The external sculptures and reliefs from nature which characterised the Raška school were also jettisoned, and a more Eastern effect was created by the use of alternate dark and light stone, creating horizontal stripes. Inside, the lives of the saints and local heroes were incorporated into the frescoes along with the more formal subjects, and so the emphasis shifted to storytelling instead of divine stillness. Churches of the Central Serbian school include Sv. Kliment in Ohrid (1295), several churches in Prizren (c.1307) and Lesnovo (1349).

After the Turks rushed into the Balkans most monasteries were abandoned, but for a while the Morava valley was secure, and during the 14th and early 15th century a new style developed. More a hybrid of the previous two than anything else, the Morava school was nonetheless distinctive in being the first style to use brick as well as stone. Typical examples of the Morava school are Ravanica (1381), Kalenić (1413) and Ljubostinja (1405).

The monastic churches almost all have one thing in common – they are set in remote wildernesses. Without your own transport it's often difficult and occasionally impossible to visit them. Notable exceptions are the clutch in and around Ohrid in Macedonia, and Mileševa near Prijepolje. Some of the monasteries in the Fruška Gora (see *Vojvodina*, p.50) are also accessible to walkers in the area.

Niš

The first time I came to Niš I found it so depressing that I left again the same day. The second time I wasn't so lucky, and was obliged to stay in one of the gloomy and expensive hotels before I could catch a train out. Should you be stuck here, there are things to do and see, despite the air of grey, grim abandonment this industrial city carries with it.

Most famous of these is the grisly Ćele Kula (tower of skulls), just over 3km out of town on the road to Dimitrovgrad. In 1809 the members of an uprising against the Turks found themselves cornered here, so, preferring death to dishonour in a characteristically Slavic fashion, their leader lit their gunpowder barrels, killing himself and all his men – as well as a good many Turks – in the process. The Turks had the heads stuffed and sent over a thousand of them off to Constantinople. This still left them with a largish pile of skulls, so they built a five sided tower with each containing 14 rows of 17 skulls (how

Lamartine made the total 15,000 I'll never know). Most of the skulls have since been removed by macabre souvenir hunters, but there are enough left to worry most visitors.

Niš's other 'attraction' is, if anything, even more upsetting. Crveni Krst was a transit concentration camp during the Second World War, with the way out leading either to the death camps or to immediate execution on the hill of Bubanj out of town. Huge numbers of people passed through here, and it's known that at least 12,000 were shot on Bubanj in a last ditch effort by the Fascists to cover their tracks. On 12th February 1942 nearly 200 prisoners tried to escape over the wall, and more than 100 did succeed – but the rest were shot down. You can still see the scars on the wall. The camp is a terrible place, empty now save for faded pictures of the occupants. It's a salutary reminder.

Practical Information: The bus station is tucked away behind the fortress, in the town centre more or less, but the train station is a bus ride away. Accommodation is a disaster, with the town having no private rooms and only expensive class A or B hotels. Apparently the town of Niška Banja, 8km towards Dimitrovgrad, has both private rooms and a campsite, but I didn't want to risk the possibility of being stuck in Niš for a second day, so I can't verify this. I stayed at the Partizan hotel, and paid £22 for the privilege. It's the cheapest hotel in town.

Titovo Užice

The modern, businesslike town of Titovo Užice is an important Serbian transport hub, being on the main Belgrade-Titograd-Bar railway, and also on the main road from Niš to Sarajevo. The bus and train stations are right next to one another, so you may not need to go into the town at all, but if you're lucky you'll have a few hours to kill, since there's a quite exceptional museum here; if you're unlucky you'll have to spend the night – and your only option is the Hotel Palas, breathtakingly expensive at £29.

In the autumn of 1941 the Partisans rose up in Užice and declared the first free republic, and Tito created a vital headquarters here, complete with a Munitions factory and printing presses. Inevitably, the Germans took offence at this, and 67 days after the uprising retook the city, killing the remaining Partisans to the last man. It was the first, and one of the most serious defeats of the whole war.

The museum to the events of that autumn is simply called Uprising 1941 (Ustanske 1941), which details what happened, as well as presenting a complete picture of how the Partisans lived and worked. It's about ten minutes walk from the bus station, across the river and turn right after one block – then keep going until you reach it. Although the museum's captions are all in Serbo-Croat there's an English booklet on sale at the entrance, which explains things pretty clearly.

This was one of the first places in Yugoslavia where the sheer bravery and courage of the Partisans was brought home to me. There are photographs here of horrific reprisals, including a whole row of civilians roughly strung up, still wearing their hats, and next to this a young Partisan with frighteningly defiant eyes being tied to a tree by a German soldier. The museum also has a collection of Partisan's weapons, including handmade rifles and pitchforks. The surgical instruments they made for themselves look absurdly inadequate. Tito's office here is preserved as it was, an austere room with blacked out windows, a single chair, desk, inkwell, map and field telephone, and in the corner a rifle rack.

Outside there's a large, disturbing, concrete sculpture of a man falling onto three spikes, and the fence running along here is made of guns, bombs and a single German helmet. Behind all this is the Munitions factory, a large arched concrete hall full of echoes. The original lighting is still here – two wires and light bulbs slung between them – and the broken machines that were used to make bombs and bullets are left here in unmarked rows. It's a very frightening place, particularly alone on a Sunday morning.

If you're in Titovo Užice for the evening then head for the notional town centre, Partizan Trg, where you'll find a greatcoated Tito frowning across the square and most of the town's entertainments. There's a cinema which seemed to be showing excellent films next week and last week but four varieties of pornography and violence just now, and a theatre up in the corner which puts on musicals. I didn't get as far as eating out here, but there didn't seem to be any shortage of restaurants should you want to do so.

Prijepolje

The small town of Prijepolje wouldn't normally get a mention – it's a small, provincial, Turkish looking town, with a fairly ordinary church and mosque side by side – but it is the best place from which to visit the monastery at Mileševa, one of the best in the whole country.

Prijepolje is conveniently situated on the Belgrade-Bar railway, but there are several stops marked Prijepolje, so be sure to alight at the right one. It's also on the Titograd-Belgrade highway, so reaching it by bus is no problem. Unfortunately neither station has a left luggage office, so you'll have to take your bags to Mileševa with you. From either station find your way across the river on the perilous suspension bridge and you're in the town centre.

The post office by the bridge will change money; for some reason the bank here won't. Tourist information is decidedly sketchy but should you need to stay then your only real choice anyway is the Hotel Mileševa, a relative bargain at £17 for a double with bath. Running parallel to the river is the main street, at the northern end of which you'll find the church, the mosque and an excellent village-hall sized restaurant. Food seems to be available at all hours, and they're just as happy if you do nothing but drink beer while you're waiting for the rain to ease off.

The monastery is situated about 6km east of Prijepolje, on the main road to Sjenica and Novi Pazar. Carrying your bag it takes about an hour and a half to get there. There are also something like four buses a day along this road, so you may be able to cut out at least half of the journey. When you get there you'll see a spectacular castle on the other side of the river: I wanted to climb up to it, but time suggested otherwise.

Since the monastery was only restored during the last century, the frescoes inside were exposed to the elements for well over two hundred years, and it's extraordinary that it's been possible to restore them to their present condition. Look carefully above the familiar angel at the tomb, and you'll see an Annunciation, one of the finest frescoes in Yugoslavia. If you've been to the fresco museum in Belgrade this one ought to be especially familiar.

VOJVODINA

For the most part Vojvodina, the northern autonomous province of
Serbia, is entirely flat, stretching from the Danube up to the
Hungarian border in an immense fastness, only broken by the river
Tisa, itself nothing to write home about. But south of the Danube the
monotonous landscape is relieved by the rolling hills of the Fruška
Gora, which rise up to above 500m and contain some fine possibilities
for walking and a whole clutch of interesting monasteries.

The area is home to the widest racial mix in Yugoslavia, numbering
Hungarians, Romanians, Swabians and Slovaks among its twenty or so
minorities. Being an autonomous province each has the right to
education in its national language, and the culture here is
correspondingly more diverse than in the rest of the country.

Vojvodina grows enough grain on its fertile plains to feed the whole
country, and is one of the most prosperous regions – this is evident in
the busy cities of Novi Sad and Subotica, as well as in the more modest
towns and villages scattered across the Pannonian plain. Tourism is
still fairly low key, though a number of people stop off here on their
way to and from Hungary – Novi Sad is on the main line from
Budapest to Belgrade.

Novi Sad

Vojvodina's capital is a bustling and cosmopolitan city with a
population rapidly approaching a quarter of a million. Once the
picture of Austro-Hungarian elegance (though not the 'Serbian
Athens' it's been dubbed), Novi Sad is now thoroughly modernised
with only the old centre and the fortress across the river to remind you
of its grand past.

Trains and buses will deposit you a little way from the centre – catch
a number 8 bus from outside the train station to the centre of town. A
friendly tourist information office at Dunavska 27 (near the river) will
provide you with a town plan and can arrange accommodation. But be
warned that private rooms tend towards the suburbs while the city's
hotels are uniformly expensive. If you have a tent then camp at the
Ribarsko Ostrvo site, on the peninsula of the same name; it has a
sandy beach, though when you see the grubby barges cruising upriver
you may be less tempted by a dip.

The old town centre is attractive enough, with solid baroque the
prevailing flavour, but the city's most interesting sight is probably the
Matica Srpske Gallery, a collection of interesting and varied art from
the region.

Across the river is the fortress of Petrovaradin, one of the strongest
defensive positions on the Danube. Originally intended to be the last
ditch defensive stronghold of the Austrians against the Turks, it took
the best part of a century to build, and by the time it was completed it
was redundant. It never saw defensive action and was only used in
earnest by a group of upstart Hungarians who shelled two thirds of

Novi Sad to destruction from here in 1848. The fortress was built to a grandiose French design and has no less than four underground levels, containing over 15km of tunnels and some 18,000 defensive loopholes. An irregular tour leads through some of the passages and it's well worth tagging along. Up above ground there's a smartish restaurant and bar; the price includes the excellent view across to Novi Sad.

Eight kilometres south of Petrovaradin is the historical town of **Sremski Karlovci**. This became the seat of the Serbian Orthodox Church after the signing of the 1699 treaty in which the Turks gave up a large part of their empire, and still contains the Patriarchal Palace, considered by some to be Vojvodina's grandest building – though not Rebecca West, who mentioned that apart from the conference room she found the interior 'faintly bizarre and sometimes not that faintly'. She also summed up her description of the outside with the comment that 'there is a suggestion, in fact, of every kind of bad taste known to Western civilization'; vitriolic stuff, even for her. Sremski Karlovci is the best place from which to explore the Fruška Gora, not least because the national park office is situated here.

Subotica

Vojvodina's second city (pop. 150,000) has little to recommend it, though tours could be laid on to the gaudy town hall as an object lesson in excess. Situated just 11km from the Hungarian border, it's not surprising that the population and first language are Hungarian. In town don't miss the exterior of the archaelogical museum, if anything even wilder than the town hall.

Should you be stuck here (and there's no good reason why you should be – trains leave for Budapest, Novi Sad and Belgrade, and frequent buses head south) then go 8km out of town on one of the regular buses to Lake Palić. Palić isn't exactly breathtaking, but it has a campsite and makes for a pleasant dip. It's also a considerable improvement on Subotica.

The Fruška Gora

As pretty as they are unexpected, the hills of the Fruška Gora rise out of the Pannonian plain up to a height of 539m (Crveni Čot) and stretch on an east-west axis for nearly 80km. Much of the area is now a national park, and the hills are rich in medicinal herbs (some 700 varieties), forests (Europe's greatest concentration of lime trees) and wildlife (wild boar, mouflon, marten etc.). Some very drinkable wines and over a dozen monasteries complete the attractions.

If you're planning to walk in the Fruška Gora then go to the National Park Office in Sremski Karlovci, a short bus ride out of Novi Sad. They will suggest various itineraries and should be able to furnish you with maps and other information. The walking is less strenuous than in Yugoslavia's mountains, but none the less picturesque for it. Unfortunately I only had time to visit two of the monasteries: Vrdnik and Krušedol.

For the better part of three centuries **Vrdnik** was home to Serbia's most treasured mortal remains – those of Prince Lazar (of Kosovo fame). In 1687 they were moved here by the monks of Ravenica, who then upgraded the existing monastery. When Rebecca West passed by in 1937 she shook Lazar's hand, something you won't be able to do, even if you go to the Orthodox cathedral in Belgrade, his current resting place – the Partisans shifted the body there to avoid its fall into Uštase hands. These days the monastery is an asylum and hospital; visit the rather charming church, completed in 1811, which sports a fine iconostasis.

Krušedol, not far away, was founded in the 16th century, but the rather crowded frescoes mostly date from the 18th and later. Its recent history is much more gloomy: the monastery was used by the Uštase fascists during the last war as a place for torturing and executing Partisans.

If you want to see a selection of the monasteries without too much effort this can be done by going on one of the regular and well organised excursions from Novi Sad or Belgrade. Ask at any travel agent in either city. On the other hand if you're walking in the Fruška Gora you can combine this with visits to another half dozen of the more inaccessible monasteries.

KOSOVO

The autonomous province of Kosovo covers the southwestern corner of Serbia. Until the 14th century it was one of the most important parts of the Balkans, spawning Serbia's great dynasties and a spate of monastery building which has never been equalled. But in 1389 Lazar lost the critical battle against the Turks at Kosovo Polje (the field of Kosovo), and the little that was left of the Serbian peoples and culture headed north. Shifting Albanians filled the vacuum, and even now nearly 80% of Kosovo's population is Albanian.

The area remains the poorest in Yugoslavia, despite massive cash injections from central government. It has also been fraught with political troubles, arising from its status as an autonomous province rather than a full federated republic. Inside Kosovo the argument runs that the area should have the same rights as neighbouring Montenegro and Macedonia. Outside, the feeling is that given full republic status Kosovo would secede from Yugoslavia and join Albania, a bad precedent for the country as a whole.

In 1968 serious rioting led to an increase in local rights, most important of which was the recognition of Albanian and Turkish as official languages, equal to Serbo-Croat. Kosovo now has Albanian media, an Albanian university and bi-lingual signs. But in 1981 further riots broke out, and this time the army was sent in to quell them, in direct conflict with Yugoslavia's policy of minimal state intervention.

The latest problems (in 1988) have been caused by rioting Serbs in the province complaining of unfair discrimination by the Albanian majority. With massive support from Serbia on one side and centuries of only recently ended repression of the Albanians on the other, the situation remains understandably tense.

Over 400 of Kosovo's dissidents are still in prison, and there is often a palpable air of resentment and hostility in the province, most notably manifested in a contradictory air of abruptness to strangers and absolute hospitality to guests. It's likely to remain a Yugoslav trouble spot, not least because the very name of Kosovo signifies the battle that ended Serbian independence for the best part of five centuries – Serbia is unlikely to risk giving this up.

Kosovo is also the region of Yugoslavia least visited by foreigners, and there are few concessions made to tourism here. Private rooms seem non-existent, campsites are sparse, public transport is sporadic and information is frequently ambiguous or inaccurate. A trip here can be quite hard work, but is compensated by some of the finest of the Serbian monasteries and the most generous of Yugoslavia's many hospitable peoples.

Geographically Kosovo is centred on a large and fairly uninteresting plain, but is fringed by mountains on its Albanian, Montenegrin, Serbian and Macedonian borders. The Šar Planina range, with summits up to 2748m, is a superb area for walking, but suffers from a frustrating lack of publicly available information.

Priština

Kosovo's grubby capital isn't the sort of place you'd stop in by choice. If you're arriving on a long distance bus you'll be dropped unceremoniously at an anonymous bus stop on the main road some way out of town; from here there are spectacular views of Priština's homogeneous grey city blocks rising from the plain.

A closer inspection reveals that the uncompromising modernity of the city conceals a level of poverty and inefficiency that I didn't see anywhere else in Yugoslavia. Kosovo's huge subsidies must have been spent on these concrete showpieces, and they can't be of much help to ordinary people. Even in the better hotels and banks the quality is only surface deep, with a dismaying lack of maintenance leaving even the newest buildings looking cracked and decayed. Behind the new facades Priština has an old town with shacks and shanties as convincing as anything you'll see in Turkey – as are the appalling living conditions. The Moslem faith and their mosques are in decline too, and I found the decrepit air of the place at best depressing.

Practical Information: Accommodation is something of a problem, with private rooms being non-existent, and the hotels all fairly expensive for what you get. I avoided the issue by arriving in the morning and leaving in the evening. Food, by contrast, is cheap and plentiful. The old town is littered with places not unlike soup kitchens where you can get nourishing bowls of stew which don't bear too thorough an investigation... More traditional grills and *bife*s are also thick on the ground. Your best source of tourist information is one of the travel agents – there doesn't seem to be a more formal body. If you're in town then don't miss the *corso*, which is good, probably by default: there isn't much else to do here.

The real reason for a trip to Priština is that it's only a 10km bus ride from one of the very best Serbian monasteries. Gračanica is an excellent example of the Raška school, with five domes rising in a pyramid above the Greek cross plan. Inside are a series of truly exceptional frescoes, dating from 1321: late medieval comic book realism, if ever I saw it.

If you're back from Gračanica in time I'd recommend leaving Priština on the next bus, and heading somewhere less gloomy, like Prizren or Peć.

Peć

In the northwestern corner of Kosovo, near the entrance to the Rugovo gorge (one of the more spectacular routes into Montenegro) lies the town of Peć. At first sight it's a run down place which looks as if it'll stay that way. Second and subsequent impressions cast it in a better light, and a fine day can work wonders. And the Turkish habit of diverting water to run freely through the town makes for a fresh and clean atmosphere – if incredibly muddy pavements. If you can make it here on a Saturday then you'll see the brilliant market, at which some of the better genuine crafts of the country are sold by peasants in a marvellous assortment of costumes, ranging from traditional Albanian to almost prim Catholic.

Unlikely as it may seem now, Peć was once of European importance. When Hungarian pressure built up in the north, in the 13th century, the seat of the Serbian church was moved here. Unfortunately all that remains of the patriarchate now is three churches 2km west of town, but these are well worth a visit for their original frescoes and a fine treasury.

If you take a bus to the village of **Dečani**, 10km south of Peć, you're within walking distance of the famous monastery of the same name. This is situated 3km west of the village, on the road to Belaje, and contains some of the best unrestored frescoes in the country, dating from 1348. Apparently the monastery escaped the usual Turkish conversion job when an imam checking out the possibilities was killed by a piece of falling masonry here – an appealing story, if not for the imam. The frescoes are beautifully bright, and detail stories from the golden age of Serbia, when kings were real kings etc... The church is particularly unusual in that both Moslems and Christians come to the tomb of the founder here for its restorative powers.

Accommodation in the area is available in the monastery dormitory, or rather more conventionally in the motel a few hundred metres upstream, which I'm told also has camping possibilities.

Prizren

Just 18km from Albania is Prizren, home to Turks, Albanians, Catholics and Dervishes. Shabby, but endearingly so, the town is as diverse as anything in Bosnia, and even goes so far as boasting Turkish as its first language and Albanian as its second – with Serbo-Croat coming a rather lame third. Its Wednesday market is excellent, with people coming in from miles around with their wares.

The town's other attractions include the walk up 100m above the town to the fortress, from which there are fine views across the surrounding area, and a couple of rather battered mosques, but the main pull is the church of Bogorodica Ljeviška. Its frescoes must once have been of the first order, but when redecorating the Turks gouged out chunks of the existing wall so that the fresh plaster would hold. The restored and somewhat frustrating result is a mess of white scars on the walls, though they nonetheless merit a visit.

If you're in the area on 6th May make an effort to go and see the Dervishes do their stuff at their annual festival. This includes ritual singing and chanting to the point where they can put pins through their skin, apparently without pain or drawing blood. Contrary to public opinion the Dervishes are a quiet peace-loving people who have the festival as a way of letting out their unhealthy aggression in a controlled way. Catch them if you can.

The Šara National Park

Situated on the northern slopes of the Šar Planina mountains, and ranging in altitude from 1000m to 2640m, the Šara National Park offers superb walking in a virtually untouristed area. Because of this it's difficult to find precise information, even when you're there. The ski station in the National Park boasts a hotel at 1750m, but they didn't have a map or any other specific information. Back in Belgrade I discovered that the area is home to unusual alpine roses, white pines, mountain yews, lynxes, bears and mountain goats. With a good map the park would rank amongst the best in the country

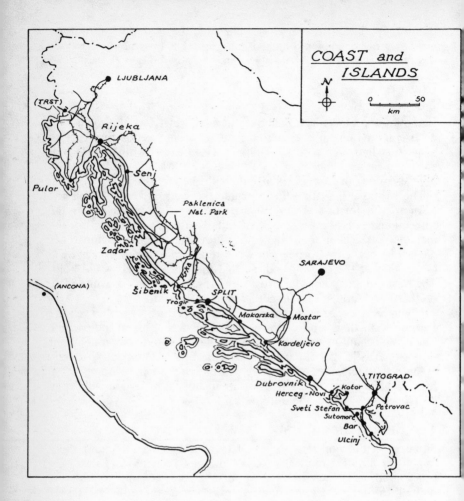

COAST and
ISLANDS

N

0   50
km

LJUBLJANA

(TRST)

Rijeka

Senj

Pular

Paklenica
Nat. Park

Zadar

SARAJEVO

(ANCONA)

Šibenik

SPLIT

Trogir

Makarska

Mostar

Kardeljevo

Dubrovnik

Kotor

TITOGRAD

Herceg - Novi

Sveti Stefan

Sutomore

Petrovac

Bar

Ulcinj

The Coast and Islands

Although four of the six republics have access to the sea, mountains separate the coast culturally and geographically from the rest of the country – and the thousand or so islands are simply the peaks of submerged parallel ranges. Until recently the only effective way of travelling along the coast was by boat, but the pan-Adriatic highway, finished in 1965, has changed all that.

The coastline is over 2000km long (6116km including the islands), but only 628km as the crow flies (1035 by road). It is home to over 200 resorts and is visited by well over 10,000,000 tourists annually, most of whom come for the sun and sea alone. (The sea, incidentally, is wonderful along the Adriatic – 12°C in February, 26°C in August and cleaner than anywhere else in the Mediterranean.) Roughly speaking the coast is less crowded from north to south, but Dubrovnik and Budva are notable exceptions.

Croatia has the lion's share of the coast, with Bosnia Hercevinia having just 10km at Kardeljevo, Slovenia a little more, near Trieste, and Montenegro extending from Hercog Novi southwards.

ISTRIA

Of a heavily visited coast, Istria, the northwestern peninsula, is by far the most touristed. It holds no great appeal for me, mainly because of the crowds, which even by Mediterranean standards seem excessive. Although the interior is wooded and hilly, with a few well-preserved medieval villages, the peace tends to be shattered irreparably by busloads of excursioners. Admittedly the coast does have many picturesque coves, Venetian towns and Roman ruins, but these can all be found without the crowds in other parts of the country.

Working round the peninsula anti-clockwise, the first town after the Italian border is **Koper**. Italian until 1944 and not entirely Yugoslav until 1954, the town still has a good proportion of Italian speakers and the architecture of the old town (thrown into sharp relief by the concrete behind) is wholly Venetian. **Piran**, although smaller, has a similar glut of modern expansion overshadowing its old town, while **Novigrad**, with its pleasant concrete beaches, heralds the start of one of the busiest stretches of coast I've ever seen.

Poreč is now the most touristed resort in Istria, and is at the heart of a series of hotel complexes, autocamps and campsites that left me

The Roman amphitheatre in Pula. (Photo: Janet Cross.)

dizzy. Just down the coast is Europe's largest naturist resort, at **Koversada**, near Vrsar. It can cater for a staggering 12,000 nudists, but book soon if you want to go – incredible though it may seem it's full all summer long.

Parts of the coast from **Rovinj** to Pula are inaccessible by road, which means that if you make the effort to get there you might just avoid the crowds.

Offshore are the beautiful **Brioni** islands, made famous by Tito – he lived there from 1949 until his death. In 1984 they were declared a national park, and though not worth a long detour, visit them if you're near Pula. The easiest way of seeing them is on a daytrip (from Pula), though the first century ruins, an old basilica and a 1,600 year old olive tree are more attractive if you see them independently.

Pula has a wonderfully preserved Roman amphitheatre (used for concerts, and film screenings during the crowd-pulling film festival in July) along with another half dozen Roman ruins worth visiting. It also has a large industrialised port.

From Pula to the concrete resort of **Rabac**, near Labin, the Istrian coast is at its least visited. In many places cliffs make it literally inaccessible, though occasional footpaths do lead down to remote coves. There is little or no public transport here, and, as yet, no signs of development. By contrast the coast is very crowded from Labin to Rijeka, with the busiest spot being Opatija. Now more nouveau-riche than chic, the town was the first major resort in Yugoslavia, fashionable in the 1890's with well-heeled Austrians. If you're here and have transport take the old road (not the tunnel) towards Pazin, stop at the Učka Pension and walk from here to the top of the mountain (1394m) – it takes about two hours round trip, and gives you an excellent view over the islands of the Kvarner Bay.

A last word of warning about Istria: except in Pula, *all* accommodation is full from late June until mid-September. That includes campsites, autocamps, private rooms and hotels. This makes spontaneous summer visits nearly impossible, though Pula does have rooms to spare and isn't that expensive.

RIJEKA

The busy industrial town and seaport of Rijeka (Fiume until 1945 – both names mean river) hardly sounds attractive, but as the major transport hub of the northern coastline it still draws large numbers of visitors. Few remember now that between the wars the Italian border ran through the middle of the city, the result of the hot-headed writer d'Annunzio persuading Italians to invade and capture it.

If you're stuck here wander up the 500 odd steps to Trsat castle for a fine view across the bay to Cres. Nearby is the church of Our Lady of Loreto, where Mary and Joseph's house stopped off (it's claimed) for three years on its way to Loreto in Italy. Despite the dubious story it's a moving place, and well worth the visit. Back down in the town, if your boat's still not ready to go, take in the 13th century cathedral and the Church of Sv. Vid from 1631.

The train station, bus station and ferry terminal are stretched along a 1km stretch of the front, and travel agents along here can find you a private room if you need to stay. Buses from Rijeka go to most points in Yugoslavia, trains run to Ljubljana, Zagreb and points onward, ferries run to the islands in the Kvarner Bay and flights connect to all domestic and many international destinations.

THE ISLANDS OF KVARNER BAY

The four largest islands of Kvarner Bay (Krk, Cres, Lošinj and Rab) are well known and fairly heavily visited. Apart from Krk, which has a bridge connecting it to the mainland, they are served by ferry and hydrofoil from Rijeka. They can also be reached from Senj, further down the coast.

Krk is the largest and busiest of the four islands, home to industry as well as tourists. The southern end is nonetheless very attractive, and if you want to see this then the boat from Senj to Baška is your best bet – you can also, conveniently, catch a boat to Rab from here. Baška has a long beach. There are excellent stark mountains nearly 500m high to the north of the town, and these are virtually unpopulated. If you go into them take plenty of water: there is almost none there.

Cres and **Lošinj** are two islands separated only by a man-made channel. Both are much less busy than Krk, which isn't to say that they're deserted. Lošinj is the more touristy of the two. Ferries and Hydrofoils run from Rijeka to both islands, and there is also a local service from Brestova in Istria to Porozina in northern Cres. If you want to get even further away then there are connections from Cres town and Mali Lošinj to the much smaller and less populous islands of Unije, Vele Strakane, Susak and Ilovik.

Apart from the oases of the small resorts and Lake Vransko (the islands' only water supply), Cres is nearly barren. The lack of water supplies seriously limits any potential for walking that either island has.

Rab the town, capital of Rab the island, is a harmonious place best seen at least once from the sea. Its four campanili stretch in an even and strikingly beautiful line, and the island is probably the most visited of Kvarner Bay. Despite this you should see it if you're in the area. The touts at the bus station should fix you up with a room, or failing this the tourist office on Maršala Tita Trg has a selection.

Connections to Rab town are fairly regular from Rijeka, Zadar and Split; there are also boats from Baška on Krk to Lopar in the north of the island, and from Jablanac on the mainland to Mišnjak on Rab's southern tip. Buses from Lopar and Mišnjak are regular but don't necessarily connect with the boats.

Take time to wander round the town, and do this early morning or late evening to avoid the day trippers – if you aren't one yourself. There are a number of superb 13th and 14th century churches, palaces and other buildings of interest, all built on fine Venetian lines. This makes it easy to forget that Venice was responsible for denuding the island of its precious timber, for limiting essential supplies of salt (fish preservative) and for generally keeping the population both poor and subdued for the best part of four hundred years.

SENJ

Going south along the coast from Rijeka you can safely skip Crikvenica and Novi Vinodolski, package resorts both, and press on to Senj. Most people here are on their way to or from the Plitvice Lakes (see *Inland Croatia*), but the town merits a stopover, even if you're not changing buses. The tourist office has private rooms. Visit the dilapidated old town and take time to see the superb Nehaj fortress. This was built by the Uskoks, a group of fearsome Serbs who had single-handedly held the Turks back from the coast from 1532 to 1538, only to abandon their position on the strength of false Venetian promises. They settled in Senj and were forced to live by astonishingly daring raids on Turkish – and subsequently any – shipping for the best part of a century.

Their exploits attracted swashbuckling types from all over Europe, and when a party was hanged in Venice in 1618 there were no less than nine Englishmen amongst them, of whom six were apparently of noble birth. But more unwilling pirates there can never have been: repeatedly, for fifty years, they asked for land in the interior which they could till peaceably, and repeatedly they were turned down by Austria and Venice. A small and oddly coincidental war between Venice and Austria destroyed the Uskoks, and the survivors were transported inland – as they had wanted all along. They disappeared without trace.

PAG

Pag, although an island, is connected to the mainland by a road bridge at its southern end, and access to Pag town can be had by bus from Zadar, or ferry from Karlobag (the better route). Ferries also run from Jablanac and Prizna to the busy northern resort of Novalja.

Pag is one of the most barren of all the Dalmatian islands, and is quite awesome in its still aridity. There is virtually no vegetation here, and the island supports a tiny local population, who produce salt, and salty sheep's milk cheese. The old town is still very attractive, and despite the development at Novalja, the island is still comparatively untouristed. But the dry torpor can be oppressive.

PAKLENICA NATIONAL PARK

Going south from Senj you can speed straight past **Jablanac** and **Karlobag** – neither town merits a stop unless you're catching a boat out to Rab or Pag. 45km south of Karlobag (an hour by bus) is the Paklenica National Park, famous for its twin gorges and for some fairly hard climbing. Even better is the walking, of which there is plenty of all standards, and enough of it to keep most hikers happy for between one and two weeks.

The park was opened in 1949, and is unusually interesting for both climatic and physical reasons. Situated under the highest peak of the Velebit massif (Vaganski Vrh, 1757m), the area experiences three distinct climates – coastal, continental and sub-alpine. The rock is Velebit Karst (of which more in a moment), and walking is possible from sea-level up to the top of the massif.

Most of the lower reaches are heavily forested with deciduous trees, while higher up mountain pastures support sub-alpine flowers and herbs. The wildlife is excellent, though the rarer animals, such as the brown bears and white vultures, remain well hidden.

Location: Paklenica is situated about 2km inland of the pan-Adriatic highway, almost exactly halfway between Karlobag and Zadar – it's an hour from either by bus. There are three bus stops which serve the park (from north to south): Starigrad Paklenica, Hotel Alan and Seline. Most of the walking and accommodation is centred on the Alan, a naturist hotel and campsite facing onto the sea.

Accommodation: The hotel (reserve via JTP Turisthotel, Zadar, 57000) has accommodation for around 400 people in double rooms costing £25 a night in July and August and £15 off season. The autocamp and the several campsites here and nearby all cost between £4-5 a night for two people, and accommodate another 2500 visitors. Private rooms take another 2200, for £13 in Class I doubles with bath and £6 in Class III doubles with shared bath. Both prices run from mid-June to mid-September – outside of this you ought to be able to bargain them down by up to 50%.

I stayed in private rooms in May and paid £7 for a double with an excellent family called Parić, right by the road leading to the park. Be warned that in July and August most of the accommodation will be full, though the majority of people here are sun and sea holidaymakers, with only a small fraction venturing into the park. Of the park's visitors most are climbers rather than walkers, so the trails are uncrowded, even at weekends when Yugoslavs from the area come to stretch their legs.

There are dozens and dozens of places offering private rooms on the stretch of coast from Starigrad Paklenica, a small town of 1,200 inhabitants 2km north of the Hotel Alan, to Seline, the village 4km south of it. If you have your own transport then the best ones seem to be those in Seline, many of which have sea views; if not then those across the road from the Alan are better, since you won't then have so far to walk to and from the park.

There are three refuges in the park, though these aren't open all the time. The main refuge, Borisov Dom, has accommodation for fifty and is definitely open at weekends from May to September. For other times and the other refuges (nearly a dozen along the massif, including the three in Paklenica) ask the man who takes your money at the main entrance. The refuges cost about £1 a head and Borisov Dom has essential provisions as well as a dormitory.

Facilities Everything you will need can be found in or near the Hotel Alan. There is a supermarket with plentiful stocks of water, juice, chocolate, nuts and biscuits etc. They also sell the principal makings of picnics (bread, tinned fish, beer, some cheese) but don't have much in the way of fruit. The two kiosks next door sell fruit and fresh meat, but have unreasonable opening times – ie. only when you're out walking; the supermarket appears to be open all the time, including on Sundays.

For meals there are several tourist restaurants, an indifferent pizzeria near the autocamp and a couple of cafés at which you can get snacks. Most of the food on offer is aimed at a German audience, with *schweinfleisch* in abundance, but there is also excellent – if expensive – fish to be had. The *zubatac* (bream) at the restaurant on the corner of the entrance to the park is exceptional, as it ought to be at £12 for two. Food based round soups, salads, omelettes and spaghetti is cheap and cheerful, Dalmatian wine goes down easily and the service is friendly, especially if you try out your newly acquired Serbo-Croat.

If you want a swim after walking there are beaches on either side of the Alan, with the better of the two being opposite the park entrance – follow the track past the rubbish tip.

A reasonable 1:50,000 map of the area with 1:25,000 inserts of the park and other places of interest can be bought at the autocamp or at the main entrance for around £1 (it goes under the title of *Južni Velebit*). The walks and footpaths are clearly marked, but the contours can be misleading since they're only at 50m and 100m intervals. A French source (1983) mentioned that there was an accompanying topographical guide in English, but on-site enquiries met with polite denials of it ever having existed. A German climbing guide to the cliffs in the park is also available, but only in Germany.

Paths indicated in red on the map are marked in reality with a white dot in a red circle, or a red and white flash. These are usually painted on rocks, though in the undergrowth you may find them on trees. It's very rare that from one mark you can't see the next. Some of the less regularly used paths have very faded markings; others will amaze you with their freshness and regularity. A series of other paths are used by local people, and these are marked as lines of dashes on the map.

A word of warning: In Paklenica it's advisable to stick to the paths marked on the map. Karst (see below) is very difficult terrain to cross, and you'll find it extremely wearing, both mentally and on your clothes and your hands. The shallowest slopes will confront you with jagged rocks, and climbs or descents of even 2m are difficult.

A marked path up Aniča Kuk took me three hours including an ascent of 700m. The same descent, just 4km across fairly shallow karst, took nearly seven hours. I was never in danger of being lost, since everything was clearly visible, but the rock is nearly impossible to cross, and my fingers were worn to all but the last layer of skin by the end. For a week I couldn't touch a hot cup. Fortunately it's not a mistake you make twice.

Assistance in emergencies is rather hit and miss. French climbers in September 1985 found nobody in the park at all, and heard a story of a two hour wait for the police after a windsurfer drowned. But in May 1988, when I was there, doctors were at the scene of a climbing accident within half an hour. There is, however, no official mountain rescue, and you may have to rely on the goodwill of other walkers and climbers.

The National Park:

The park is dominated by the Velebit Massif, a range of dry limestone mountains stretching for 200km along the coast. The geological term Velebit Karst came from the rock formations of this area, and karst is now used to describe any similar terrain – this includes most of the coastal mountains in Yugoslavia, stretching from Istria to Montenegro, and large parts of the interior.

Karst is grey, wild and very dry. It is formed by the absorbtion of water into porous limestone, which then corrodes and finally erodes the harder limestone underneath. Young karst is characterised by small fissures in the rock, while more developed areas contain long underground caves, rivers that appear from the rock and disappear again almost immediately, and highly porous rock which is completely dry only a few minutes after rain has fallen. The rock is irregularly sculptured into sharp and wild shapes, and is extremely abrasive.

Yugoslavia's karst was almost entirely covered with vegetation, but large parts, particularly on the islands and along the coast, were denuded of their trees and then lost the soil from wind, erosion and overgrazing, and is now known as naked karst. It's incredibly poor land, on which it seems unlikely that anything could survive – but people do live here, and somehow eke a living of sorts from the wilderness.

When an underground cave collapses the surface is flattened, and soil gradually accumulates here. This is then cleared of rocks, walled in and then cultivated by peasants. One of the hazards of this type of field (known as a *polje*) is that they don't always drain as quickly as they fill up, creating lakes of a few days' or weeks' duration. Every so often you'll be surprised by a boat at the edge of a field or pasture. It's also the reason why the houses are never built on a polje, but always to one side. Paklenica is unusually well forested for karst, with over 50% of the terrain being covered.

The National Park's geomorphology consists primarily of a long horizontal valley running between the Velebit ridge and the sea. Two gorge valleys, Velika and Mala (large and small) Paklenica, with cliffs over 400m high in places, cut through to the sea, and there are also several networks of subterranean caves. The most famous of these is Manita Peć, which has been explored for over 175m and contains beautiful rock formations and two large halls.

The park provides a habitat for many rare mammals, including brown bears, wolves, wild boar, martens, wild cat and roe deer. Birds of prey, including eagles and rare white vultures can be seen in the higher regions. Several varieties of harmless snake live near the valley floor, and after rain you are likely to see these and large green and brown toads. Lizards, including a large green variety, are also common.

Because of its triple climate the weather is unusually variable. It's the only place I've ever walked where I've been drenched by rain, then sunburned and finally hailed on – in the same day. Prepare for all weathers, especially in May and early June, when there is still snow on north facing slopes above 1500m. In summer the inner parts of the park can be fearsomely hot, though above 1200m the air is fresher. Even when the sun is shining along the coast localised storms can exist in the park, and you should be ready for them.

Access: There are dozens of ways into the park, via old paths, over the mountains, or even across the karst, if you dare. There are also two official routes in. The main entrance is about 300m south of the Hotel Alan, and clearly marked *Nacionalni Park Paklenica*. This gives access to the Velika Paklenica canyon. The other entrance is from the village of Seline, which leads towards Mala Paklenica.

At the main entrance, a brisk kilometre up an unmetalled road (15 minutes on foot) there is a hut, and a man who'll sell you an entrance ticket (around 75p), a map (about £1) and postcards. The entrance money is used for park and trail upkeep – please don't avoid paying. Another kilometre on, the road ends in a car park, and all of the main trails start from here (35 minutes from the main road).

The entrance to Mala Paklenice is about 4km south of the main one, just after the small church of Sv. Marko (an unremarkable hour on foot). Turn inland and follow the track towards the clearly visible canyon. At the end of the track (perhaps 2km from the main road, half an hour on foot) there's some space for car parking and apparently there is someone here to take your money, but neither time I came to this entrance in May was there any sign of life.

Park rules: These rules have been established not to hamper your holiday but to protect the park and its inhabitants. You are asked: not to pick flowers or other plants, or to damage trees and undergrowth; not to damage any stalactite or other rock formations in the grottoes; not to hunt or carry weapons with you in the park; not to camp or make any kind of fire. Apparently permission to camp may be obtained from the park administration in exceptional circumstances, but normally you should use the refuges if you need to stay overnight.

Typical karst formations near the summit of Anića Kuk in the Paklenica National Park.

TRAILS IN THE PAKLENICA NATIONAL PARK

With the exception of the last couple of suggested trails, these are all one day trips, taking from four hours (Manita Peć) to over ten (Velika Golić). Most can be reduced by over an hour if you drive to the car park at the main entrance (it takes over half an hour to walk each way), but the timings given here include this walk since I had no car at Paklenica. It is even possible to climb Vaganski Vrh, the highest mountain in the area at 1757m, in one day, but you should allow at least 14 hours for the round trip. It's much more satisfactory to break the journey at the refuge.

Mala and Velika Paklenica

This is a circular walk, and includes both gorges and some excellent views. It runs from Starigrad to Seline, up Mala Paklenice, across the wide ridge between the canyons and then down Velika Paklenica. Although it can be done in reverse, the route suggested here is better paced – Mala Paklenica is a tougher walk in either direction than Velika Paklenica, and it's better to do it early in the day while you're still fresh.

The walk takes about nine hours, including the hour along the road between the two entrances. The only way of avoiding this is if you can get a lift between the two. Taking your own car doesn't help, since the trail ends up at the opposite entrance from the one it starts at.

From the Hotel Alan there are two ways of getting to Seline – straight along the flat coastal road or along the path running through the string of villages just inland, Škilići, Jurline and Jukici. The coast road is easy, and takes an hour if you stop for a quick Turkish coffee at the local bar on the outskirts of Seline. Turn left after the village of Seline, opposite Sv. Marko, and follow the dirt road towards the canyon ahead.

The footpath to Seline starts just after the bridge, 300m from the main park entrance. There may or may not be water flowing under this. Go to the left of the church and bear right towards the village ahead. The path through the villages is fairly clear, and if in doubt just ask for Seline or the next village on the way. The path is shorter on the map, and slightly quicker than the road – if you make no wrong turnings. The two routes leading to Mala Paklenica meet nearly a kilometre inland, where you should see clear red and white flashes marking the way to the canyon.

The entrance to the canyon is about half an hour from the main road, where the dirt track peters out. The way up the first part of the gorge is pretty obvious but not very clearly marked. The best path, of several used by goats, seems to be that on the left above what was, in May, a dry gully. The track starts by rising above the gully floor and then levels off to join the floor of the gorge and finally crosses it, just after a small tributary runs into the main part (also dry from May to September, except after exceptional rain).

Herds of mountain goats graze the scrub on the sides of the lower part, before the walls become steeper as you enter the canyon proper. The path is increasingly obvious after a while, partly because of improved markings and partly because there is only one way that it can go and that's along the floor of the gorge. Even in midsummer this doesn't get too much sun, so the going isn't too hot, though it is fairly steep in places, and becomes more so after the first hour.

When you reach the first big boulders the path climbs to the right – this is clear, if not well marked, and assisted with cables and secure pitons where it crosses the rock. Don't be put off: it's not difficult. After this there are very clear markings for the next two hours. These are best followed precisely, as they indicate the easiest way of crossing the boulders and rocks. The first part after the cables ascends sharply until you're about 200m above the sea, when the floor of the canyon levels out.

This stretch is one of the best I've ever walked: the views back down the gorge are marvellous, the rock has been formed into brilliant shapes and textures, small trees and flowers grow tenaciously from pockets in the cliffs and the boulders stretch you without being either dangerous or too difficult. After a while a few puddles become evident, and as you go uphill gently these metamorphose into a rivulet which finally becomes quite a busy stream. This is wonderfully refreshing. Follow the stream up, turning left when the canyon branches in two. The path crosses the stream regularly, but you shouldn't get wet feet since the crossings are marked with conveniently placed stepping stones.

Twenty minutes after the gorge forks, the trail leaves the stream – but only after a couple of false alarms where you dive off into the woods and rejoin it fifty yards upstream. The walk from Seline to here took me about four hours, without pushing the pace. The path now heads steeply uphill in a zigzag until you're at 650m – an ascent of perhaps 200m. At the top there is a rock in a dry stone wall clearly marked Sv. Jakov, though there is no obvious church on the site. This junction is also easy to pinpoint on the map.

Take the left hand of the two paths, marked Starigrad and Jivile. The path is now indistinct and runs across low mountain pastures. Red and white markers on the occasional rocks on the ground help you; if you lose these head west-northwest until you join the marked path which comes in from your right. The path now goes down a rocky gully with a base that's quite difficult to walk on (especially in the pouring rain). This divides in several places, but the proper path is indicated clearly each time. Eventually you arrive at a small farm, with three or four houses and some walled pastures.

Go through the farm on the leftmost of the tracks and immediately afterwards fork right along the marked path. From here there are clear indications all the way to the valley floor, which you won't even need if you follow the donkey droppings – the path from here onwards is the farm's access road. At first it continues more or less flat and then you arrive quite unexpectedly at the top edge of Velika Paklenica, with an exceptional view. To the right you should be able to see the ridge of the Velebit Massif, with Vaganski Vrh indistinct among the jumble of points above 1700m. Across the valley is the peak of Vidakov Kuk (866m) and the long ridge of Velika Golić (1285m). It's an ideal picnic spot.

The path zigzags down steeply from here (about 650m) to the valley floor (250m), and is a good test of knee strength. At the floor of the valley the trail crosses the river and joins the wide gravel path which leads to the top of the canyon. This is the most travelled road in Paklenica and has been properly built and cemented to avoid erosion. It's an easy walk from here down to the base of the climbing walls of Anića Kuk to your left (400m high). The views down the gorge as you leave it are excellent.

From the car park it's only half an hour or so to the main road, completing the circuit. It took me nine hours in weather which started off good, turned very wet across the shoulder between the two gorges and rained twice more on the way down Velika Paklenica. I probably stopped for a little over an hour altogether, and wasn't in a hurry to reach anywhere – the walk could doubtless be done in six hours by the competitive.

Manita Peć and Vidakov Kuk

This trail takes in the grotto of Manita Peć and the peak above it, called Vidakov Kuk. Although this is only at 866m the view is excellent since it's one of Paklenica's nearest summits to the sea. The second part of the walk involves some scrambling and a good sense of balance, but it's not as difficult – or dangerous – as rock climbing. As far as Manita Peć the walk is sometimes steep but never difficult.

If you're fit it shouldn't take much more than two hours to Manita Peć from the main road. From Manita Peć to Vidakov Kuk you should allow about an hour and a half up and an hour back. Count in some time to explore the grotto, and take a torch with you – when I was there I had the impression that there must be some artificial lighting somewhere, but it certainly wasn't switched on. Without some form of lighting you won't see more than the first five or ten metres of the cave, which has actually been explored for over 175m.

Start at the main entrance and make your way to the toll and car park. There's only one trail from here, and this follows the floor of the gorge. Much of the path up through the canyon, up to where it levels out at a little over 200m, has been properly paved, and two concrete bridges have been put across the torrent that cascades refreshingly down. The trail isn't especially pretty, but it does help preserve the rest of the rock, which is full of interesting formations and patterned with the kind of colours that go into natural dyes.

When the path levels out it changes from paved to grit (an hour and a quarter from the main road). 300m from here there's a sign on the left of the path marked Borisov Dom (the refuge) 1h15, and 230m later is where the path starts towards Mala Paklenica (see the previous walk). Ten minutes further on there's a clearly marked path to the left, signed Manita Peć 40', and that's almost exactly how long it will take you to walk up the long path that zigzags twice before reaching the cave at 540m.

Like most caves, it isn't especially inspiring from the outside, and when I was there I didn't have the chance to explore very far inside – what I did see was some beautiful stalactites and other calciferous rock formations. Later I met a party of Germans who had explored the cave in depth with proper caving lights, and they thought very highly of it, mentioning two halls, one of which they reckoned to be over 30m tall.

The trail from Manita Peć to Vidakov Kuk is posted by a combination of very fresh and very faded markers. When in doubt follow the fresh ones. The path starts obscurely from the right hand side of Manita Peć (looking into the cave), going down one or two metres to start with and traversing a steep and fairly insecure scree-like slope before gaining a shallow scrub forest.

The trail continues consistently upwards and closer to the cliff, drifting right as you look at the ridge. Eventually a way up through a steep split in the cliff is marked, and it's here that you need to be fairly agile, with the terrain rocky and mostly unassisted. As you attain the ridge the summit is only about fifty metres above you, to your left. There isn't a marked trail to the peak, but there are several fairly easy ways to reach it. You should make sure that you have secure hand and footholds, since the rock is unusually friable in places. The view from the top looks out across the sea and the barren wastes of Pag.

The marked trail continues fairly gently from the base of Vidakov Kuk to the farm at Ramići, where you can either go down to the valley or up towards Velika Golić (see the description under the Velika Golić heading). There is apparently a way down the back of Vidakov Kuk which leads to the village of Tomići (see separate heading) and thence to Starigrad – I failed to find this, but met two Austrians who had negotiated the route in three hours.

Anića Kuk

This is certainly the most climbed peak in the whole national park. There are something like 25 routes up the west and north faces, and these are all serious climbs which shouldn't be attempted without ropes and proper climbing equipment. There are reports that some of the pitons and belay points are no longer secure, but I haven't personally confirmed this – instead I took one of the two walking routes to the top, which makes an excellent six hour return trip (under five if you have a car).

Anića Kuk is only 712m high, but it's an isolated, exposed peak and is the nearest major summit to the sea. The side facing into the gorge is a near vertical drop of 400m; don't stray too close to it.

Both walking routes follow Velika Paklenica upstream past the car park and then up the paved zigzag path until a sharp uphill left hand bend, hard on the river. This is about half an hour from the car park; just over an hour from the main road. Cross the river and follow a mixture of yellow flashes and red and white markers towards the base of the cliff which comes down to a flint shaped point.

The yellow flashes mark the route to the right of this. This isn't marked on the map, though a party of unequipped Germans who left at the same time reached the summit only a quarter of an hour after me, with no apparent difficulty. There are some assisted and fairly tricky passages on this trail, but you don't need ropes.

The marked route starts to the left of the base of the cliff – follow it diagonally upwards across loose scree until you see the red and white marks, which are clearer as you enter the wood. After this there are fewer people around – most of those you've seen so far are climbers not walkers. The path zigzags up steeply for nearly an hour, at which point it meets the ridge.

From here the path curves round the back of the mountain through woods and scrub, before coming out onto the rock. From this point it's a fifty minute climb (half an hour if you've done any rock climbing) to the summit. The way is well-marked, but not always easy, with naked karst under your hands and feet. A good sense of balance is a great help here, as is a lack of vertigo, though anyone can make the summit. This is well worth the effort, with really excellent views in all directions waiting for you.

There are two ways down, easiest of which is to return the way you came. The other way includes the assisted path used by climbers, and is sporadically marked in yellow. Start by heading down the slope towards the gorge and then turn left along the ridge and reach the summit marked by the yellow flag – on the way along the ridge look out for (and through) the hole in the shoulder of the mountain behind you. From this summit (clearly visible from Anića Kuk) the path leads down to the valley.

It was this path that I missed, and there that I made the mistake of not going back the way I'd come. Instead, since I could see the sea and various obvious landmarks, I decided to cross the shallow karst and take a short cut home. The journey down was fairly nightmarish, with brambles and heavy undergrowth where there wasn't raw karst. With unremitting regularity the jagged rock dropped away in three metre cliffs ending in thorn-bushes. Sunburn, ants nests, a succession of snakes, inadequate water supplies and bleeding hands didn't make the journey any more pleasant. Take my word for it: if you don't find the path, go back the way you came.

I found out later that the best way of doing the circuit is to go up the yellow trail and back down the well-marked red and white one. This way you climb rather than descend the assisted trail, and have an easier walk home.

Velika Golić

Some of the more spectacular views in Paklenica can be had from the long ridge of Velika Golić. There is an excellent walk lasting about ten hours which includes this, and then returns via the refuge.

The first hour and a half is exactly as for Manita Peć, but instead of turning uphill to the cave continue straight on, following the river and indications for Borisov Dom, the refuge. After about half an hour you'll reach a water trough and a sign indicating Borisov Dom 30'. The main path branches up to the left and just under ten minutes further on along this there is an unmarked path branching steeply uphill away from the river. Follow this up its zigzags for about forty minutes, after which you'll come across single red dashes – these become normal markings at a dry stone wall.

The trail now leads to Ramići, a farm surrounded by pastures and dry stone walls (note that there is another Ramići in the same area – the small settlement by Borisov Dom). The marked path that goes straight on, through the farm, leads eventually to Vidakov Kuk; the route to Velika Golić is a hard right hand turn, almost behind you as you arrive at the farm.

From here, after skirting between a series of dry stone walls, the path rises steadily and you're soon quite a long way above the farm. The ground becomes rougher as the route skirts the 903m summit of Čelinka and crosses a rocky wood before surfacing on an open pasture. This leads directly to the corner of the ridge, level with the top of Čelinka. It takes about two hours from the river to this point. The view from here is excellent, looking down to the refuge below, down the canyon and onto the tops of Anića Kuk and the surrounding ridges, and across to the sea.

The ridge is an extraordinary formation, consisting of a series of parallel broken limestone ledges 40 degrees steep. The valley side of this is nearly a sheer drop, but the side from which you've approached is relatively shallow, as is the gradient of the ridge itself, which takes the best part of two kilometres to rise from 900m to 1285m. There are a whole series of frustrating false crests to this, each of which is utterly convincing. Progress along the ridge is effected by scrambling and hopping from rock to rock, and is, fortunately, well marked – on taking a wrong turning I found myself staring more or less straight down some 400m.

The summit is a superb viewpoint and merits the five hours or more it takes to reach it. But do take warm clothing – it was on this ridge that I was hailed on in late May.

The best way down from here is to continue along the ridge after the peak, climbing a secondary summit of 1160m before the marked path curves back and down towards Borisov Dom. This should take two hours, but I wasn't able to check this out – I was too busy cowering in the hail and rain, waiting for the thunderstorm centred on the summit to go and play somewhere else.

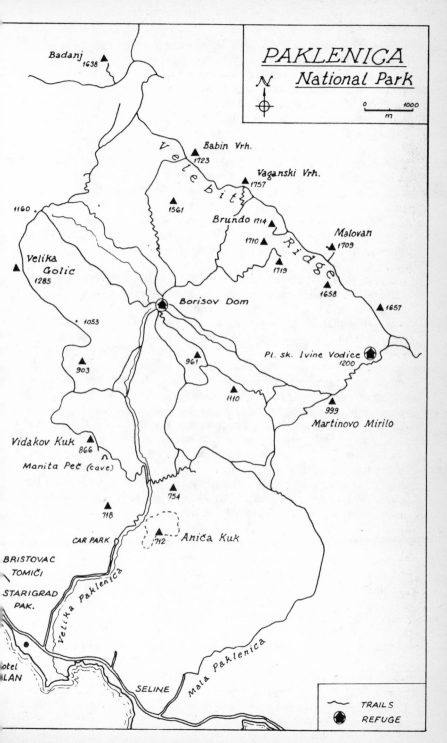

Bristovac Tomići

There are a number of tiny villages in and around Paklenica, only accessible by country track and cut off from the rest of the world. Most of these are now deserted or inhabited by only one or two old couples. If you chance upon one and there's anyone at home then you'll probably be welcomed in and force-fed home brewed *šlivovice*. This happened to me just two or three kilometres from Starigrad, in the village of Bristovac Tomići (the locals leave off the Bristovac).

The start of the track is fairly well concealed – the best way of finding it is to start at the tourist office in Starigrad (opposite the new bus stop) and walk down the road 100m or so towards the Hotel Alan. Before you reach the large restaurant on the right there are two impermanent looking kiosks, also on the right. Opposite the point between these is a tiny road marked Zadarskog Odreda. Follow this for 30m, when it jinks right and then left, and continue straight inland up the concrete path.
   When this path runs out continue on the unmarked donkey trail and follow this uphill until you reach the white shrine at the crest. From here you can see a dry stone wall, and the path continues to the left of this – the map is rather vague at this point. The wall leads to the village, which consists of half a dozen houses and some pastures round it.
   An old man called Parić and his wife came out to greet me, and offered me too much to drink and a couple of hours of mime, laughter, doggerel and digging through my dictionary. It's in situations like this that pictures of home and American cigarettes (dozens of cheap local brands are available, but Winstons and Camels make a better gift) really come in handy. These two people, neither of whom are much under seventy, live on their own in a place which can have snow in every month of the year, with no water supply, no electricity, no central heating and the nearest shops and other people over an hour away. Their children – and all the other people from the village – have moved away to a more comfortable life.

Other walks

Paklenica contains a wide variety of other walks, though I was limited by time and weather to the ones described above. I particularly wanted to climb Vaganski Vrh, but the unpredictable weather made it impossible. I had positive feedback from other walkers on the following pair of longer walks:

Vaganski Vrh. Obviously walkers will want to reach the highest point in the Velebit Massif, though anywhere along the upper ridge will give you a similar view – there are another half dozen points over 1700m. Fanciful descriptions of the view mention being able to see Italy on a clear day, but there are only a few occasions a year when this is possible, and these in winter.

I met a young German couple who had climbed the mountain a week earlier – it took them a straight 14 hours from the Hotel Alan campsite. They went along Velika Paklenica to Borisov Dom (two and a half hours) and then followed the signs, taking the right hand of the two paths available, and then forking at the junction marked left to Vaganski and right to Babin Kuk. From here the path was less well marked, and sometimes difficult, but they never had to resort to technical climbing (though they did have the right equipment). It took them five and a half hours from Borisov Dom to the summit, and four to return to the refuge. They looked excessively fit and healthy.

An older couple I spoke to had taken twelve hours to go from the car park to the summit and back to the refuge, where they had stayed the night. The following day they went from the refuge to **Babin Kuk** (1435m), and back to their car in eleven hours. They rated Babin Kuk very highly – Vaganski Vrh's only advantage is that it also gives a view inland over the rest of the mountains in the Velebit Massif. They mentioned, finally, that they had found two litres of water per day per person insufficient in hot weather.

Velebit Ridge. This is one of the best – and hardest – walks that Paklenica has to offer. You must have the right clothing and equipment (survival bags etc.) to attempt this, and a man I spoke to had been obliged to spend a night at 1600m, in the open, just under the ridge. He reckoned that his space blanket had saved his life. You will need to check that the Ivine Vodice refuge is open, and ideally plan to spend the first night there and the second in Borisov Dom.

The route starts by going up Mala Paklenica until you reach the stone marked Sveti Jakov (as for Mala Paklenica, above). Take the right hand of the two paths and follow this until you reach a branch marked left for Borisov Dom. Turn right here (my source had forgotten how the right hand path was indicated), and climb steadily towards the peak of Martinovo mirilo (999m) – the path skirts to the left of the summit.

Soon after, the path becomes more clear as it joins the route between the two refuges, and from here it's a reasonably steep climb to the refuge, at 1200m. Estimates vary widely between six and nine hours from Seline to the refuge.

The route up to the ridge is quite clear, quite steep and quite spectacular. Along the ridge there are a number of summits which can be attempted – my source rated the following very highly (with rough timings from the refuge): Malovan (1709m, 4h), Brundo (1714m), Vaganski Vrh (1757m) and Babin Vrh (1723m, 14h). He did, however, get stranded by nightfall on his way down from Babin Vrh towards Borisov Dom. It might therfore be prudent to attempt only one or two of them, in which case Malovan and Vaganski Vrh are the obvious choices.

ZADAR

Zadar is the economic and transport centre for northern Dalmatia. It's thriving and modern but also has a fairly quiet old walled town on a peninsula. Most of Zadar was damaged in the war and the unpretentious rebuilding is unusually inoffensive. There's plenty of accommodation here, most of which is handled by travel agents in the old town, less than five minutes from the bus station and ferry terminal.

The old town merits a half day exploration if you have the time, with highspots being a pretty good archaeological museum, a handful of churches from the 9th century on and a very fine collection of church relics, housed in their own museum.

Boats leave Zadar for most of the nearby islands, the nearest of which is **Ugljan**, just a half hour away. Excursions also run from here to the **Kornati archipelago**, a national park consisting of 109 uninhabited islands. The park is managed from Murter, a small town half way between Zadar and Šibenik, and there you can find out about real survival holidays – they have small huts with the bare essentials, for rent, as well as a number of more comfortable ways of seeing the islands.

Šibenik, the next major town southwards, didn't impress me greatly, but is the springboard for trips upriver by boat or bus to the Krka falls (see *Inland Croatia*). You can also catch boats to most of the nearby islands, and these are generally less busy than the ones further north.

SPLIT AND TROGIR

Trogir is one of the better places along the crowded Dalmatian coast. Most buses won't go into the town but will drop you off five minutes away, on the main road. Cross the stone bridge onto the small island (under half a kilometre long) and ignore the busy port on the shore; you must leave your car here if you have one. The town has a pleasantly uncorrupted medieval feel to it, partly because it's not bursting with tourists, partly because it houses an authentically jumbled wealth of pleasing architecture, including a fine 13th century Romanesque cathedral.

Most of the sights and facilities can be found on or near the main square, Narodni Trg. Tourist information has a good supply of reasonably priced private rooms, and will also tell you which of the old and famous buildings you should see. Don't miss the cathedral, which has some excellent 15th century sculpture by Nicholas of Florence, and even more by truthful but immodest local boy Radovan ('by Radovan, most excellent in his art').

Split, just 26km down the coast from Trogir, is one of Yugoslavia's best known tourist attractions. Diocletian, who built the palace that everyone comes to see, may have had a monster ego, but even he can't

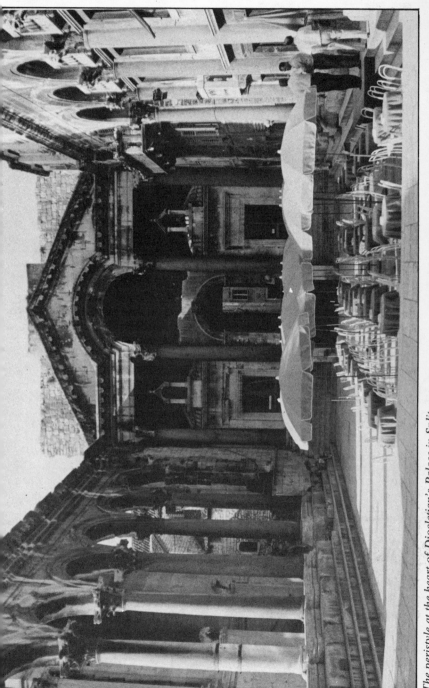

The peristyle at the heart of Diocletian's Palace in Split.

have imagined that his palace would be so popular.

Despite its sprawling suburbs the centre of Split is surprisingly small, and the ferry terminal, bus station, train station, Diocletian's palace and the tourist facilities are conveniently situated along the seafront. If you get offered a room at the bus station (and the chances are that you will be) bargain strenuously and take it – for a short stay you'll certainly have to pay more at a tourist office or travel agent. One tip: dump your bag at left luggage, so that you have the freedom to reject a room if it's too far, too expensive or not up to scratch. You can always collect your bag later.

As long as it stands, Split's main attraction will be Diocletian's Palace. Diocletian was from this area and wanted to retire here, so from 295 until 305 he had the palace built on his native shores and lived here for the last eight years of his life. The palace must have been a wonder in its complete state: it covers a surface area of 48,000 square yards, has massive walls, and included huge chambers, soldiers' quarters, temples and arcaded corridors.

When the Roman empire collapsed, the palace fell into a state of disrepair, but refugees from Salona moved in and converted archways into houses, and corridors into streets, using the defenses to good effect against invading hordes from the north. Even now the old town houses a considerable number of people and is at least as full of locals as visitors.

A fine view of it all can be had from the campanile; the Christians were also responsible for doing ₁ conversion job on the mausoleum next door and making a very small cathedral out of it – look up and you'll see some pagan-looking sculptures and even the heads of Diocletian and his wife, it's said. Diocletian himself was moved out by the builders and hasn't been seen since. On no account miss the chance to go round the underground chambers which are the only whole rooms remaining from the palace – it's the only way you'll get a real impression of how big the palace must once have been.

Split is also home to the Meštrović Gallery, the palace the sculptor intended to retire to. If you're remotely interested in him then go and see the comprehensive collection on show here. Failing that buy the excellent book (in English, with reasonable colour pictures, under £1) at any bookshop.

If you know your archaeology then you won't miss the chance to wander round the extensive ruins of **Salona** (now called Solin), once the most important Roman town in the area, and now a short bus ride or dull half hour walk north of town. The ruins are still 90% unexamined, but what there is leaves a tremendous impression – most of the area is desolate and genuinely dilapidated, and a hot dusty afternoon stroll round here works wonders on the imagination.

ŠOLTA

The island of Šolta lies an hour away from Split and is easily reached
by boat. There aren't many roads, and outside of the villages at which
the boat stops there are very few people. This makes the island one of
the better ones to explore, particularly if you can reach the largely
uninhabited south coast, a crenellated 15km (as the crow flies) of
inlets, coves and tiny bays, as yet untainted by tourism.

The island is only 5km wide, perhaps 10km on foot, and efforts to
walk across it ought to be amply rewarded. There are around 200
private rooms scattered over the island, but avoid the new holiday
complex at the once-upon-a-time village of Nečujam. There's no
official campsite on the island, so discreet freelancing shouldn't be a
problem.

BRAČ

Like Šolta, Brač is an hour from Split and easily reached. That's where
the similarity ends. Brač is busy, popular and famous for its white
marble (samples in Washington's White House, Diocletian's Palace
etc.). If you find yourself here try reaching the almost deserted
southwestern coast. Along from here is the resort of Bol, above which
is Vidova Gora (780m), justly famous for its sunset views.

MAKARSKA

Continuing down the coast from Split you can ignore the windblown
town of Omiš, and continue rapidly past the string of resorts that make
up the Makarska Riviera. Makarska itself is a small but busy town,
tastefully restored in stone after the 1962 earthquake. It makes a
conveniently sunny stopover if you're feeling travel weary and
footsore, having over 2km of pebble beach, a good vegetable market
and plenty of private rooms (though these disappear fast in summer)
and reasonably priced restaurants (away from the palm studded
seafront).

If you want walking there are a couple of excellent summits in the
Biokovo mountains behind the town. A marked path starts from
Makarska: it's indicated, in red, 1425m – 3h. On your way up you'll
find the refuge Dom Vosač (1370m), which also marks the start of a
trail leading to Sveti Jure (1762m), apparently a much harder climb.
More information on these can be had from Tourist Information in
Markaska.

KARDELJEVO

Kardeljevo wouldn't be worth a mention, but it is an important
transport hub. The railway from Sarajevo terminates here, buses go to
all coastal destinations and head into the interior, and ferries run

regularly to Trpanj on Pelješac (the best route to Korčula). The town is of no interest, so it's fortunate that the ferry terminal is only a short walk from the bus and train stations, which are amply furnished with snack bars.

HVAR

Hvar is one of the greenest and most pleasant of the islands, with a fine uniformity of 16th century Venetian architecture in the towns and gorgeous vegetation along the long thin coastline. Unfortunately it's one of the Adriatic's worst kept secrets, and has most of the negative aspects of any well – some might say excessively – developed resort.

KORČULA

Korčula is similar to Hvar in many ways, though perhaps attracts slightly fewer people. Even if you ignore the rest of the island however, the old town of Korčula is well worth a visit. It's most easily reached from the port of Orebić on the Pelješac peninsula – regular boats make the crossing in about fifteen minutes.

Korčula old town is surrounded by stout walls and appears more medieval than Venetian. This impression is confirmed inside, where a leaf-veined network of narrow streets protect the town from strong north winds. Crammed into a space that's obviously too small is a charming cathedral, and near this is a house that purports to have been Marco Polo's. Whether it is or not, the great traveller probably was from Korčula, and probably lived in this sort of palace. If you can, catch the town in the light of very early morning.

PELJEŠAC

This peninsula is more like an island than a stretch of coastline. Running down the middle of the narrow spit of land (only 6km across at its widest point) is a superb mountain ridge which is over 900m high for much of its length. There are few finer sights than making the two hour climb from Orebić before dawn and then watching the sun rise over the mainland.

Orebić is increasingly crowded, and has all the facilities you'd expect, including private rooms which go fast in summer. Catch the boat to Korčula from here; return to the mainland by bus, or by boat from Trpanj to Kardeljevo, which saves a long detour.

MLJET

Mljet is one of the most attractive islands in the whole Adriatic. Despite being unusually beautiful, and entirely unspoiled by deforestation, it remains relatively unvisited. This may be because it

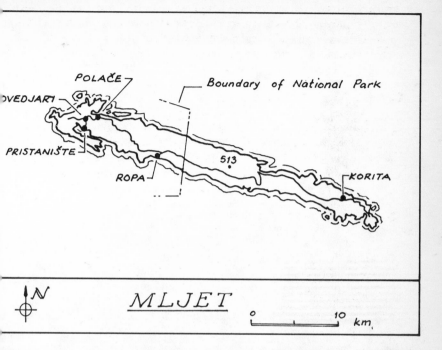

Dubrovnik's old town. (Photo: Janet Cross.)

has no town of any size, and few architectural gems or famous ruins.

Most visitors are day trippers from Dubrovnik, and they only therefore have time to see the most obvious attraction – a pair of large salt water lakes. A deserted monastery on an island in the larger of these has been put to practical use as a hotel, and is used as the luncheon venue for excursions. Avoid it between midday and 3pm.

The entire western end of the island, including the lakes, has been declared a national park, and the office running this is in Govedjari, a village 2km from Polače, the island's port. Both villages have private rooms, and this is your best accommodation bet. Access to the island is easiest from Trstenik, an hour away on Pelješac, though there are also boats from Korčula and Dubrovnik.

Mljet is the only place in Europe where you can find mongooses in the wild. Apparently they were originally brought here from Africa to try and keep down the snake population, which is still, it should be mentioned, significant.

The island's walking isn't especially strenuous (the highest point in the park is under 400m) but is nonetheless rewarding. Excellent bathing can be had in the lakes, there are still numerous unexplored coves in the island's northwestern tip, and apart from the occasional incursions by day trips there are few people to contend with. A day or two here makes a pleasant complement to some harder mountain walking on the mainland.

DUBROVNIK

Dubrovnik is by far the most visited place in Yugoslavia, with annual figures now approaching three and a half million. Of these the British (814,000) and Germans (805,000) account for nearly half.

Obviously people come here for a reason, and though I wouldn't go as far as Byron (who described it as the pearl of the Adriatic), it must be admitted that the city has its attractions, not least of which is the ease of finding accommodation (20,000 private rooms alone), places to eat and people who understand you. The obverse of the same coin means that you'll be unlikely to want to spend more than a day or two here.

The city state of Ragusa (the name was only changed to Dubrovnik in 1918, on the grounds that Ragusa sounded too Italian by half) was one of the most devious of all independent republics. While Venice was at war with Turkey, Ragusa managed to stay chummy with both, accepting the protection of one and paying tribute to the other.

Ragusa rose to fame at the end of the 13th century, and was a long way ahead of its time in political thinking, establishing a health service as early as 1432 and the principle of free education in 1435. The city was an asylum to those who asked it, and centuries before slavery was abolished in Europe it was outlawed here. Many slaves subsequently had their freedom bought by Ragusan patricians.

It was nonetheless a hypocritical society, that saw no contradiction in strong Christian values and dealing with the Ottoman empire, and in accepting profitable trade with the enemy whenever it could. Oddly enough no art other than literature was countenanced until the republic fell, and it wasn't until the Austrians had been in control for half a century that the city's first theatre was built. In 1950 Dubrovnik managed a spectacular *volte face* with the inauguration of an annual summer festival, now world famous, which runs from early July until the middle of August.

Ragusa was almost entirely destroyed by massive earthquakes in 1667, so most of what you see now only dates back to the end of the 17th century, and more than you might imagine is late 20th century restoration, a process continuing even now.

The two best ways of seeing the city are from outside – either walk round the top of the massive town walls or take the cable car to the top of Srdj (403m). This last could also be done as a fairly uninspiring walk up the dry hillside: unless the queue is really daunting you're better off buying the £1 ticket and saving your legs for Lokrum (see below) and walks further afield.

Once you've seen Dubrovnik from above, the city should be approached carefully: after 9am it becomes 90% tourists and 10% atmosphere. Early evening is also a pleasant time, with soft light treating old and new stone alike, kindly. The evening stroll up and down the main street, Placa (once the strait between mainland and island), is now more tourist than local, but you can still catch something of the original atmosphere in the steep and narrow streets off this.

Dubrovnik doesn't lack sights, though the city itself is as interesting as most of the crowded museums and palaces. Make the effort to see the cathedral, not for its rather spartan interior but for its treasury. There are some really superb pieces here, including a large number of spectacularly grisly reliquaries. On display prominently is also the pitcher and ewer that Rebecca West described so fittingly, 'Nothing could be more offensive to the eye, to the touch, or to common sense ... It has the infinite elaborateness of eczema'. Note the pre-Dali lobsters and an abundance of tortoises and snakes.

Practical Information: Accommodation shouldn't be a problem – at the bus station, near the port of Gruž, anyone looking remotely foreign is positively surrounded by offers of private rooms. Check location and price carefully: this is easier if you've already equipped yourself with a map from the tourist office 100m uphill of the bus station. If you're flying in then JAT buses should drop you at the JAT terminal, just round the corner from the bus station, and there's also an excellent daily market for fresh fruit and vegetables nearby.

Flat fare Libertas buses cover the whole town (1, 2, 3 and 6 go from the bus station to the old town, marked Pile), and the surrounding areas as well. Finally, there's a good tourist office right inside the main gate (Pile) of the old town, just after Onofrio's famous fountain and next door to an expensive but exquisite ice-cream parlour, where cornets are served acrobatically.

LOKRUM

When you're in Dubrovnik keep at least half a day free for a trip to Lokrum, the town's own offshore nature reserve. Visited unwillingly by a shipwrecked Richard the Lionheart in the 13th century, you can now reach it in 15 minutes by a half hourly boat from the old town quay.

The sub-tropical island of Lokrum hasn't yet been 'developed' in the conventional sense, and makes a wonderful break from the crowds gawking at Dubrovnik. One of its many positive points is that even when the boats arriving are full the 2km island can easily absorb all comers, leaving an impression (away from a small central part) of tranquillity, only punctuated by the cries of birds and the fluttering of butterflies.

A network of footpaths criss-crosses the island and provides access to the sea and into the dense woods. There are several rock beaches, and these are cleaner and fresher than Dubrovnik's (excepting those owned by the better hotels in Lapad, the peninsula suburb above the bus station), as well as a very warm salt water lake, just opposite the point where the boat arrives. This has a 10m cliff which encourages the more reckless to dive off it, apparently without harm.

The island's main attraction, though, lies in its enormous variety of vegetation, which is even more astonishing when you realise that there is no fresh water supply – hence the absolute ban on making fires of any kind, or even on smoking. If a fire were to start here then the whole island would be razed. When you're wandering along the paths look out for the numerous species of butterflies and birds: in June I saw white admirals, several unusual fritillaries, and some beautiful, nervous, large yellows.

In the middle of the island there's an old botanical garden, most of which seems to be like a series of wonderfully unmaintained secret gardens. Amongst slightly dilapidated walls there grow palms with soft furry trunks, trellises of twisted vines and crippled trees supported on crutches, while broken cloches sprout thyme and basil and lettuce run to seed. In the heavy silence and deep shade there's an agreeable air of mystery which is shattered fairly unceremoniously when you round a corner and discover the restaurant and bar, and a small natural history museum, all within the structure of what must once have been a large Benedictine monastery.

Finally, it was from the northern tip of Lokrum that I realised what it was that I'd found vaguely unsettling about Dubrovnik all along – it has the air of a film set. It's easy to imagine people building and living in the new town, but the old town, with its squeaky clean buildings, giant clapboard walls and throngs of admiring visitors, looks as if it's a display piece, only there to be looked at.

GULF OF KOTOR

Continuing down the coast from Dubrovnik there are a string of resorts, largest of which is **Cavtat**, once a watering hole for wealthy Austrians and now package tour country. Its only point of interest is Meštrović's bizarre mausoleum for the Račić family, a very Slavic reflection on death. It's an odd fact that the whole family died off as soon as the building was finished.

The stretch from Cavtat to **Igalo** isn't wildly inspiring, and neither is Igalo itself unless you need one of its very costly mud cures. Igalo marks the start of the Gulf of Kotor the nearest the Mediterranean gets to having a fjord.

The huge natural harbour – parts of it are 30km from the open sea – allowed the development of unparalleled maritime skills in the Middle Ages, which evolved naturally into piracy by the 15th century and later gave the seas internationally renowned navigators and naval engineers. The gulf is surrounded by steep grey mountains which plunge into the sea, and is dominated by the bulk of Lovčen (1749m, see *Montenegro*) above the town of Kotor.

Hercog Novi (New Hercog) is the first town you'll come to in Montenegro, though it was built in 1382 to give Bosnia an important access to the sea. Its strategical position was then bitterly fought over for the next five centuries. Now it has nicer flowers than most resorts, but is nonetheless just that – a resort.

A ferry plies the isthmus from Kamenari to Lepetane and if you're in a tearing hurry you can save an hour to Kotor by taking it, but you'll miss out on several interesting attractions. In the past this gap was closed by a chain in times of war to prevent shipping from entering the inner gulf.

Just 9km along the bay is the resort of **Risan**, apparently one of the oldest towns in Yugoslavia. Why it should be popular is hard to ascertain, since apart from a couple of Roman mosaics there's nothing here of any interest.

Perast on the other hand is in a state of charming decay. Its falling-down Venetian architecture is fine (best seen from above; head up the crumbling streets leading away from the shore) and the town also offers access to the overly photographed but undeniably attractive islands offshore. A fine illusion makes these sail up and down as you drive past them. Private rooms are available but the supply is slightly smaller than the demand.

Unless you're on an excursion the most convenient way of seeing the islands is to hire a boat. Beautiful cypresses adorn Sveti Djordje, whose only building is a heavily restored 12th century Benedictine abbey. Next door is Gospa od Škrpjela, an artificial island constructed on a submerged rock. There are several legends about why and by whom, varying from the daunting to the wildly imaginative. The fairly ordinary baroque church has an interesting collection of some 2,000 votive tablets and a beautiful green marble altar.

At the furthest extreme of the Gulf, the town of **Kotor** once came a close second to Dubrovnik as an attractive walled city. That all changed in 1979, when an earthquake almost levelled the old town, and even now they are still busy rebuilding – the work is being undertaken excellently in fine stone, but Kotor is, for the time being, something of a ghost town smelling of fresh mortar. Glances into boarded up buildings more often reveal glimpses of rubble and sky than anything habitable, and the full extent of the devastation can be seen from the fortress above.

Accommodation is plentiful – book private rooms from the kiosk outside the main gate to the old town, and be prepared to bargain. Food is strangely difficult to come by in the whole Gulf, but Kotor does have a couple of restaurants, though they're neither obvious nor especially cheap.

The town's main attractions are being repaired, so you may not be allowed to see the Cathedral of St. Tryphon, or the Church of St. Luke, both of which merit visits. See the treasury in the former, which amongst a whole collection of goodies houses St. Tryphon's head, bought from a passing relic-laden boat in 890 by a town in need of a patron, it seems. The Maritime museum would be a rainy day only attraction, were it not for the excellent 1:25,000 scale relief map, made in 1931 and complete with marked footpaths of the period. Make sketches and head for the hills.

Kotor's finest attraction is the fortress of St. Ivan which dominates the town, and embraces it with huge walls which date in places from the 9th century – though repairs were made as late as 1940. Although there is a proper path up to the top there are two more interesting ways of reaching it. The best of these is to leave the town by the small west gate and cross the pair of bridges just outside the walls. Turn right along the bank of the gully, keeping to the right of the works, and cross the wooden fence. The path is then a clear terraced zigzag leading up the mountainside. Going up this can be negotiated straight, but if you come down this way it's easier to stay on the path. Watch out for a couple of very savage dogs on your way – when I passed both were chained, but dangerous-looking.

On the way up you pass a couple of houses before arriving at a tiny ruined church. This is full of mud, its windows are smashed and it's only used now by cows. The damp remains of frescoes are still clearly visible, but irremediably damaged, and the cemetery is ragged and overgrown. It's a sad, touching place.

At about this level you can make your way across to the castle, and enter the walls through the leftmost of a large pair of windows. Once here you're back on the official path up inside the fortress. The zigzag path also goes on up from the church, and eventually leads to the valley behind the ridge above the gulf. There are a number of villages along here that are now deserted or only partially inhabited, and there is apparently a route that leads to Risan (18km away by road, a little further by this path).

The other route up to the fortress starts at the base of the leftmost walls and follows them up by a disused sentry path. This is exciting in that it's not completely safe, but the views are more spectacular than on the official route, and the chances are that you won't meet anyone here, since it's barred at the bottom by a small tree. The views from the top of the fortress, however you choose to get there, are excellent and well worth the steep walk.

THE MONTENEGRIN COAST

The coast from Budva down to the Albanian border remains the least developed in the country, but that's changing fast. Resorts are springing up everywhere, and in five years it will probably be as crowded as Istria. See it now.

Budva's old town, like Kotor's, was trashed by the 1979 earthquake. It's now been completely rebuilt and gives a fair impression of the city as it was, though obviously it hasn't the same lived in feel of the original. In a rather perverse way I preferred the ruins, which were dramatic at any time, and positively eerie in the evenings. Now Budva is Montenegro's biggest money spinner, and is filled throughout the season by package tours, who come here for Yugoslavia's sandiest beaches. Be warned that the bus station is always inordinately busy.

Avoid the ugly resort of Bečići and the expensive one of Miločer, and move on to **Sveti Stefan**, the much-photographed island fishing village attached to the mainland by a beautiful sandy causeway. Stay on the shore if you want to avoid the disappointment of discovering that it's not a village at all, but a De Luxe hotel complex – the original village was deserted after the war and enterprisingly converted in the 1960s.

The small resorts of **Petrovac** and **Sutomore** are unashamedly there for their beaches. Both are busy in summer, Sutomore more than Petrovac because it's on the Belgrade to Bar railway. Both can be skipped in favour of Ulcinj, the last town before Albania.

Just after Sutomore is the town of **Bar** which you might well visit in transit – ferries come here from Italy, Greece and points north in Yugoslavia, and it's the terminus for the new and wonderful Belgrade railway line. Catching buses or trains to or from here in summer is hard work: it's essential to reserve ahead as far as possible, but even then you may find yourself stranded here, and Bar isn't a place you'll want to hang around in for long. Unlike Kotor and Budva there wasn't anything interesting to rebuild after the 1979 earthquake.

Although it's no great secret **Ulcinj** is a pleasant place to be, at the head of the aptly named 12km Velika Plaža (big beach). The town is Turkish to the rest of the coast's Venetian, and has ample private rooms. If you want a beach this is probably it.

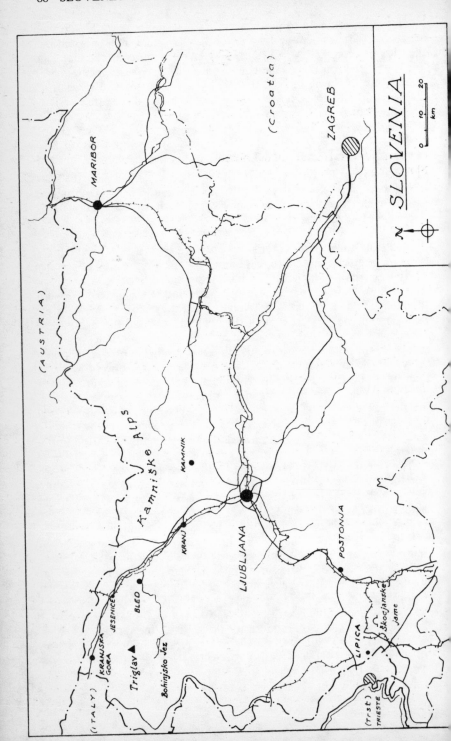

Slovenia

The Slovenes arrived with the Slavic hordes after the collapse of the Roman Empire and have stayed in the northwestern corner of the Balkans ever since. A thousand years of Austrian (mis)rule has obviously had its effects, most notably in town architecture, but the Slovenes remain culturally independent from both the west and the rest of Yugoslavia. In the mountains, where the weather is unreliable, unusual wooden racks (*kozolec*) are used for drying the hay – and in the Julian Alps a positive art form has been made out of these when they're built together to make open ended barns, known as *topolars*. Mountain pastures still contain tiny wooden villages where cheese is made in the summer, and people live here in one of the most harmonious balances with nature I've witnessed.

Economically and industrially Slovenia is way ahead of the rest of the country, with earnings over double the national average and a proportion of foreign cars and well stocked shops that's a shock after a visit to Macedonia or Kosovo. The Slovenes will tell you that this is due to their industriousness, and though it's true that they're the best organised, and most helpful and efficient of all Yugoslavs, they also profit from an advantageous geographical position, tucked up against the Italian and Austrian borders.

In recent years the republic's evident prosperity has caused political clashes with Belgrade, leading to a series of show trials in the summer of 1988, when the government accused Slovenia of wanting to leave the federation. The Republic defended itself with a call for a more commercial, forward thinking and upmarket brand of socialism. In their persistence and pride, at least, the Slovenes are notably Slavic.

The Slovenian coast is short and to my taste overdeveloped, but this is more than compensated for by the beautiful countryside and exceptional mountains, which offer some of the best Alpine walking in Europe. Geographically similar to the Austrian Alps, those in Slovenia have a unique charm which is only enhanced by the Slovenes, a friendly, hospitable and mountain loving people.

This national enthusiasm for the mountains has meant that Slovenia is well mapped, trails are clearly marked and there is room for over 6,000 in 163 mountain refuges, most of which are surprisingly comfortable and well-equipped. The area is also crossed by no less than three long distance walking paths, two of which are parts of the European network (E6-YU and E7-YU). The third is the superb Slovenian Alpine Traverse, a 300km route that takes in around 80 high spots. The mountains are well looked after, and nowhere more so than in the only national park, named after Yugoslavia's highest mountain, Triglav (2864m).

LJUBLJANA

Slovenia's capital is a lively and prosperous city that oozes Austro-Hungarian elegance – which is hardly surprising considering its background. It also boasts some pretty unappealing tower block suburbs, but that too isn't so unusual given a population of over 300,000, and a reputation for being the place that Yugoslavs would most like to move to.

Practical Information: The compact city centre spans the river Ljubljanica, with an old town underneath the castle on one side, and solid 19th century baroque on the other. Titova Cesta is a big boulevard that divides the city in two, with the river on the east side and the opera and museums to the west.

Buses and trains arrive on the north edge of town, a healthy quarter of an hour walk from the centre – head down Titova Cesta and you'll find a wonderful tourist information centre (TIC). Opposite this there's a post office on the corner of the pedestrian street which leads to the heart of the city, Prešernov Trg.

The ever friendly people at the TIC will provide you with maps, information and the necessary help with accommodation – private rooms are in short supply and out of town, the campsite's not very appealing and hotels are expensive. The cheapest, at £11 without bath, is the Park, which has an ambience midway between prison and long term institution. The student rooms and dormitories are much better value if you're there in summer. Better than staying in town is to make Ljubljana a daytrip – it's under an hour away from a whole heap of smaller towns, and is very well connected.

Food and evening socialising is centred on Prešernov Trg, where you'll find bars, terraces, pizzerias, grills and unexpectedly large numbers of people just out and about. Ljubljana often seems to be one festival after another, and it's a place where dancing in the streets isn't unusual. Prices are higher on average than you'd expect to pay in the south, but nonetheless not extravagant. Up by Titova Cesta there are fairly regular, if impromptu, new wave/punk gigs by local hopefuls, while more sedentary entertainment is on offer at the fine opera house on the smart side of town. Some of the best classical music in the country can also be heard here.

Ljubljana's sights are all within easy walking distance of the centre. Head up to the castle for a view across town, and up to the fine eleventh floor bar on top of the biggest building on Titova Cesta for an even better one (take the right hand lift; the left hand one's a decoy).

Down in town the Franciscan church and the cathedral are both big and baroque, though the cathedral's in better shape, probably the reason why I prefer the other. Between the two you can hardly miss the rather fanciful triple bridge across the river; unnecessary, but pleasing. Behind the cathedral there's an excellent daily market. By contrast Ljubljana's museums are fairly disappointing, and unless it's raining you can avoid them.

Before heading off to the mountains a visit to the **Slovene Alpine Association** is a good idea. It's situated at Dvoržakova 9, off the west side of Titova Cesta, before the station. They have a good selection of maps and guides and although not officially a retail outlet (try the Mladinska Knjiga bookshop, Titova Cesta 3, on the second floor) they can give you pointers about good places to go, how to get there, and even local weather forecasts.

They also have up to date information on the refuges and their opening times. (For the record most are open from June to September, and weekends only in May and October. Some are open at weekends only, a few are open year round.) An essential purchase is *How to climb Triglav* (in English, 75p), even if you're not going up that far (see p.102).

THE KAMNIŠKE ALPS

Forty kilometres north of Ljubljana lie the Kamniške Alps, one of the most interesting places for walking in Slovenia. Although virtually unknown to foreigners, the area is popular with Slovenes, especially at weekends, and has a dozen refuges and numerous marked trails. The Slovene Alpine Association publish an excellent 1:25,000 scale map of the area (Grintovci), which includes full details of the refuges and the principle trails, with (enthusiastic) timings. They also publish a less detailed map (1:50,000).

Practical Information

Access: The Alps can be walked from the south facing (Ljubljana) side, or more interestingly from the north, coming up from behind so that the summit you reach gives a view 50km across the plain, over 1,500m below. The southern side is much easier to reach – or leave – however, whatever your means of transport, so the best way is probably to start from the northern side and then work your way across the mountains to the south, staying at a refuge (or refuges) on the way. The range can be crossed in three places; each has a refuge nearby.

The northern point of access is the village of Solčava. This is reached via the small towns of Kamnik, Gornji Grad and Ljubno, and takes around three hours from Ljubljana, given good connections. Buses run from Ljubljana to Kamnik three or four times an hour; change here for Ljubno (two or three buses a day – only one on Sundays), and there for Solčava (two a day).

Kamnik isn't a bad place to be stuck in: it's a pleasant town with good fresh fruit stalls and a couple of great bars. Gornji Grad is even better (buses tend to break the journey here) – it has a cathedral-sized Baroque church, with some superb *trompe l'oeil* (look carefully at the eye-deceiving painted picture frames) and a wonderful atmosphere of airy disuse. There's also a bizarre pension here, off the main road, which has clean double rooms for an inexplicable £4 – the rather folksy

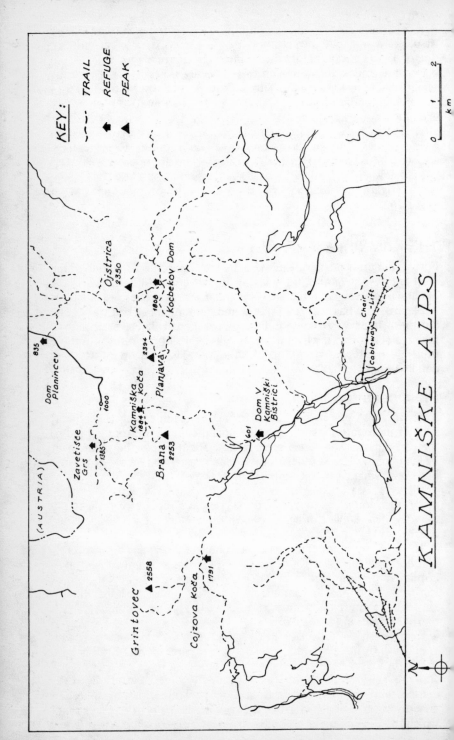

main road pension charges £16 for rather less. If you're here for the night the restaurant opposite the expensive pension is wonderful; full meals for two at about £5, no menu.

Once you've made it as far as Solčava (or as far as the bus goes – you want to go on up the valley as far as you can) keep heading upstream another three kilometres until you reach the refuge of Dom Planincev (800m). This is a friendly, well-equipped place with rooms for two, four and six people and also dormitories. They serve fairly cheap food and drink, and charge around £4 a head for the double rooms. A fairly amateur attempt was made to overcharge me here (on the grounds of my being the only foreigner for miles, I suspect), but I ended up paying around £12 for drinks, dinner and a room for two, which seemed reasonable.

If you can't face the several bus changes necessary, then the area is best accessed from the south. Go to Kamnik on a weekend and then catch one of the ten buses a day (three on weekdays) to Kamniški Bistrici, 13km up the valley (at 600m). There's a small refuge here, and it's only about four hours to either of the two nearest crests (both at around 1800m), which each have refuges with around 100 places.

Food and Equipment: Food shouldn't be any problem – refuges are never more than five hours apart and they seem suspiciously well stocked with food and drink at very reasonable prices (rarely more than it would cost in a town, and you're including a transport surcharge). Obviously survival food is a good idea (nuts, mintcake and the like), especially if you're going to be walking above 1800m – and take a litre of water per person.

You also need a good range of clothing: walking up a thousand metres in summer sunshine often requires shorts, but when you get there (up to 2500m) it could conceivably snow. Don't underestimate the incredibly changeable weather. From July onwards there's no real ice or snow left, but before this you may have to traverse occasional patches above 2000m. These paths are usefully marked 'very difficult' on the map. Anything marked 'rather difficult' implies a rocky or assisted part, and is easily manageable if you have any experience of simple climbing or scrambling.

Assistance: Here, as everywhere else in Slovenia, the voluntary mountain rescue service, GRS, does a fine job (see the *How to climb Triglav* booklet for more details). You can help them find you in the event of trouble by signing the visitors book at each refuge you pass and noting down where you came from and where you're headed.

Trails in the Kamniške Alps

If you don't have much time then the most interesting route is to come across the Alps, starting on the northern side, climbing one of the easier peaks on the way. The most popular of the three crossing points is Kamniško Sedlo (the Kamnik Saddle), at 1865m. This takes about four hours – the signs offer you a competitive three – from Dom Planincev and is an excellent walk (see below). To the west of the saddle is Brana (2253m), a not too difficult hour away, while to the east stands the considerably harder summit of Planjava (2394m). The walk between the saddle and Kamniški Bistrica takes nearly five hours either up or down – there's a vertical 1250m between the two.

The western crossing point, Kokrsko Sedlo (1791m), is hard to reach from the northern side, crossing at least one part marked 'very difficult' by whichever path you choose. But from Kamniški Bistrici, on the south side, it's an easy (if steep) four hour walk. From the refuge here, Coizova Koča, there's a good deal of reputedly excellent walking, including one or two very severe climbs but also an easy access to the road up to Jezersko, a resort near the Austrian border which is well connected with Ljubljana.

On the eastern side of the Alps there's a col called Škarje, at 2141m. An hour south of this stands Kocbekov Dom (1808m), an excellent starting point for a good range of easy and medium walks in the eastern Alps. From the northern side there's a path starting from Dom Planincev: cross the valley and follow the marked path to Koča Pod Ojstrico (a little over an hour). The rightmost trail from here leads up to Škarje, soon after which the path branches right for the refuge and left to the summit of Ojstrica.

The refuge is also accessible from a path a kilometre south of Kamniški Bistrica in a little over five hours. The last half hour is moderately tricky. From Škarje or the refuge it's under an hour and a half to the splendid peak of Ojstrica (2350m) – although this is well secured by pitons and cables be prepared for some fairly vertiginous views on the way.

From Dom Planincev to Kamniško Sedlo: This walk could be done in three hours, especially if you have your own transport or can cadge a lift as far as the parking area at the end of the road, some three kilometres from the refuge, and nearly 200m up from it. Allowing four or more will make things considerably easier – I found it quite hard work after a month or so with nothing more strenuous than a dash to the shops, and took a little under four hours.

If you have to walk along the road it's no bad thing – a gently winding way up along the valley floor towards its head, with the obvious jagged cut of Kotliči (1974m) in front of you. Kamniško Sedlo is the next dip to the left of this, as you look up the valley.

The metalled road ends in a parking place with a small chalet café. Fifteen minutes uphill from here you reach a waterfall, Slap Rinka, which although not especially voluminous does fall a clear 50m onto flat rocks, creating a wonderful impression on a fine day. From here onwards the path is steep, winding up to the top of the waterfall and then following the course of the stream as it tumbles down from above with authentic rushing water noises.

At Kamniške Sedlo. (Photo: Martine Simon.)

The trail then heads into a steep and rocky wood and emerges an hour and a quarter from the parking place at Frischaufov Dom (simply marked Koča on the signs), a beautifully situated refuge currently being further upgraded so that it will have 120 places by 1989. This is situated at 1305m and is used as a starting point by weekend walkers who come up here from Ljubljana on Friday night and start walking seriously on Saturday morning – it can get crowded, especially in August and early September. Facilities are less luxurious here than at Dom Planincev, but are nonetheless good (rooms at £2 a head, 50p in dormitories; filling meals at about £3).

From Frischaufov Dom upwards there are consistently superb views. The upper part of the route starts by making a long traverse around the head of the valley, cutting across an exposed scree slope on a wide trail before approaching a very steep zigzag leading up to the lower rock face of Brana. The rocky part of the climb is eighty minutes from Frischaufov Dom and starts at 1700m.

The trail now cuts across the rock face diagonally, and would be very exposed were it not for more than adequate cable and piton assistance. At the top of this part there's a rather gravelly section which isn't aided, but with a clear head and not too many glances downwards it isn't difficult to negotiate. The last section cuts across a precipitous slope, somewhat shallower on its upper than lower side, but the path is flat and wide enough to walk steadily across.

The trail comes out quite suddenly onto the saddle at nearly 1900m, a smooth slope covered in tufty mountain grass. The views both north and south from here are really excellent – look down at the now miniaturised Slap Rinka on one side and across towards Ljubljana (and beyond, on a clear day) on the other.

Kamniška Koča, a friendly, airy refuge, perches on the hump of the saddle and provides first class soup. Rooms here go for £3 a head, beds in dormitories for £1.50. It makes a fine place for climbs to the nearby summits, and can be used as the launchpad for the spectacular ridge walk east to Ojstrica (several parts are 'rather difficult', but none 'very'), or for the eastern traverse to Kocbekov Dom, which stays below 2115m. The western route to Coizova Koča takes at least seven hours, and is 'very hard' in places. Only for experienced mountaineers.

Just to the west of Kamniško Sedlo stands the impressive pointy peak of Brana. This is marked as being another hour, but unless you're out for a quick jog and in a hurry to finish the course then I'd recommend an hour and a half – it's a vertical 400m. The start of the route to the summit is a rather nerve testing traverse across the upper end of a scree slope which gives you the very real impression that if you were to slip it would be a long long while before you stopped. The steep path then crosses a rocky spur but is well assisted all the way and although marked as being 'rather hard' it feels safer than the lower portion. The view from the summit more than justifies the long journey up.

The eastward path from the saddle skirts around the lower shoulders of Planjava, before approaching its second peak. The trail is exposed for much of the way, and routes to the top all require some serious mountaineering experience. If you have this then these two, and the summits of Grintovec (2558m) and Skuta (2532m) are all supremely good places to be; if you haven't, then content yourself with the very worthy Brana or Ojstrica.

BLED

Ranking alongside the Postojna caves as one of Slovenia's top tourist attractions, Lake Bled is undeniably one of the most beautiful places in Yugoslavia. True, the atmosphere can be marred by crowds, but walk round the lake at dawn and you'll see a fairytale prettiness. At times this tends towards Disneyland artificial – right down to the mountain backdrop, the castle perched up on its bluff and an Alpine church on a small island in the middle of the lake. I prefer the wilder, more outdoor-looking Lake Bohinj, but since you have to pass Bled to get there, it would be foolish not to take in both.

Bled's main sight is the crystal lake, along with its castle and island. A walk round the perimeter is as pleasant a way of seeing it as any, and if you really dawdle can be made to last nearly two hours. Another hour can be usefully consumed at the oars of a rowing boat (for hire from several places around the lake, about £1 an hour). Row out to the island as early as you can and see the church before the noisesome restaurant there starts up. The church itself is no big deal, but situation counts for a lot, and if you follow the guides you'll toll the bell and say a prayer, which is good for the concentration whatever your beliefs.

Back on shore you'll find the castle a short steep walk up to an overpriced restaurant with a view. There's an unusually disparate collection of uninteresting material in the museum here. Better by far is to walk up a path on the lake side of the castle to the crag next door – same wonderful view, no people.

One of the biggest attractions in Bled, in a villa on the shore beneath the castle, is the Triglav National Park office. A new centre has recently opened here with the admirable aim of increasing the general awareness of mountain ecology, conservation and local wildlife. They also sell local maps and guides, including an excellent hardback book on the park (in English), which is worth every penny of what at first seems a steep £6.

Practical Information: Reaching Bled is no problem – hourly buses come from Ljubljana and take an hour and a half. Everything else is as easily arranged, though you'll have to expect a price tag commensurate with its popularity.

For accommodation most people will want a suite with a lake view at the Grand Hotel or Bled Villa (once Tito's rather fine summer house), until they find that this costs £90 a night. They'll then head for Alpetour or Kompass, both on Ljubljanska (the main road heading up away from the lake), who have private accommodation for over 4,000. I had a really beautiful room in a splendid house called 'Anna', just off the east side of Ljubljanska, near the bus stop (£14 for a double with a wonderful breakfast). A cheaper option is the campsite at the opposite end of the lake, though this is fairly often full up (hardly surprising), and attracts a crowd that seem content lying on the small beach in front, like stranded seals.

There's nowhere particularly cheap to eat in Bled unless you picnic or go to the dive opposite the bus stop at the upper end of Ljubljanska, which makes you feel like an extra from *Barfly*, only the drunks here are noticeably less violent. Various and quite edible fare of the chicken and chips variety, but not recommended for romantic dinners by candlelight. Excellent lake trout can be had from the second restaurant past the Grand on the left (rather smart, on the shore). Meals at around £15 for two. If you go round the left hand side you'll see your dinner innocently swimming round beforehand.

Hribarice, in the Triglav National Park.

THE TRIGLAV NATIONAL PARK

Triglav is the best organised, most accessible and highest of Yugoslavia's national parks, and contains some of the best – and best documented – walking in the country. The park is named after its highest mountain, Triglav (2864m), literally 'three heads', which has been a symbol of Slovenian independence and ideals since ever. Although the area is well known amongst the Alpine climbing fraternity most of the people you meet walking here are Slovenes.

After the sensitive frontiers in this area were finally rationalised in 1954, the Triglav National Park was set up in earnest, with an area greatly increased from the original 1924 mountain reserve. It now stretches nearly as far as the Austrian border to the north, the Italian border to the west, Lake Bled to the east and includes Lake Bohinj to the south. The rapidly expanding winter and summer resorts of Kranjska Gora and Bovec are just outside the park limits, but both offer alternative access points.

The Soča Valley

The Sava, Trenta and Soča valleys all cut deep into the landscape, and if you get the chance to drive along any of them (even by bus) you'll be rewarded by a series of suitably neck-craning views. The Soča was the scene for some of the most vicious fighting of the First World War, with each side losing over a million men. Suitably graphic descriptions of the events can be found in Ernest Hemingway's *A Farewell to Arms* – he was an ambulance driver here during the thick of it, and wrote of what he witnessed at some length.

Much of the fighting took place around Kobarid (Caporetto), though to pass through the pleasant village now you'd have no idea. Just north of here (4km west of Bovec), as the river takes a sharp bend, look out for Boka Slap, a voluminous 60m waterfall on the north side of the road. You can walk up to the base of this in ten or fifteen minutes, and brave the heavy spray: it's especially impressive after rains or during the spring melts.

The Vršič Pass

The road from Bovec to Kranjska Gora crosses through the Triglav National Park and goes over the superb Vršič Pass at 1611m, having come up from below 500m. There are 50 numbered hairpins on this narrow road, and going along it in an old bus on a cold, wet and windy day is as scary a way of passing the time as any mountain climbing.

A number of good trails start from the pass, and there's a useful refuge just off the road. A two day walk from here would take you to Triglav via the harder north approaches, allowing you to come down the other side, to Bohinj, in three to four days in all. It makes a spectacular alternative to the milder south side.

Bohinj

Slovenia's largest (just over 4km long) and most appealing lake is less than an hour away from Bled, but attracts well under half the visitors and is considerably less developed. And even though some 85,000 tourists do visit annually (20,000 from abroad), the lake and its surrounding villages have more than enough room to cope.

The area has an untamed yet pastoral feel to it, and even with the tourism remains a poor farming community. Surrounded by uncompromising mountains and under snow for over three months of the year, it's a difficult place in which to make a living from the land, and yet the people here somehow manage, using a combination of potatoes, small crops, cheesemaking and forestry.

Winter tourism is also on the increase, with excellent cross country skiing in the area. In the harder winters the lake freezes over and makes a pretty good skating rink – though since the verger and his son went fatally through the ice after the war the locals haven't been so keen. Customs here reflect the area's long term isolation and superstition is alive and strong, with the moon and the weather at least as influential on people's lives as the church. On death an unusual custom persists: mothers are mourned for two years, but fathers for only 18 months – this may be a legacy from a more matriarchal society.

Local lore backed up with hard facts provides the text for a superb book of pictures of Bohinj by one of Yugoslavia's best photographers, Joco Žnidaršič. It's most easily found in bookshops in Ljubljana.

'We will endeavour to render you exceedingly agreeable' runs the message in the local brochure, and as a statement on how I took to Bohinj it couldn't be more accurate.

The sights in the area are low key, often natural phenomena: and waterfalls and mountains, weather changes and the way people live are more interesting here than any museums or picture galleries. A notable exception is the rather small-time Gothic church of Sv. Janez, at the head of the lake where the Sava starts its long journey down to Belgrade. It possesses some interesting frescoes dating from the 15th century, although the church is older. Look out for an unusual white devil, perched insidiously on a shoulder; far more credible than the cloven-hooved black chaps toting pichforks.

Across the bridge and round the corner you'll find a statue of four fairly heroic looking men pointing at the horizon. Follow the finger and you'll see that they're looking up at Triglav – these are the first four people who climbed the mountain in 1778. Look closely and you'll see that their clothing is hopelessly inadequate and their rucksacks have wooden frames.

Whatever your personal aspirations to higher things (like Triglav, for example), take the time to walk around the lake, a beautiful 12km tour that takes between three and four hours. Going clockwise from the bridge at the eastern end, follow the road along the southern shore until you reach the campsite. A left hand turn here leads to the ski lift up Mt. Vogel, one way of avoiding a 1,000m climb. If you're going walking into the mountains anyway save your money for later.

At the western end of the lake, and centred on the Hotel Zlatorog (named after the mythical mountain goat who guards Triglav's golden treasure), is a smallish resort. This is within an hour of the famous Slavica waterfall, where the river drops down 50m, just after its source. The river then runs down to the lake, and leaves at the other end as the Sava.

The walk along the northern shore of the lake is gorgeous, following a country footpath under the cliffs, with views across the lake to the upswinging slopes of Vogel. If you only want to walk half way round then you can walk the northern path and catch a bus back to the eastern end from the Hotel Zlatarog.

Practical Information: Despite being up in the hills at the end of a valley Bohinj is easy to reach, and eight buses a day make the 30km run up from Bled. Stop at Bohinjsko Jezero, the lake itself, rather than any of the several Bohinj villages on the way. A hundred metres back up the road to Bled, on the right hand side, is a tourist information office, an exchange bureau, a souvenir shop and a very ordinary if cheap restaurant.

Tourist information will find you a private room (£8-£14 for doubles, depending on class, location and season), but if you're staying for less than three nights they'll sting you for a surcharge. If you have the time and energy then wandering up the road to Stara Fužina (across the bridge, and about a kilometre past Sv. Janez) and knocking on doors where rooms are advertised will net you a cheaper one. The second house on the left, 500m from the lake, has some of the most comfortable beds I've ever slept in and serves copious breakfasts (£10 for doubles, £8 if you forgo breakfast).

Hotels aren't that expensive, at £18-25 for quality doubles, but with private rooms in abundance you don't need to bother. The same goes for camping, which runs to £7 a night (£9 in season) at the site on the south side of the lake (room for 600). I took a private room for the nights before and after walking, and otherwise stayed in refuges.

Food around Bohinj is generally good, with the Hotel Jezero's restaurant dishing up some of the lake's really excellent trout (full meals at around £8 for two). It makes the perfect post Triglav celebration, and you can eat out on the terrace if the evening's fine. They also serve 'Both with egg', 'Mincedard' and 'Been Soup', if the menu's to be believed.

If you're going walking for a few days then make sure you change enough money (in the Bohinj tourist office) for refuges and food – I took £60 for two people, for two nights and three days, and managed to spend most of it.

Maps, Books and Guides

A number of maps and guidebooks to the Triglav National Park are available, and if you speak Slovenian or even German there is a wide variety. The National Park Office in Bled has a full selection (see *Bled*) and most of these can be picked up in Ljubljana at a bookshop or the Slovene Mountain Association (see *Ljubljana*).

The most important investment is the pocket guide *How to climb Triglav* (75p), even if you're not going to – the guide has useful information on climbing and walking in Slovenia generally and the Triglav National Park specifically, and also contains important details of mountain rescue and a superb glossary of the Slovenian terms you might need in the event of an accident.

The hardback guide to the park is more of a general publication than a walking guide, though for anyone interested in mountain life, wildlife and some superb pictures, it's £6 well spent. Budding botanists will also want the *Protected Plants* booklet (£1).

The area is well mapped out, though in truth you could cover it without maps if you follow the red and white markers and stay on the trails. In practice most people will feel safer with a map, and that of the Triglav National Park (1:50,000) is one of the best available. Also published by the Slovene Mountain Association is a two sheet 1:50,000 scale map of the Julian Alps. For Triglav you'll need the eastern half.

Wonderful, and more detailed, are the pair of 1:20,000 maps covering Bohinj and Triglav, and at £1 a go you can probably afford to splash out on these two as well as the one of the whole park. Freytag and Berndt publish one of their 1:100,000 *Wanderkarten* of the Julian Alps, which can be bought in Stanfords in London (£3) – this gives you a pretty good advance idea of what to expect, but isn't really detailed enough on site.

For most walking in the Julian Alps, and almost all in the Triglav National Park, you won't need a mountain guide – paths are well marked and secured, and refuges are regularly spaced. Nonetheless, you'll probably get more from the mountains if you do take a guide – they know the flowers and plants indigenous to the area, and can explain the bewildering variety in the geomorphology, as well as leading you to places you wouldn't think of going alone.

Compared with neighbouring countries there is a shorter history of tourism here. One of the results is that there aren't any full time guides in the Julian Alps. Instead local experts take time off from their normal employment to act as guides (they nonetheless have to pass strict exams to do this), and this can be arranged through the national park office in Bled or the tourist office in Bohinj. Rates start at a very reasonable £10 a day for gentle walking, and high mountaineering off the trails costs about twice that. Compare this with French Alpine prices of £60 a day and upwards.

I didn't take a guide, partly because I already had lots of expert advice from the Slovene Mountain Association about which way to go, and partly because I wanted to check that climbing Triglav was possible without too much outside help.

Food and Lodging

Although you would normally take a considerable amount of food with you on an expedition that could easily last three or four days, there's no need to when you walk in the Triglav National Park. Altogether there are 35 refuges, and these all serve hot food of some description. A nourishing soup at a refuge is far better than eating something out of a heavy tin, and provides just the right balance of heat, nourishment, salt and liquid for walking. Refuges are never more than five hours apart, and it's usually only a couple of hours between them. Nonetheless, I did carry some emergency supplies, and private goodies like nut bars, chocolate and mintcake, and was grateful for these. And take a litre of water – you can refill this at the refuges, which all have a clean water supply.

Camping is strictly forbidden in the park, so your options are to return to base each evening, or to stay in the refuges. In any case, with single day ascensions of up to 2000m you don't really want to be carrying your camping stuff about with you. Refuges cost about £4 a head in rooms of four or six people (perhaps half that in dormitories), and are convivial places where friends are quickly made and notes cheerfully exchanged. Bedding is provided. Although you can't book refuges in advance they'll find you a place even when they're full.

There isn't much choice of food, but you can always get something warm, tasty and filling, and there seems to be no shortage of beer, wine and *vinjak*, even when this has to be helicoptered up. An allowance of £10 a day all in (food, drink and accommodation) should be more than adequate. The refuges within the national park are all open from the last week in June until the end of September, with some being open outside these times at weekends, and a few in permanence.

Assistance

The Slovenian Mountain Rescue service (GRS) is a voluntary organisation which is as well supported here as in the rest of the republic. See *How to climb Triglav* for more information. Don't forget to sign in at the refuges you pass and note down your destination and where you've just come from – this helps the GRS trace you in the event of trouble.

Park Conduct

The following suggestions are supplied for visitors by the National Park Office in Bled – they're all pretty self-evident, but they nonetheless bear repeating: keep to the marked trails if you're inexperienced; take adequate bad weather clothing; don't harm animals or plants; take your litter away with you; close gates you open; don't damage Alpine cottages, signs, visitor's books or altitude stamps; prevent forest fires; don't cause rockfalls; greet other mountaineers; respect the nature and cultural wealth of the park.

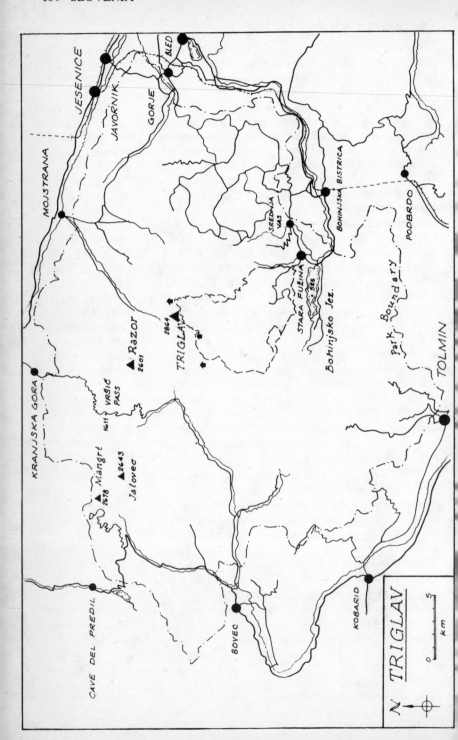

Weather

The variable weather in the Triglav National Park is probably the single biggest danger. Sunny days can quickly turn to snowstorms (temperatures can fall by over ten degrees in half an hour, and snow falls above 1800m in every month of the year), and the opposite effects of warm winds coming down the valleys (like the Swiss *foehn*) cause dangerous avalanches in the spring.

Temperatures in the park tend towards the cool (above 2200m the annual average is below freezing), with the highest and lowest recorded temperatures at Kredarica (2515m) being 18°C and a fresh -28°C. The July average here is under 6°C. Down in the valleys the picture is brighter, with Tolmin (180m) having all time highest and lowest recorded temperatures of 38°C and -18°C. The July average here is a healthy 20°C.

Precipitation is medium to heavy, but again very variable – occasionally over a metre of snow arrives in two days, and at 2500m over a centimetre of the stuff falls on an average 269 days of the year. After the middle of October any snow that falls at this altitude stays until the end of June.

Storms and high winds are also a danger, particularly on exposed ridges where lightning finds its favourite targets. Winds of over 200kph have been recorded and 150kph isn't exceptional. If you're caught in an early afternoon summer storm after a sunny morning then you should find or make a shelter – it will pass within two hours. Don't push on through the storm, and avoid exposed ridges.

The best weather occurs in September and the first fortnight of October, when you'll have the lowest rainfall, the least storms and the most sunshine. August is particularly prone to storms, but is otherwise a second best, particularly if you avoid walking between noon and 3pm. Precipitation is at its highest in the mountains in June and July.

Flora and Fauna

Those interested in the nature and wildlife of the Triglav National Park should invest in the hardback guide, which has a superb section, complete with colour pictures and full Latin names. What appears here is just an appetiser.

The tree pattern, and in particular the tree line, is complex. In some places larch and spruce grow highest, but where it's regularly too humid then beech will be at the upper limit.

Throughout the park beautiful and unusual flowers are to be found. There are a number indigenous to the area, and some which are only found on and around Triglav itself, which are of special interest. Above 2200m flowers must adapt to a fierce climate, where the summer temperature cycle has a daily range of 26°C (-10°C to 19°C). The result is tiny, tenacious and unusually colourful flowers, most famous of which is edelweiss, found here in the mountains in the northern part of the park.

On Triglav you should look out for the Triglav rose and the Triglav gentian, both of which have tiny flowers and even smaller leaves, which grow like moss. The Triglav rose is thought to have survived the last ice age. Less common is the sky herald, which looks at first sight like tightly bunched forget-me-nots.

Yugoslavia's highest flower is the Julian poppy, whose blossom looks just like the conventional variety, but with white petals and a yellow heart. One was spotted right on Triglav's summit a couple of years back.

Lower down various species of saxifrage are found, here almost always in common with the Zois bellflower, named after the eighteenth century botanist who discovered it nearby. Also common are the Frolich gentian, which might be a crocus were it not for its flowering in August and September, and the large yellow gentian, used widely for medicinal purposes.

The Triglav National Park has a well documented and varied animal life ranging from rare fresh water sponges in Lake Bohinj to pairs of golden eagles. All of the Alpine mammalia are found here, from marmot and marten to mountain hare, red and roe deer, ibex and chamois. Bears pass through occasionally, but don't live here.

Smaller creatures include a variety of lizards, a few snakes (harmless if unprovoked) and the black salamander, a curious amphibian that gives birth to live young and only comes out in wet weather, spending the rest of its time hiding under rocks. Buzzards, kestrels and sparrowhawks are all fairly common, and it's possible that you might also see capercaillies, black grouse or ptarmigans. It's unlikely that you'll spot the area's most unusual bird, the eagle owl, which in Europe is only found here, in the national park. It's the largest of the owl family, with a body up to 70cm long.

Climbing Triglav

Each year, on the first weekend in September, a hundred Slovene women climb Triglav. With them go the top ten guides, and the sight of 110 people strung out on the ridge between Triglav and its lower peak is unforgettable. Be warned that the refuges are crowded the night before.

There are over twenty ways of approaching Triglav, all of which have their merits. The best dozen of these are detailed in *How to climb Triglav* (the information provided in this section is sufficient for climbing Triglav, but the pocket guide has useful supplementary details of the Slovenian language, mountain rescue, etc.). Generally speaking, approaches from the south are less tricky (and perhaps less spectacular) than those from the north.

I was advised by Danilo from the Slovene Mountain Association, and had an excellent three day hike, comprising two complete routes and parts of two others suggested by the pocket guide (for reference, 3A, 1D, 3F, 3D). This was a circular trail, beginning and ending in the village of Stara Fužina, one kilometre away from the eastern end of Lake Bohinj, and is described below.

A final word: Don't climb Triglav alone. If you're not in company it's strongly advisable to team up with people at the first refuge you reach and walk with them. Triglav is steep and can be dangerous, and although there are enough people around to make the chance of an unseen accident unlikely, the mountains are big enough to hide whole groups, let alone solitary figures – especially in bad weather.

Timings: Without rushing excessively at any point the whole journey took 26 hours, split as follows: Day one – up 1950m, 8 hours; Day two – up 650m, down 1500m, 11 hours; Day three – up 100m, down 1200m, 7 hours. By the timings on the signs (which don't, in any case, count breaks) it would take 20 hours. An hour (and 100m down and up) of the second day was spent investigating a path we didn't eventually take, making the real total 25 hours.

All roads going north out of Stari Fužina join up where they level out at 640m, after a steep gravel kilometre-long approach. On the morning we went in early September we started off in dense lake fog, but found ourselves in hazy sunshine as soon as we were 100m up and half an hour away from the village.

The path now continues for quite a while along the course of the river, undulating very gently and passing small summer pastures. As the pocket guide points out, the only disadvantage of this route up is that it's a long time before you see Triglav at all, and a good hour and a half before you even start to climb properly. This isn't really a problem, as it gives you a chance to warm up your muscles and look around. Keep to the left of the river, following signs for Voje. You pass a small refuge half way up the valley on the right that still looked pretty sleepy when we went past at 8.30am. Ignore the left hand turn soon after this, and follow signs for Vodnikov Dom.

When the path starts going uphill it does so with a vengeance. Remember not to walk too fast – from this point to the refuge for the night (Triglavski Dom) is more than a vertical 1800m. The way zigzags up through deciduous woods on a rocky path that gradually becomes less rough underfoot. The forest here is really beautiful, with a deep tranquillity aided by the deep and sound-absorbing beds of old dry leaves which stay from one year to the next.

Eventually (an hour from the valley floor) the path crosses a small pasture (1150m) with over-bright green grass after the depths of the woods. This is the first point at which you can see how far up you've come – over 500m. After a hundred metres the path goes back up into a forest with glimpses of incredibly steep slopes and the occasional cliff.

At about 1400m the trail finally gets less consistently steep, and allows you to look around more instead of doggedly ahead. It also comes out of the thick forest definitively, and skirts along the base of a cliff along one side of a high valley. As this narrows it encloses a patch of quite scary wasteland, with blasted land filled in with loose rocks and skeleton trees, tufts of earth and scrubby vegetation. Doubtless our appreciation of this was enhanced by the clouds building up in the distance, the enclosed feeling of being surrounded by very close, very high mountains and the heavy buzzing of late summer flies.

Through all this the trail winds a constantly unpredictable path, gaining altitude in a series of unexpected loops around and over rocks that take on a more and more definite look of karst – further below there's enough topsoil to hide its character.

After four and a half hours (from Stara Fužina) you should be at about 1650m. From this point you'll come across a series of false crests leading towards Vodnikov Dom, a refuge at 1815m. Each of these reveals Triglav (just left of straight ahead), with the little refuge of Planika Dom (2408m) below its summit. In silhouette, on the right hand shoulder, you can see Triglavski Dom (2515m). They both look closer than they really are.

When Vodnikov Dom comes into sight, about ten minutes before you reach it, you can see the small mountain village of Velo Polje 100m below you on the left hand side. If you have the time or energy to make a detour then you can go down to this and see cheese being made the old fashioned way. With another 700m to climb you may prefer to go to one of the villages lower down, on your return from Triglav.

Vodnikov Dom is a small refuge by Triglav standards, with space for about forty people, if pushed. Most visitors use it as a stopping off point, taking in some of the quite wonderful soup and coffee served here as a pick-me-up before the afternoon's walking. It's situated at the junction of a number of paths, and although generally busy it's rarely crowded.

It was after 1.30pm by the time we left here, and the weather looked as if we would be lucky to reach the refuge dry. At first we had planned to go to Planika Dom, the traditional point of attack for people climbing Triglav from this side, but given the dodgy weather and the fact that Triglavski Dom has its own weather station, we decided to take the more eastern route.

From Vodnikov Dom the routes to both refuges stay together for the first hour, traversing some very steep and unsecured slopes – the path isn't steep, but the gradient you're cutting across is. Where the path itself is steeper or obviously dangerous it has been secured by pitons and occasionally with metal rope cables. As you approach a saddle at 2020m look out for the violent forms of the karst on the left hand side.

At the saddle there's a meeting of paths. Dom Planika is clearly signed to the left; follow the right hand markings for Kredarica, the name of the mountain that Triglavski Dom sits beside. From here onwards (and for most of the next two days) the views are unreservedly spectacular.

As you cross the saddle you can suddenly see down a great distance to the right, where long steep cliffs run alongside the south side of the valley running down to Krma, highest of the access points by road from Bled. To the west is the summit of Triglav, with steep scree and shale slopes leading towards the lower of its two peaks.

You need to be sure-footed from here all the way up to the refuge, a steep and occasionally slippery hour or so, with several assisted parts. A narrow ledge with cables and pitons was made less than easy for us by the surprising appearance of 40 sheep using the same path to come down. Towards the top we suddenly found ourselves enveloped in damp fog, and finding the next red and white markers was quite a job – especially when some miserable wind-chilled rain started down on us. We were fortunately only 20 minutes from the refuge.

Triglavski Dom is one of the best equipped and most friendly refuges I've ever stayed in. Accommodation is provided in rooms of four and six beds, and also in a couple of large dormitories. I couldn't ascertain whether there were rooms for less than four people. Food is nourishing and wholesome, and coffee is served in large cups ideal for starting you off in the morning.

We set off at 8am, in a bitterly cold wind and with the top of the mountain shrouded in worrying looking cloud. The weather forecast however was generally good, especially for the morning. The whole of the climb up the last 350m from Triglavski Dom is pretty exciting, with steep rock faces to be crossed and a gusting wind to divert your attention from the increasingly giddy views down the mountain. This side of Triglav is more impressive than the ascent from Planika Dom, since you can see straight down to the Trenta Valley, a near vertical 2000m below.

The climb from the refuge is a marked hour, but we took it gently and arrived in an hour and a half. The last section, after the paths from the two refuges meet, is one of the most spectacular I've ever walked. The trail runs along a ridge, in places well under a metre wide, and isn't always secured. To the north there's a drop of over a thousand metres, while to the south a clear 400m separates you from the plateau on which you can see the Planika refuge. Altitude euphoria isn't uncommon up here, but be warned that it can also make you careless. And with ice-covered pitons and freezing winds you do need to be careful.

The peak of Triglav isn't a disappointment, though I must admit the table with the visitor's book on it looks a little out of place. It's hard to imagine anyone carrying it up here. There's also a small and rather bizarre rocket-like structure perched on the top. This apart it's pure joy, standing at the highest point, with mountain ranges stretching away beneath you in all directions – as we climbed up, the clouds came and went and finally swept away altogether.

From Triglav it's almost all downhill. The path we took starts by going down the south face, the least steep of the immediate approaches. This isn't to say that it's a gentle slope – a considerable part of the route down to the col at 2659m is assisted, with good reason.

At the col the path splits in two, with the left hand route going down to Planika Dom and the right hand route going over the pass and down to the west. The next section isn't easy, with gravelly rock crumbling underfoot on a very steep path. Fear of slipping is the main problem – there's nothing much to break your fall for several hundred metres.

An hour and a half from the top should see you safely down onto a more or less horizontal path not much above 2400m. This is surrounded by wild, sculptured rocks and punctuated by clusters of tiny Alpine flowers. This is all dominated by the bulk of Triglav, which looks quite unassailable – even knowing that you've just come down from its summit. After a typical karst crest you suddenly arrive at the upper edge of a valley which ends in a col, a suitable home for Tržaška Koča (2152m), the ideal lunchspot (around four and a half hours from Triglavski Dom).

After another fine soup we decided to take the path which avoided the steep climb between Dolič (2164m) and Čez Hribarice (2358m). This leads down from Tržaška Koča on the path to Luknja, and then branches left, signed for Prehodavica, the entrance to the seven lakes valley.

Having gone down a fair way we discovered that the route led across about 50m of snow before traversing a dangerous looking slope on an unsecured path, part of which seemed to have been washed away. With two members of the party inexperienced (and unwilling) on snow, we decided to head back after all. That night we spoke to two Germans who scoffed at our caution, having walked the path upwards the same day – though later they admitted it wasn't easy.

The trail from Dolič up to the pass into Hribarice is indeed steep, and by this time (nearly 4pm) we were getting tired. Nonetheless none of us regretted making the effort – Hribarice is incredible, something between desert and blasted moonscape, an utterly dry karst bowl with miniature flowers somehow surviving amongst the devastated rocks.

The path crosses this wild and windy place and comes out at the head of the Seven Lakes Valley. Just before this a sign indicates that the Seven Lakes Refuge (signed 7J) is two hours away – it's better to allow three. A steep, winding path leads down to the first, and least impressive of the seven lakes. Soon afterwards we chanced upon two wonderful groups (six and eight) of chamois, high up on a scree slope. Apparently this is an unusual sight – certainly judging by our friends' reactions in Bled and Ljubljana.

The Seven Lakes Valley, through which we were now walking, is an unlikely combination of Wild West cliffs on one side and karst on the other, with lakes spread out in the middle. All very attractive under the setting sun, although we were flagging after ten and a half hours of walking: 'more bloody karst' appears at the end of a badly scrawled page in my notebook.

Coming down from the summit of Triglav, looking south.

Koča pri Triglavski Jezerih (1685m) is neatly situated between two of the valley's smallest and most attractive lakes. The refuge is one of the most popular in the national park, and prone to crowding in high summer and at weekends – even at midweek in September it was busy. Their coffee wasn't a patch on Triglavski Dom's, but the staff were at least as cheerful and friendly. And if you're much over six foot you'll find the bunk beds far too short. Petty complaints; it's a great place.

The following morning we set off at around 8am in clear, cold and sunny weather. The route we decided to take back to Stara Fužina cuts across the plateau between 500m and 1000m above Lake Bohinj, before coming down through forest and running along the upper edge of the cliff on its northern shore.

After leaving the refuge, keep to the left hand side of the lake along its whole shore. About twenty minutes from the refuge you reach a signpost – take the left hand branch, signed Plovčarija and Stara Fužina.

The trail now leaves the valley floor and cuts round to the left before coming out onto mountain pastureland after nearly an hour. In the middle of this there are a few wooden buildings and signs in four languages offering milk to the right – this is the turning for Pl. Viševnik. It's not that obvious, and we went straight on, towards Pl. Dedno Polje, cutting across a small path between the two eastward routes on realising our mistake.

After walking for two and a half hours from the refuge we had reached the small mountain village of Pl. Viševnik. On the way here the route is constantly varied, with different karst forms in strong evidence, including sinkholes, large depressions where underground caves had collapsed (*poljes*) and the classic sculpted and carved shapes in the rock.

Pl. Viševnik is situated on a small plateau only accessible on foot, and has the unspoiled, slightly deserted look of any tiny village this cut off. Some of the houses had been recently repaired, but more looked as if they had been long abandoned, bearing witness to the continually decreasing numbers of people who live the traditional life, spending the summer months in the mountains and wintering in the valleys.

The 100m high slope leading out of the village is the last real ascent of the journey. After this the path then runs across a high meadow, with grasses and trees that wouldn't look out of place in Hampshire were it not for the flying grasshoppers and the backdrop of hard grey mountains.

At a small karst pass, half an hour from Viševnik, you can suddenly see as far as Stara Fužina several kilometres away. From here it's all downhill. At first the trail goes down steeply through deep evergreen forests with the occasional deep pothole in the rocks, until after an hour it joins a clearing at the end of a forest road. This occurs at the just the point where the pine trees turn to luxurious deciduous, and makes an excellent spot for a picnic – if you've got any food left.

The path continues on the other side of the road and cuts down gently to the edge of the cliff overlooking Lake Bohinj. On the other side the ski resort and the Hotel Vogel can be seen at about the same altitude, while the lake 800m below glitters superbly. Enjoy the view before going on down the long steep path through the forest. At one point the path crosses an unexpectedly large field of deep rhubarb before plunging back into the woods.

It comes out at an idyllic place, full of grassy banks, meadow flowers, small chalets and wooden farmhouses overlooking the lake. It's not far beyond here to the Planina Dom Vogar, a large and solid looking refuge with tables outside. On spotting a sign claiming an hour to Stara Fužina and after an austere two days we permitted ourselves a beer here before walking down the last part of the route. This is steep and in places made difficult by rocks and roots on the path – though this may have been attributable to tiredness...

In any case the hour sign is accurate, and you'll soon find yourself back on the path you started out on nearly three days beforehand. Check into a private room, take a shower and head on over to the Hotel Jezero for a bite to eat.

Other Trails in the Triglav National Park

There is almost unlimited walking in the national park and in the surrounding area. If you read Slovenian, German or Italian there are a number of walking, climbing and mountaineering guidebooks available, and even with a good map you can see something of the range.

Favourite peaks include the breathtaking summit of Mangrt on the Italian border (2678m), the blade-sharp ridge of Razor (2601m) and the needlepoint of Jalovec (2643m), but there's also a huge variety of walking which doesn't include climbing up to the tops of mountains – the beautiful valleys, forests and pastures aren't there to be ignored. A huge range of lower summits are also available, for those who want to stand on the tops of mountains without having to go above 2000m.

THE TRANS-SLOVENIAN LONG DISTANCE WALK

One of the most interesting holidays that Slovenia offers is the walk from Maribor in the northeast, to the coast near Trieste. Although no literature is available in English, German speakers are fully catered for by a pocket guide published by the Slovene Mountain Association (available from them, in Ljubljana, £1.50). This guide provides enough information and maps for anyone to follow, even without German.

There are refuges along the whole route, which covers some of the most impressive mountains in the republic, including (naturally) Triglav, but also Grintovec (2558m; the highest point in the Kamniške Alps), Razor (2601m) and Jalovec (2643m). The whole length of the walk would take a fit person 30 days at eight hours a day, so most people opt for a section of it, usually near Triglav. The route is clearly

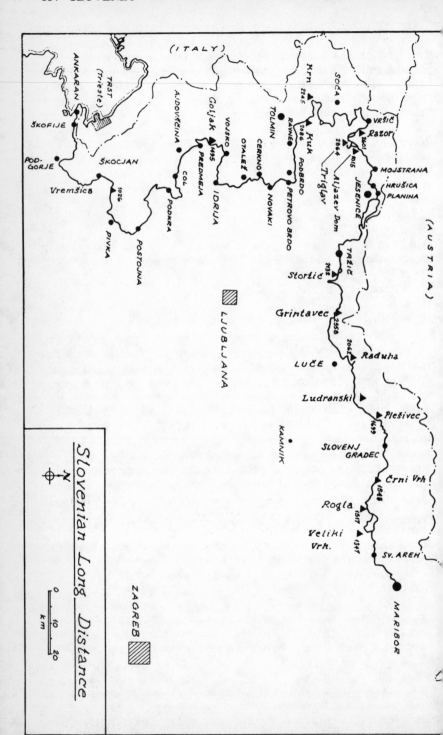

Slovenian Long Distance

marked throughout by red and white markers and is denoted on maps by a circled 1.

Eighty checkpoints with rubber stamps allow you to fill in the route in a little booklet made specially for the purpose, and the German guide includes full details of the refuges, the times between points and the difficulty of the route.

THE E6-YU AND E7-YU ROUTES

Parts of two of the European walking routes cross Yugoslavia, and these make a viable alternative for those wanting to walk across meadows and through forests rather than scaling the country's highest mountains. The E6 runs from the Baltic to the Mediterranean; the E7 from the Atlantic to the Black Sea.

Although there is no information in English on either route there are 1:50,000 scale maps available and the routes are clearly marked on the ground. You need to be determined to read the Slovenian or Serbo-Croat guides. A detailed explanation of both is due to be published in German, but again this isn't of much use to the average English reader.

E6-YU

The last 230km of the E6 (of a total 2000km) lies in Yugoslavia. This part runs from Radlje, on the Austrian border, to Opatija (just west of Rijeka), on the Mediterranean. In 1976 the path was reconstructed and has now been marked clearly by distinctive red circles around yellow spots.

The Yugoslavian part of the walk can be done in 12 to 14 moderate days, and since there are 36 checkpoints with food and lodging you'll find no problems with accommodation and eating. The route goes along country roads and across meadows, avoiding towns of any size at all, and where the path uses normal roads those carrying the least traffic have been selected.

Up to date documentation, including a brochure of 1:50,000 scale maps, can be obtained from Mladinska Kniga, a bookshop in Ljubljana (see *Ljubljana* for details), or you can try the ever helpful Slovene Mountain Association (Planinska Zveza Slovenije, Dvoržakova 9, Ljubljana, 61000) for further information.

E7-YU

In September 1986 the Yugoslavian section of the E7 was opened. This starts off far away in Lisbon, crosses Spain, passes through Nice, Genova and around Lake Como before arriving at Robič on the Yugoslav-Italian frontier. It then runs through the Soča valley, and crosses Slovenia, fetching up at Kumrovec on the border with Croatia. Going on eastwards through Yugoslavia, it bypasses Belgrade and then travels through southern Romania to Constanta on the Black Sea.

The Yugoslavian portion is 370km long and takes a good fortnight at a moderate pace. It's well marked with the standard yellow dot in a red circle, and the route has been made and is maintained by the Slovenian forestry organisations.

A first guide to the E7-YU is currently being put together in Slovenian, so it'll be a while before there's a German or English one available. The Slovenian part is mapped out, however (in 1:50,000 scale), and a booklet with some general information and spaces for the checkpoint stamps has already been published. Further information ought to be available from the two sources above (see E6-YU) by the time you read this.

I walked along the part of the E7 running through the Soča valley, using Hemingway (*A Farewell to Arms*) as an out of date guide, and found it more stimulating than the E6, partly because the route was overshadowed by mountains. I was also lucky enough to be blessed by better weather than I had on the short section I walked of the E6.

CAVES AND LIPPIZANERS

Slovenia's biggest tourist pull isn't Triglav, or even Lake Bled, but a cave 50km south of Ljubljana. One of several of interest in the area, Postojna is the longest, largest and most famous, and it has the advantage of being within striking distance of Lipica.

Postojna and Škocjan

Regular buses whizz down from Ljubljana to Postojna, and once you're in town you won't miss the signs for the caves – or the throngs following them. Over a million people a year visit, and the management claim a fairly astonishing 24 million since they were discovered early in the last century. These days the crowding has reached such levels that a 2km railway is needed in the first part to avoid jams.

Tours go round every half hour in season and you should remember to dress warmly – the temperature never exceeds 8°C. The caves are about four million years old, and extend for 27km, though you won't see more than a small part of this. The rock formations are indeed as spectacular as the brochures imply, but for my money I'd rather see something smaller and less crowded – such as Škocjan.

Although the caves at Škocjan are nothing like as large as those at Postojna they're no less impressive – perhaps because of the lack of a railway and the smaller crowds that visit. Reach them on the bus to Koper – they're not far off the main road.

Lipica

The tiny village of Lipica is far more famous than its size or position would imply. First created as a stud in 1580 it became for a long while the sole supplier of the famous Lippizaner horses to the Spanish Riding School in Vienna. Historical upsets and frequent changes of address have meant that there are now several breeders of 'genuine'

Lippizaners, but it's true enough that these were the first, even if there were only 13 left here at the end of the last war.

The place now thrives as much as a tourist attraction as a stud farm, and you can even go on a riding holiday on some of the finest mounts in Europe. Spanish Riding School dressage goes on show twice daily, and here you can witness the famous spectacle of white horses dancing to Viennese waltzes. Reach Lipica by bus from Sežana (on the Italian border) or Divača (on the main road down to Koper).

Lippizana horses on display at Lipca. (Photo Yugoslavia National Tourist Office.)

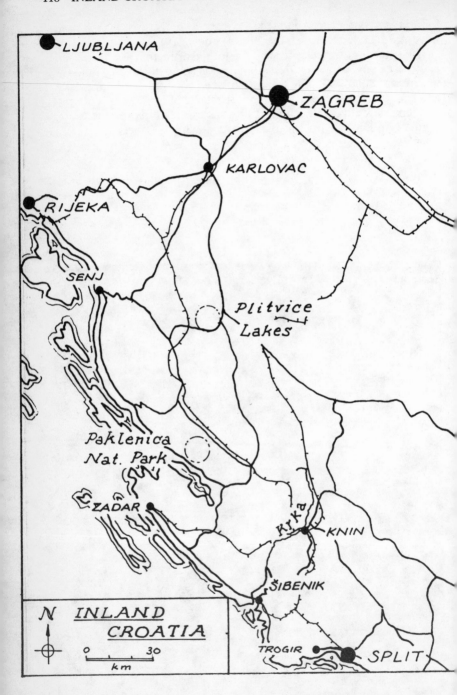

Inland Croatia

The Croats first arrived in Yugoslavia in the 6th and 7th centuries, as subjects of the Avars. By the 8th century independence had been achieved, and in 924 they established their first kingdom.

Never a strong country, and always prone to outside intervention, Croatia subsequently affiliated itself with Hungary, switching its allegiance to Austria in 1527, then back to Hungary and finally to the Austro-Hungarian empire, before being granted some autonomy in 1868. The coastal part of Croatia stayed in Venetian hands until Napoleon 'liberated' it, only to be ceded subsequently to Austria.

In 1918 the republic became part of the new Kingdom of Serbs, Croats and Slovenes, but independent sentiments, encouraged by Mussolini, led to the assassination of King Alexander in Marseille by Croatian nationalists. The independence movement degenerated into the Uštase fascists, who for a short while led a separate puppet state during the last war, before falling to the resistance movement.

After 1945 Croatia was established as one of the six republics, and with its long stretch of coastline soon began a rapid economic recovery, heavily based on tourism. Nationalist sentiments resurfaced strongly in the early 70s, with many people being reluctant to fund the poorer republics, and had it not been for Tito, himself Croatian, Croatia would probably have seceded from Yugoslavia.

Everywhere in Croatia is noticeably more affluent than in the south, and prices tend to reflect this. Its proximity to Austria and Germany ensures a steady flow of tourists and the cash that comes with them, and inland it has also been blessed with some unusual natural wonders, including the famous lakes at Plitvice and the Krka waterfalls. The hills and villages of the Zagorje are still beautiful despite being well known, and the area boasts over a hundred castles, many of them ruined. The area is vaguely reminiscent of Tuscany, in the way that most of the countryside has managed to stay unspoiled despite large numbers of foreigners passing through. Finally, there is the capital, Zagreb, one of Yugoslavia's finest cities.

ZAGREB

With a population of nearly a million Zagreb is Yugoslavia's second largest city, but in many ways ranks alongside (and even above) the capital. Belgrade has been razed and rebuilt so many times that it's now a jumble of styles predominated by concrete. Zagreb is one of the better examples of clean and solid Habsburg architecture, tending towards palatial elegance and large squares from which to view it. The city is also particularly strong on classical culture, with regular opera, ballet, theatre and classical performances of international standard.

Until the early 19th century Zagreb was two small hill towns, the religious community of Kaptol, dominated by the cathedral, and the secular one of Gradec, above and beside it. The two are still separated clearly by Radićeva, a south facing street which runs down to the new town. Most of the city is within walking distance of Trg Republike, a large square faced with department stores. The cathedral is off to one side, the old town is directly behind it and most of the museums are nearby.

The main part of the old town is centred on Radićev Trg, which is dominated by St. Mark's church. The roof has been gaudily tiled with the Croatian coat of arms, in the fashion of seaside resorts with clock flowerbeds. It was in this square that Matija Gubec, leader of the 16th century peasant uprising, was put to death – the Austrians held a coronation for him with a crown of red hot iron. Inside all is modern Croatian art which is more or less successful, depending on perspective. I admired the Meštrović crucifixion, but little else.

The cathedral makes a strong contrast with this – an almost empty, very spacious building with some fine inlay on the choir stalls. The tablets containing the ten commandments are written in Glagolitic, which was kept here as a liturgical language despite the people being Roman Catholic rather than Orthodox.

Zagreb has a number of fine galleries, including the newly opened Mimara museum, a catholic collection ranging from ancient Greek pottery to a rather touching Degas pastel. For a more coherent collection see the Strossmayer old masters. Strossmayer (1815-1905), whose fine statue by Meštrović sits on Strossmayer square, was the strongly pro-Croat Bishop who, amongst numerous other good deeds, created the University of Zagreb. He also collected art very seriously, and his private collection must have been one of the best anywhere.

If you have a taste for Meštrović then visit his Atelier, now a simple, fairly small collection, which is less intimidating than the one in Split, if also less comprehensive.

Practical Information: Zagreb is a popular city and accommodation can therefore be a problem if you're on a tight budget – there are plenty of hotels, but none of them come cheap. Private rooms seem to be in very short supply, and are generally located some way out of town, so your best bet, if you have a tent, might be the campsite. The city plan marks one on the river Sava, tram 4, 5 or 14 to Mladost, reports of which are good, but the 1988 camping guide doesn't list this. Check before you trek out there.

Food is less of a problem. Zagreb has restaurants for all tastes – and budgets – and also has a wonderful seven day a week open market in

The church of Sv. Marko, in Zagreb, with the arms of Croatia and Zagreb in tiles on the roof.

the square just opposite the cathedral. Peasants still come here to sell their half dozen cabbages and underneath it, in the basement, you can buy home made pasta and cheese – and turn a blind eye to the cartloads of skinned sheep's heads.

Tourist information is fairly heavy on the ground and most offices and travel agents will furnish you with a good map. There's an office in the train station but if this is shut then try across the square in front of you, or on Trg Republike, a ten minute walk directly away from the train station.

Public transport is crowded but effective, and trams run through Trg Republike and past the train station, which has a left-luggage office. The bus station is a very dull fifteen minute walk due east of here, which can be avoided by a quick ride on tram 2, 3, 6 or 8. At the bus station you can buy advance tickets and make reservations, but be warned that they have been known to *triple* book seats to Plitvice.

Finally, if you want a breath of country air, take tram 8 or 14 to the cable car station and then the half hour ride up to the 1035m peak of Sljeme. From here there's some pleasant, not too strenuous, walking to be had. And in winter you can ski down.

THE PLITVICE LAKES

Yugoslavia's most popular natural attraction is a series of 16 lakes which fall from one to the next in a series of steps. They are set in superb deep forests which are still populated by bears, wolves and wild boar, and are all the more unusual for being found in the middle of a typically dry karst region, where surface water is hardly ever seen.

The area has been very carefully exploited, and although it can get very busy (10,000 people a day pass through at the height of the season) the crowds are usually tolerable. Wooden walkways have been built in many places which serve the dual purpose of avoiding erosion and allowing people to walk over, under, across and alongside the waterfalls, and around the lakes.

The whole park ranges from 380m to 1280m, but the lakes are all situated between 483m and 696m, with the largest single waterfall being nearly 70m high. The combination of running water and altitude makes the park wonderfully refreshing almost all through the summer, though cold and gloomy in winter. April and October are the best times to visit, the former because the water flow is increased by the melting snows, and the latter because of the fabulous autumn colours.

The lakes were created and are maintained by their unusual vegetation – the mosses, algaes and other freshwater plants absorb the calcium in the water and then deposit it as calciferous mud. This can be seen clearly as a white coating on submerged tree trunks in the smaller lakes. The water flow causes this calciferous mud to be carried to the lips of the lakes, and deposited there, with the long term effect that the whole lake system is gradually gaining altitude.

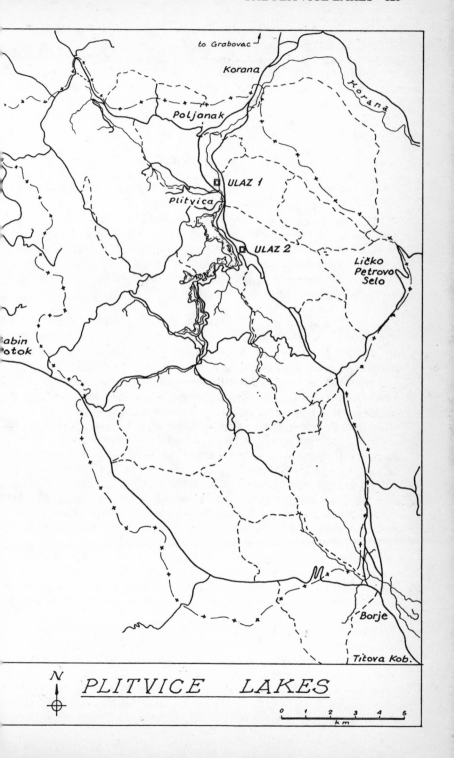

PLITVICE LAKES

In the short term, the effect is that thousands of people are keen to come and see Plitvice, and life has been organised so that this is as easy as possible – to the extent that there is a panoramic train ride, a couple of boats on one of the largest lakes, and a series of itineraries from one to ten hours long which take in the most scenic parts of the park. This is active socialism: everything should be accessible to everyone.

After the initial impression of being too looked after wore off it was replaced by something akin to euphoria – the lakes *are* beautiful, after all, and you'd have to be very determined not to be impressed by that much moving water. You begin to see why people who live in these conditions start believing in water gods.

Each of the lakes seems to be a different colour, ranging from turquoise to emerald through every blue and green you could imagine. In places the lakes seem as still and reflective as a cathedral, elsewhere they run away fast, frothing through steep gullies and shooting out from fissures in the rock. And the magical noise of falling water drowns out even the most persistent children. On the less frequented paths it's easy to imagine the bears and wolves, as you walk across a deeply shaded bed of leaves which crunch underfoot.

You should allow at least two days (ie. three nights) to see the whole park, but you can get a good impression of it all in a single day. Try anyway to give it more than the statutory three hours allotted to the coachloads ferried up from the coast.

Apart from the marked itineraries, which lead you round the best known sights, there are many other paths open to the public in the national park. Unfortunately the staff at the park offices will rarely do more than tell you 'the red route leads to the boat, then over to the big waterfall and return by the panoramic railway', and one woman (in the Zagreb office) even insisted that only the official itineraries were open to tourists – this is not true.

Luckily there's a map available from these same offices, for about 50p, which includes a 1:50,000 scale map of the whole area, a 1:25,000 map of the lakes and a large schematic view of the park, as seen from a plane. With the aid of this you can easily find a couple of days' walking in the area, none of which is too strenuous.

It's inadvisable to be in the wilds after nightfall – the bears and wolves avoid the crowds and the main paths, but do patrol at night. The wolves are only normally seen in winter, but a hungry bear (or one that thinks you're too close to its children) may be inquisitive. There have been no incidents in recent years involving tourists, but local people are understandably cautious, and discourage the idea of camping out in the woods. Walk in the daytime and stay on the paths marked on the maps and you'll be quite safe – there are no wild animals here that will attack in the daytime unless they're seriously provoked.

The Plitvice Lakes.

Practical Information

The lakes are situated a little over half way down the main road from Zagreb to Zadar. Regular buses run from both, and also from Senj. The park has two entrances, wittily called *Ulaz 1* and *Ulaz 2*. In theory Ulaz 1 serves the so called lower lakes and Ulaz 2 the upper ones, but for most people Ulaz 2 (the southern entrance) is the more useful. It's here that you'll find the ticket office, tourist information, private accommodation, a post office, a shop and a self-service restaurant, and it's also within easy reach of both the lower and the upper lakes.

At the tourist office at Ulaz 2 you can buy a map and obtain multilingual information on the park. You can also change money. Beside the office there's a small and slightly overpriced supermarket, and nearby there's an open air grill bar, with trick bitumen on the seats just waiting to stain your clothes. If you have your own car there's adequate parking at both entrances.

Accommodation is expensive here, with private rooms starting at around £10 and going up to over £18. Price is determined by location rather than quality – which is universally good. The room I stayed in was one of the more expensive (£14 in May) but was only a couple of kilometres from Ulaz 2; cheaper rooms are anything up to 15km away.

Hotels are about double the price of private rooms and are often full at the height of the season. Camping is a problem if you don't have your own transport. The nearest site is at Korana, about 9km north of Ulaz 1. There's another one at Grabovac, 3km beyond Korana, and a third at Borje, 15km south of Ulaz 2. They all cost around £7 a night.

Food is also not as easy to come by as you might imagine. A good, cheap, self-service restaurant is open from noon to 4pm at Ulaz 2, but in the evening there's nothing within 3km of the southern end of the park, so if you haven't got transport you're in for a fair hike. The 'Texas' restaurant in the village of Mukinje, 2km from Ulaz 2, is only meant to be for park staff, but apparently it's possible to eat here – in May I failed to do so, dismally. The first night I was at Plitvice I ate a wonderful supper cooked for me by the family I was staying with, since all the restaurants were shut, and thereafter I made picnics from provisions bought at the small shop.

Buy your entry ticket to Plitvice by the car park – it's a steep £7.50, though it does last for as many days as you want. As far as I know this is only verified on the boat and the panoramic train, but you ought to buy a ticket as the money goes to the park's upkeep and protection. On the ticket is a wonderful series of hieroglyphs explaining the park rules, most of which go without saying: don't pick flowers, make fires, engrave trees, steal nests, throw litter or break stalactites. Some of the others aren't so obvious: don't leave the paths, sleep rough, go paddling in the lakes or dance wildly to your ghettoblaster.

If you're in the area on the last Sunday of May there's a folk wedding held by the largest of the waterfalls in the park. This was once no doubt a very traditional affair, but now has the air of being very much staged for the tourists. Nonetheless, even cynics should be impressed by the traditional costumes, the falling water which all but drowns out the songs, and the folk dancing and festivities which are held afterwards.

If you don't have your own transport, *leaving* the park may be much more difficult than arriving. Regular buses pass through on their way to Zadar, Zagreb and Senj, but if these are full, or the driver doesn't like the look of your bags, they have a habit of cruising on past. Testimony to this is borne out by the graffiti in the bus shelter at Ulaz 2, a selection of which is included here, in the unlikely event that you won't have plenty of time to read it yourself.

'The only natural wonder we saw was the fog and the rain – still waiting at 2.30 for the 1.40 bus' (May '88), 'It takes two hours to get to Plitvice – but two days to get out', 'So what, no bus, who cares – who wants to leave this paradise? Later: I retract that – a bus, any bus!', and my favourite, 'Great tourist strategy!'.

There isn't much you can do to improve this situation, but buses early in the day do seem to be better than the ones later on.

THE KRKA RIVER AND FALLS

As if the Plitvice Lakes weren't enough, Croatia has another set of falls, which are, if anything, even more spectacular. The Krka river is short (under 80km) but contains a series of eight splendid waterfalls, the Slapovi Krke. In 1985 the middle and lower parts of the river were made a national park, and this includes the two best known and most spectacular waterfalls, Skradinski Buk and Roški Slap.

Skradinski Buk is one of the most beautiful waterfalls you'll see anywhere, and the tourist brochure isn't far off the mark when it describes it as 'the most beautiful travertine waterfall in Europe'. Travertine formations are pale limestone deposits, and these have formed seventeen steps with a difference in height of 45.7m between top and bottom. In spring the water rushes over them and creates the perfect background for the tourist poster of the chap in waders angling for trout.

Unfortunately, however, a hydroelectric plant upstream has enfeebled the river and in the middle of summer the falls can be something of a disappointment, particularly if you've had to brave the crowds to see them. In May, when I went, it wasn't busy and there seemed to be no shortage of water.

Skradinski Buk is only 16km from Šibenik, and in summer there are several buses a day right to the falls. Failing this take a local bus to Skradin and get off just after the village of Tomilja. From here it's only an hour along the road on foot. An alternative way of getting to the falls is to take one of the fairly frequent excursion boats upriver, also from Šibenik.

There's another boat ride to be had from just above Skradinski Buk to Roški Slap, a 15m waterfall that was apparently worth a visit in its own right before the hydroelectric station was built. Your reason for taking the boat now is to visit Visovac, a Franciscan monastery built on a small island. The main attraction here is the friar's superb library, which contains amongst many treasures some lovely hand-illuminated manuscripts.

BOSNIA - HERCEGOVINIA

Bosnia-Hercegovinia

The land now covered by Bosnia-Hercegovinia was ruled by a loose group of feudal lords until the end of the 12th century, when the acceptance of protection from Hungary helped unify the small kingdoms and states. Hercegovinia sunsequently became an independent duchy (the word *hercog* means duke). This period also saw the rise in importance of the Bogomils, one of the most interesting, and politically important, of Christianity's heretical offshoots. Bogomil was a tenth century Bulgarian priest who developed the ideas of the Manicheans (who had sought to resolve the teachings of Zoroaster and Christ) and came up with the interesting idea that it was the devil and not God who had created the world. It was therefore man's duty to put things to rights and to play an active part in making a bad world better.

The Bogomils were apparently great ascetics, living a simple and pure life since association with things of the flesh was necessarily contact with the devil. They condemmed marriage, icons, the consumption of meat and wine, and even churches, as being too material. There are obvious resemblances with other European heresies here, such as the Cathars and Albigensians, and it provides a thought-provoking foretaste of Protestantism. Nothing remains of the Bogomils save their tombs, and it is only comparatively recently that much has been discovered about them.

What is important is that they were predictably attacked by the Orthodox church to the east and the Catholics to the west, and on the arrival of the Turks were therefore relatively happy at being allowed to continue their religion as long as they notionally considered themselves Moslems rather than Christians. This meant that the Ottoman Empire established itself here far more smoothly than in other parts of the Balkans, and it was the existing ruling class who effectively continued to do so, only under different patrons.

Even now Bosnia-Hercegovinia is noticably more Turkish in flavour than the rest of the country, and over a third of the population are Moslem. Very few of these are of Turkish origin, most being the descendants of those who changed religion in the 14th and 15th century. White minarets dot the countryside, coffee is exclusively Turkish and the music and cuisine has a strong Eastern flavour.

After wide discontent in the last century, including a number of viciously repressed peasant uprisings, the world powers agreed that the

Austro-Hungarian Empire should be given a chance at ruling the state. This came nowhere near resolving the 'Bosnian Question', as was proved by the young Gavrilo Princip in Sarajevo on 28th June 1914.

Bosnia-Hercegovinia was the stage for some of the largest and bloodiest battles fought by the Partisans in the last war, and it was at Jajce in 1943 that the country's new constitution was drawn up by the Communists.

The republic occupies the geographical centre of Yugoslavia and is almost landlocked. In its continental interior the widest range of the country's temperatures is experienced: recorded values go from a chilly -43°C to a warm +40°C. Over 80% of Bosnia-Hercegovina is mountainous, and there are more than 50 distinct mountain regions, containing some 30 peaks between 1700m and 2386m (Maglić). There are numerous refuges and chalets, but finding the location of these and who looks after them is a trying task. Information is incredibly decentralised, and often you have to go to a place before you can find out anything about it. Nonetheless, when it's in their power the people here are among the most helpful and friendly in the country.

SARAJEVO

Sarajevo is one of the most interesting places in Yugoslavia. Famous in schoolbooks for being the scene of the assassination that sparked off the First World War, it's now a a bustling city with a population rapidly approaching half a million.

Although inhabited since time immemorial, the city didn't become important until the arrival of the Turks in the 15th century. Being at the crossroads of several trade routes to Constantinople it then expanded rapidly, and a traveller passing through in 1660 thought that it had at least 10,000 houses.

Some of the 16th century buildings remain, but most of the city was razed by Prince Eugene of Savoy in 1667. Much of what was left was then replaced by the heavy handed Austrians on arriving in 1878 (it took them three months to capture the town), and after the last war the bazaar was largely rebuilt. Since then huge building projects have continued apace, though these are mostly well away from the compact centre, the heart of which is the Baščaršija, even now the nearest you'll get to a bazaar before Turkey.

Sarajevo has numerous sights centred along the river Miljacka. This is much smaller than you'd imagine for a city so important, and is spanned by a number of stone bridges, most famous of which is Principov Most, named after Franz Ferdinand's assassin.

Between Princip Bridge and the town hall, and stretching back from the Austrian embankment, is the Baščaršija, Sarajevo's greatest attraction. The narrow streets are packed with little wooden kiosks selling everything from antique teapots and leather sandals to carpets and *kilims*.

Despite being very attractive, much of what's on show is not good quality and can be overpriced, although it may seem cheap by Western standards. I limited my purchases here to a very plain Turkish coffee set for four (£4) and some Bosnian folk music (£1 per cassette). If you know your subject there's also a fair amount of good quality, antique gold and silver. There's a whole street reserved for the metal smiths, who work at the back of the shop and display there wares out front, and the bazaar also contains unlimited supplies of *burek, ćevapčići*, and wildly sweet Turkish cakes.

A couple of the original department stores of the 16th century (*bezistans*) are still running, and there are also one or two *hans* to be seen. (*Hans* were the defensive night stops on the trading routes, the Ottoman equivalent of the *caravanserai*.)

More spectacular, and obvious from afar, are the mosques, a number of which are open to infidels. Most famous of these – it's the largest in the Balkans – is the Gazi Husrev Beg mosque, built from 1531 to 1538. It was designed by the man who subsequently became chief architect in Istanbul, and is similar to the Ali Pasha mosque there. The mosque is architecturally pure, being 26m wide, with a dome 13m wide and 26m above the floor. There are carpets here from almost every Moslem country, including a couple of beautiful ones from Iran and Turkey. And although the paintwork is in poor repair (which is odd since it only dates from 1775 and was extensively restored in 1886), the calligraphic motifs from the Koran are still clear. In the courtyard outside there's a fine fountain and a couple of tombs containing Gazi Husrev Beg and his favourite wife. Look up and you'll feel suitably dwarfed by the minaret, from which a muezzin still calls the faithful to prayer, cupping his hands and crying out above the traffic 'God is great ... There is no God but God'.

Gazi Husrev Beg had a *medersa* (Koran school) and library built at the same time as the mosque, and these are also worth a visit – the library contains 25,000 books from the 12th century on, mostly in ancient Persian languages.

A complete contrast to the mosques is found in the old Orthodox Church, a dark place full of mystery, and now a museum. To see an Orthodox service go to the cathedral, almost next door to the Catholic one. This was built in the Russian-Byzantine style in 1869 and has a huge iconostasis, gilded by Russian artists. During a service you can feel some of the mystery of the Orthodox church; everyone stands, candle in hand, plainsong is chanted, incense is burned and the priests disappear behind the iconostasis, where you can see tantalising glimpses of the altar, gilt and velvet. It's a holy affair, but outside of services the cathedral seems strangely hollow.

On the riverbank, not far from the Baščaršija, is the town hall, built rather tactlessly by the Austrians in 1892 in a pseudo-Moorish style. It earned the rounded contempt of Rebecca West, who observed acidly that 'it has little round windows all over it which suggest that it is rich beyond the dreams of avarice in lavatories'. It was here that Franz Ferdinand made his last speech.

The assassination

The assassination of Franz Ferdinand and his wife Sophie Chotek is so full of anomalies, discrepancies and coincidences that it seems both incredible that he could have imagined that he wouldn't be killed, and that he was killed. Look at just two of the facts: Franz Ferdinand had 70,000 troops just outside the town – but none to guard him. And his assassin, Gavrilo Princip, couldn't hit a moving target – but the coach unexpectedly stopped right in front of him.

That Franz Ferdinand wasn't guarded points to his fatal arrogance – he had decided to ride unprotected through a hostile town on June 28th, a day of national mourning since the defeat at Kosovo in 1389. And why did the car stop? In the town hall it was agreed that a different return route should be taken (a bomb had been thrown on their arrival), but, incredibly, nobody told the drivers. So at the point where the route changed, Potoriek, the Military Governor, shouted at the driver, who stopped – right in front of Princip, who leaned forward, and shot Franz Ferdinand. Princip aimed again, this time for General Potoriek. Sophie Chotek, trying to save her husband, jumped forwards and took the second fatal bullet.

Austria had long been looking for a reason to declare war on Serbia, and this provided it – Serbia was accused of complicity in the plot (no link has ever been proved, incidentally) and war was declared in July. Russia took offence, Germany supported Austria, seeing the perfect chance of a slice of France, and the First World War had started. That the Austrians were pushing for a fight is borne out by the evidence that Princip wasn't even put on trial until October 1914, three months after war with Serbia had been declared.

The three main protagonists were all under 21, and couldn't be executed. But by 1918 they had all died in unhealthy Austrian prisons. There is now a pair of footsteps carved in the pavement at the spot where Princip carried out the assassination, and standing in them creates a kind of historical vertigo. The corner is no different from any other, but you can feel a 19 year old's anxiety, resolve and action.

The building on the corner houses a small and touching museum to the event, and has blurred blow-ups of the conspirators who look like caricatures of Balkan leftists; what's so emotive about it all is perhaps the terrible amateurishness of the plot.

Practical Information

The bus and train stations are situated next to one another and from here it's a good half hour walk to the centre of town. Better by far is the circular tram number 1, which runs from the station along the embankment to the Baščaršija, and then back along Maršala Tita to the station. Buy tickets at kiosks and punch them on board.

Tourist information is plentiful, with a useful office being on JNA (a road parallel to the embankment and Maršala Tita) at number 50. They'll supply you with a map.

Accommodation can be a problem – private rooms are expensive and poorly located. But the Hotel Stari Grad (35 rooms at Maršala Tita 126, Tel. 533 394) is excellent if you can get in. I reserved ahead a couple of weeks from an Atlas office in Dubrovnik. It's about £12 for a double room, and has hot water, clean sheets, soap, toilet paper, the whole bit, though their breakfasts are indifferent. Failing that try the nearby Central (room for 65, Zrinjskog 8, Tel. 215 115).

Food is no problem. Sarajevo has literally hundreds of snack bars selling *burek* (which is at its very best here; try the spinach filled variety) and various grilled meats. Restaurants are fewer and further between, but good value. Although not cheap, the restaurant just off the north side of Maršala Tita, near the Baščaršija, is excellent. The 'kid cooked in sack' is recommended, as is their Trappist's cheese.

Sarajevo has more than its fair share of bookshops, theatres and cinemas, most of which show films in the original versions, subtitled into Serbo-Croat. When these aren't violent or pornographic they tend towards the excellent – I saw Bertolucci's *Novocento* (*1900*), in Italian with subtitles, at the Kinoteka, a wonderful cinema on Djure Djakovića. Entry price? 20p.
  There's a good fruit and vegetable market on the other side of the river from the town hall, and along from this, starting from Princip Bridge, there's a pleasant garden where you can picnic in the shade. If you want to get further out of the town take the cable car which starts just up from the market. It goes up every half hour to a restaurant at 1,000m, nearly 500m above the town.

The area round Sarajevo includes some excellent mountains which are widely skied in winter. They are marred, it's true, by ski installations, but there is nonetheless plenty of summer walking in the area, up to over 2000m. A 1:50,000 scale map is on sale for £1 from the Planinarsko Društvo, which is found in town by continuing north about 50m from Princip Bridge until you reach the T-junction. The mountain organisation is slightly to your left, in front of you. Their hours are irregular, but when open they're very helpful.

JAJCE AND THE PLIVA LAKES

Once the seat of the Bosnian kings, Jajce is now more famous for the undeniably picturesque waterfall which adorns a hundred tourist brochures. The town is also etched into the Yugoslav national consciousness as being the place where the second session of the Antifascist Council for the National Liberation of Yugoslavia

(AVNOJ) was held on the night of 29th November 1943. Jajce was a partisan stronghold, and somehow 142 delegates managed to attend the conference there, many of them travelling across hundreds of miles of occupied territory on foot to do so. It was here, under the unequivocal slogan 'Death to Fascism – Liberty to the People', that the new constitution of Yugoslavia was drawn up. Which is why 29.XI.1943 appears on the country's coat of arms.

Nowadays Jajce is something of a museum town, perched quietly on its hill above the place where the Pliva suddenly drops 30m to meet the river Vrbas. On arriving you won't have the best view of the town – to see what all the fuss is about head across the river. The mass of water seems to sprout from under the town, itself a charming mixture of Turkish and Bosnian architecture, with a solid looking 15th century castle rounding off the top of the picture.

Underneath the castle are catacombs or burial rooms, for which several conflicting explanations are given, ranging from secret Bogomils to tombs robbed by the Turks. Needless to say they're pretty gloomy, whatever the explanation. Not far from here is the Temple of Mithras, a remarkably well preserved late Roman shrine. Its main attraction is a 4th century bas-relief of Mithras sacrificing the traditional bull, which in death gives life (an idea not far removed from the Crucifixion). You'll have to get someone from the tourist office to show you round.

One of the town's more obvious landmarks is the tower of St. Luke. Originally some Fransiscans also guarded the mortal remains of the saint here, but when the Turks came they hot-footed to Venice. This caused a predictable conflict with the people of Padua, who also had a corpse of St. Luke (albeit headless) and had been venerating theirs for over 300 years. On taking the case to a papal trial the Franciscans won, which is odd, considering that the head of St. Luke had been in the Vatican since 580. At the same time another of St. Luke's arms was being used in Rome to cure the sick.

If you're lucky enough to be in Jajce on a Wednesday then you won't miss the weekly market. Peasants still bring local produce into the town, and it remains one of the better places in the country to buy homemade goods, such as local costumes. Jajce is small enough and far enough inland to have avoided the problems of mass tourist consumerism that have afflicted more accessible places like Mostar and Trebinje, near Dubrovnik.

About 8km west of Jajce lie the Pliva Lakes. These are beautiful calciferous formations and are famous for the rather feeble-looking disused wooden mills alongside them. The area has a campsite, which tends to be full in high season, but in late spring it's very pleasant.

WALKING IN BOSNIA-HERCEGOVINIA

There is no lack of walking to be done in Bosnia-Hercegovinia, but there is a problem in finding out exactly where you walk, what the accommodation situation is and how to get there. The most accessible and well-documented regions are the mountains around Sarajevo (see *Sarajevo*) and the Sutjeska National Park (see below).

The area southwest of Jajce was recommended to me: apparently there are four fairly easily climbed mountains in the area with summits from 1800m to 2000m. A network of well-marked paths supposedly connects them together, but my source (in Jajce) wasn't very specific, and failed to show up for a more sober meeting the following morning.

A friend in Sarajevo also highly recommended the area around the small town of Jablanica, 50km north of Mostar on the road to Sarajevo. Two of the region's most attractive mountains, Čvrsnica (2228m) and Prenj (2155), are situated near here, and though they're quite steep climbs, they both have marked paths to the summits. This area is also rich in Bogomil tombs (*stećci*), and new ones are being discovered all the time.

The Sutjeska National Park

Sutjeska has a lot going for it – two beautiful rivers, a virgin forest, Bosnia's highest mountain, a splendid 70m waterfall, half a dozen glacial lakes and an interesting past – but it's seldom visited by foreigners.

Access to the park is from the fairly well developed village of Tjentište, which is where you'll find the parks office, a campsite, and, should you want to splash out, hotels. The village is situated 24km south of Foča on the main road from Sarajevo to Dubrovnik, and is easily reached by bus from either city. In summer it tends to be full of athletic Yugoslavs, but few of these venture far into the park.

The park is genuinely unspoiled, with no mountain huts and no settlements (which obviously means no mountain rescue), and a small area of primeval forest. Apart from this one there are only two others in Europe; one 100km away, in Montenegro (Biogradska Gora), and one in Poland. The park also supports around 100 bears, as well the usual wild boar, deer and chamois.

Dotted around liberally are monuments to the Resistance, including a vast pair of winglike stones that are guaranteed to make you feel small. This is as far as most of the people who are here on an excursion get – ten minutes away the park is beautifully deserted. The monuments are there for a very good reason. The battles that took place here in 1943 were amongst the most critical of the whole war for the Partisans, and it was here, surrounded by 130,000 German troops (to the Partisans' 20,000) that Tito was wounded. A way out was discovered, but a division had to be left behind to draw enemy fire. This division was killed to the last man, as were the sick and immobile wounded. The Partisans lost more than 7,000 men in this battle alone; they are commemorated in Tjentište.

The park is centred on the Sutjeska river, with the peaks of the Zelengora range to the west of the main road and Maglić to the east. The Zelengora has excellent walking, with a number of fine summits up to 2032m and no less than seven glacial lakes; Maglić (2386m) is a harder mountain climb, but is not beyond the abilities of the reasonably fit.

Other important attractions of the park are Peručica, the primeval forest, and the Skakavac waterfall, 3km from the point where the Sutjeska and Peručica rivers meet.

OTHER TOWNS IN BOSNIA-HERCEGOVINIA

Bosnia-Hercegovinia is littered with interesting Turkish towns, any of which you are likely to pass though by bus on your way to Sarajevo or points north. **Foča** must once have been a pleasant town but it's become tainted by a kind of modern paralysis, and the only building of real interest, the mosque, seems to be closed.

For more excitement join one of the raft trips that leave from here and head down the Drina for a couple of days, fetching up at Višegrad. This is real rafting – boats made of logs tied together – and it's a good thing that the rafters are all highly proficient at their job. Contact tourist information (Foča, 71480, Yugoslavia, Tel. (073) 72204) or the Zelengora Hotel (Tel. 72036) for further information.

From Foča it's 80km down the Drina to the convenient stopover of **Višegrad**, immortalised by Ivo Andrić in his Nobel prizewinning novel *The Bridge on the Drina*. In fact the bridge is the town's only real sight, and is unusually harmonious to the eye, considering that the 'middle' has four and a half arches to one side and five and a half to the other. Private rooms are cheap, and though they aren't that plentiful, there aren't many people looking for them either.

Just 32km from Dubrovnik, **Trebinje** is the town most tourists are shown as being representative of Turkish architecture. This is much less to do with any qualities inherent in the town, and more to do with its only being an hour away from Dubrovnik on the tour bus. A once lively and traditional Saturday market has now given way to a rather tragic self-parody, with prices to match. You can do much better almost anywhere else.

Although crowded by busloads whisked up from the beach for an afternoon's Turkish culture, the old town of **Mostar** is still worth half a day of your time. It's self-consciously proud of its few attractions, and makes a brave effort to fleece the groups passing by. There's a premium on accommodation and the nearest campsite is 12km away. Add the hottest temperatures in Yugoslavia and you might consider staying the night somewhere else.

Mostar to most people is its bridge (not surprising – *most* means bridge, and *stari* means old), an elegant single span built by the Turks in 1557. The arch is 20m high and 30m wide and took nine years to finish. The architect, who had been threatened with death if the bridge collapsed, dug his own grave shortly before completion, but fled before the final unveiling. It hasn't yet shown any signs of falling down. In summer the local wideboys will dive off the bridge, which is a pretty foolish thing to do, for the right recompense. Don't encourage them.

The town is also well known for its small bazaar and has a number of goldsmiths who will cheerfully sell you recently made antiques if you're not an expert. More interesting are the town's 14 mosques, ten of which are still in use. Don't on any account miss the chance to climb the minaret of Mehmed Pasha's mosque – I haven't climbed one anywhere else in the world.

Handicrafts in the Baščaršija, the old Turkish market in Sarajevo.

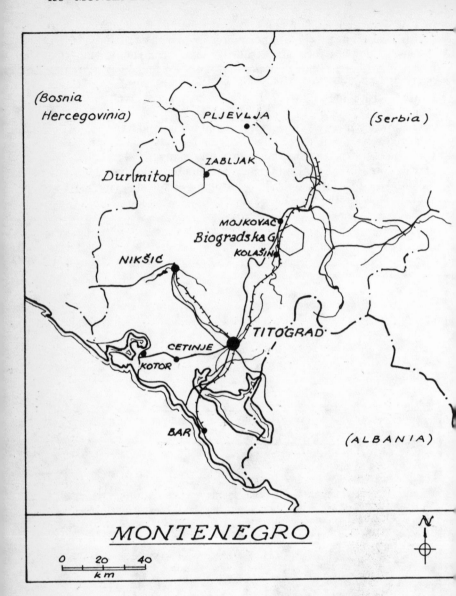

(Bosnia
Hercegovinia)

PLJEVLJA

(Serbia)

ZABLJAK

Durmitor

MOJKOVAC

Biogradska G

NIKŠIĆ

KOLAŠIN

TITOGRAD

CETINJE

KOTOR

BAR

(ALBANIA)

MONTENEGRO

N

0   20   40
k m

Montenegro

Montenegro, despite being the smallest and one of the poorest of the six republics, has some of the best walking in Yugoslavia. There are four national parks, including virgin forest, assailable mountains, one of the world's most interesting mausoleums, and a strange lake on the Albanian border. Add to this the Montenegrins – heroic, Homeric characters – and Montenegro makes a wonderful venue, not least because the interior is largely unvisited – what tourism there is tends to stay firmly on the coast (see *Coast and Islands*).

History: Montenegrins are and always have been strongly independent, and it took the charisma of a man called Ivan Crnović (John the Outlaw) to weld the state together in the 16th century. When he was succeeded by the Bishop of Cetinje, Church and State became one, and the country was ruled for the next three centuries by Orthodox Prince Bishops, with the line of succession passing from uncle to nephew.

The Montenegrins were the only people in the Balkans who weren't subjugated by the Turks, Venetians, Hungarians or Austrians. But in the early 18th century there was a serious danger of the country being infiltrated by Islam, and it took Danilo I, father of the Njegoš dynasty, to solve the problem: his answer – baptism or death.

Soon afterwards, one of history's most endearing pretenders to a throne, Šćepan the Small, arrived on the scene. Although apparently an ordinary looking – if short – monk, he allowed the rumour to circulate that he was actually the Tsar of Russia (who had in fact recently been killed) and that if they liked, he would rule Montenegro. What's extraordinary about the story is not just his audacity, but his success as a ruler. Even when denounced by a Russian delegation, sent specially for the purpose, he managed to keep his kingdom. It's sad that in the end he was defeated by his barber, who was successfully bribed to slit his throat.

The Montenegrins spent most of the 18th and 19th centuries being a mystery to the outside world. The country was virtually inaccessible, and certainly not safely so, and very few western Europeans ever made it as far inland as Cetinje, the capital. The Turks managed to reach – and raze – Cetinje on no less than three occasions, but each time fairly barbarous guerrilla warfare soon saw them off. In battle the Montenegrins would cut off the heads of their own mortally wounded rather than leave them to the Turks, and until just over a century ago you could still see the heads of Turks that had been killed in battle on spikes in Cetinje.

This habit, not surprisingly, put off foreign visitors, and Marshal Marmont, Napoleon's chief in the Balkans, took Prince Bishop Petar I to task about it. Petar replied that the custom shouldn't seem strange to a nation that did the same thing to their King and Queen. Tactics like this were the only way of keeping the Turks at bay, and though it's not a justification, the custom is nonetheless less horrific than the Turkish one of impaling live prisoners.

Petar I was succeeded in 1830 by his nephew Petar II, Montenegro's most illustrious leader (see *Cetinje and Lovčen* for more on this brilliant man). Even now, it's his portrait that hangs in many Montenegrin homes; outside Montenegro Tito's image is ubiquitous.

On his succession in 1851 Danilo II fell in love, changed his mind about celibacy, and changed the rules of succession accordingly. Fate decreed otherwise: nine years later Danilo was assassinated before arranging any suitable heirs, and it was his nephew Nikola I who succeeded.

King Nikola I was an unusually talented man – not only was he a brilliant fighter and tactician, but he was also a good linguist (he spoke French, German, Italian, Russian and some English) and a gifted politician. Unfortunately he was let down by a badly underdeveloped sense of ethics.

Nikola persuaded large subsidies out of Russia, Austria, Italy *and* Turkey. This would have been no bad thing had he not decided to pocket most of them, while keeping his population in penury. When Russia sent generous gifts of grain to relieve a famine, Nikola sold it to those who could afford to buy. Later he led a personal crusade for the capture of Scutari, which cost the lives of 20,000 of his soldiers. He then surrendered it, but not before making a sizeable killing on the Vienna stockmarket on the outcome. In 1916 he fled to France, having committed a final act of treachery in delivering Montenegro to the Austrians. He died in Nice, in exile, in 1921.

After the First World War Montenegro was absorbed into Yugoslavia, somewhat against its wishes. The grounds were fair – it, or rather its king, hadn't resisted the Austrians very forcefully. This, and Scutari, explain the inconguous First World War memorials dated 1912-21 instead of the more familiar 1914-18: before the war Montenegrins were fighting Albanians; after it they were fighting Serbs. Twenty years later Tito's call for armed struggle was answered the most strongly here, and a greater percentage were killed fighting than in any other group.

The people: Montenegrins look accustomed to heroism; a tough, handsome people, they have historically only had two occupations – fighting and poetry: indeed, until very recently *all* speech outside of the immediate family was in blank verse. They are attractive too, with

ontenegrin woman with her grandfather. (Photo: Simon Palmour.)

the men sporting fierce moustaches under straight noses, and the women regularly reaching six foot. Add good health (they're the longest lived of Yugoslavia's peoples) and excellent eyesight (the lowest rate of myopia per capita in the world), and the Montenegrins start to look supernatural.

Fortunately they have their faults, most notable of which is the other side of courage, pride. Montenegrins will never admit to being at fault, and will always provide wrong, but plausible, answers rather than appear ignorant. This can – and does – lead to havoc with the practical things in life, like public transport and accommodation, but it's not done maliciously.

A perceptive insight on the people is given by the story about a traveller meeting a Montenegrin. The traveller asks what the population of the country is, and is told 'With Russia, about 180 million'. Knowing that the actual figure can't exceed 200,000, the traveller asks again, adding 'without Russia'. The Montenegrin replies 'But we will never desert the Russians'.

CETINJE AND LOVČEN

Cetinje must have been one of the world's most unusual capitals. At its largest it only had a population of 15,000, and until less than a century ago its only access was via a mule track, despite it supporting no less than fifteen embassies. Even now the first two things you notice about Cetinje are that it's small and it's difficult to get to.

The town became capital of Montenegro in the 15th century, when a defensive position which the Turks couldn't reach was needed, and it flourished rapidly. By 1493 it had the first printing press in the Balkans, and this was used to print religious books, some of which you can see in the monastery today. Until 1918, Cetinje remained the capital, when Podgorica (now Titograd), a far more accessible town altogether, was chosen as the administrative centre for this part of the newly created Yugoslavia.

If you don't have a car the chances are that you'll be arriving by bus. All transport from the coast, including buses from Dubrovnik and Kotor, now seems to run along the new road via Budva, which means that you'll miss the best, or at least the most spectacular, route over the Lovčen pass. Never mind – the road up from Budva is itself pretty thrilling, with a superb view along the coast as you climb up over 700m from the sea, and a vertiginous panorama at the top which takes in Sveti Stefan, Budva and the island between them sliding gently into the water.

Just down from here, at 660m in the wildest karst – it's a mistake to call it barren, but it's very rough, like a volcano frozen in mid-eruption – is Cetinje. From the bus station it's two minutes to the centre of town, marked by the Episcopal Palace (the Biljarda), Nikola's Palace and the monastery.

On one side of the square is a branch of Unis Tourist, who will point you firmly in the direction of the Grand Hotel, a Class A joint aimed very much at the package tour. Insist, and they'll give you the address of a private room, which certainly looked like the only one in town when I was there, but I suppose there must be others. These are cheap (around £5 for a double), but not the height of luxury.

The family I stayed with were classic Montenegrins, with the father speaking reasonable French, three of four intelligent children having passable English, and bottles being passed round at the first intimation of friendliness. If you want little luxuries like hot running water then you'll have to stay at the Grand, which is smart, but not cheap (around £30 for a double room; all have bathrooms).

Across the road from Intours, and towards the Grand, is a small office (marked *Agencija*) with French speaking staff who have various multilingual brochures on the town. Use the Grand Hotel for exchange.

Cetinje has an abundance of bars and small eateries, many of which don't actually serve food. Make the right gestures and you'll eventually be offered a stew or whatever's being cooked up for the family. The only *bona fide* restaurant in town appears to be that attached to the Grand. Also be warned that Cetinje seems to close early, with most bars shutting at around 10pm, even at the weekend.

For a town so small it's positively jammed with things worth seeing. Most obvious are the foreign legations, which are for the most part empty. It's a pity that you can only see the exteriors of these superb mansions, of which the largest, naturally, is the Russian Legation, close by the Biljarda. On the way to the Grand Hotel is the British Legation, which looks like an outsize country house in Surrey – this like the others, was abandoned in 1916.

The monastery was the cultural centre of the town for centuries, but has been knocked down and rebuilt several times since the 15th century, with some obvious changes from the 18th and 19th centuries. Inside there's a large treasury of precious vestments, chalices and scriptures, including a book printed in 1493, barely a decade after Caxton. The collection is spoiled somewhat by your being obliged to see it as part of a guided tour delivered in a Serbo-Croat monotone. Near the monastery is a small ruined tower, of no special significance now, but it was on this that the Turkish heads used to be displayed.

In the centre, and easily mistaken for a legation, is Nikola's Palace, now the town museum. Downstairs there's a large collection of weapons, uniforms and medals, but the main interest is in the imperial apartments upstairs.

These purport to be as they would have been when Nikola was here, but what actually happened was that he cleared out with his own furniture, so the apartments have been refurnished with gifts from the great powers. There's a collection of really tacky ornaments in the state dining room as well as a dubious Chippendale table and chairs next door, and some really dreadful empire furniture, but this is all offset by beautiful parquet floors and some interesting pictures, including an old photograph of Queen Victoria and two sons, and portraits of the last Tsar and Tsarina of Russia, shortly before the revolution.

Nikola, ever the able politician, succeeded in marrying off all of his eight daughters into European royal households, leading to the joke about them being Montenegro's most profitable export.

Turn left out of here and you'll see the Biljarda, probably the only episcopal palace to be known as 'Billiards'. Before going in have a look at the massive relief map of Montenegro next door. This is something like 30m x 30m, and was built by Italian prisoners of war in 1917 under Austrian supervision. Looking at it you'll realise just why Montenegro has never been subdued.

As palaces go the Biljarda is pretty modest, which is an apt reflection of the man who built it, Petar II. He would have been an unusual man at any time, a cultured, distinguished giant of six foot eight who spoke German, French, Latin and Russian fluently and read the literatures of each in the original. He was apparently a dangerous fighter in battle, but he was also Montenegro's (and probably Yugolsavia's) greatest poet, writing such metaphysical epics as *The Mountain Wreath* and *Discovery of the Microcosm*.

Somehow he also found time to ratify Montenegro's borders with Turkey and Austria, to set up schools, and to entertain the rare visitors who came to Cetinje by shooting lemons out of the air – as Sir Gardiner Wilkinson, a passing Englishman wrote, 'A singular accomplishment for a Bishop'. Petar II Petrović Njegoš died of tuberculosis at the age of 37, ridiculously early for a Montenegrin. He's buried at the top of Mt. Lovčen, 24km out of town.

His palace is now a series of museums, including a good exhibition of contemporary Montenegrin art downstairs – look out for a seated woman by Gabro Rajčević (1912-43), which has just the right amount of Post Impressionism, and an industrial blue seaside by Bogomil Karlovaris which is near abstract.

Upstairs there's a small museum dedicated to the life of Petar II – among other things you'll find a wonderful handwritten passport, which he only used once, to go to his investiture in St. Petersburg. His investiture is here too, written beautifully on silk. At the end you can see why the palace is so called: a small, slightly battered billiard table doesn't seem very impressive, until you recollect the journey it had to make up the mule trails.

Although closed when I was there, the Biljarda also houses a very scary museum of the National Liberation, which is essentially a huge archive of photographs of the Montenegrin Partisans, many of them at the point of execution. Montenegro stayed free for almost the whole of the war, but the cost was terrible. The collection is being reorganised, but should be open by early 1989.

Lovčen

Petar II is buried on top of the mountain where he used to go and pray. The only recently completed mausoleum forms the heart of the national park of Mt. Lovčen. Access to the mausoleum is your biggest problem. Although only two to three hours away from Cetinje by foot (24km by road), I couldn't find anyone who would direct me, though I was assured that there are footpaths. With no map, no water and incredibly difficult terrain I wasn't going to take the risk, but if you can get up it should be possible to walk back, either by using bearings on Cetinje, or by taking the road (five hours, and mostly downhill).

The easiest way to see it is as part of one of the regular excursions, but it's a place that needs to be visited as quietly as possible, and I've met several people who didn't think it was worth the trip having seen it this way. There are taxis in Cetinje, and hiring one for a couple of hours is another possibility – they're open to negotiation. I talked nicely to the Grand Hotel and they let me up with the restaurant staff (yes, there's a restaurant at the top, but it's tactfully unobtrusive, built into the mountain) at 8am.

The mausoleum was designed by the ubiquitous Meštrović, but was executed by a pupil of his, Andrija Krstulović, in Split. The parts were then shipped round to Budva and hauled all the way up here for assembly in 1974.

The situation is unparalleled. The tomb is mined from the summit of a perfect mountain, with views from the top of Cetinje 1000m below, and Lake Skadar and Kotor, more than a vertical mile down. The entrance deliberately slows you down from the drive up – where the road ends, a tunnel curves gently up 651 steps 4m wide in even groups of nine. Walking up this cool, hushed, almost dark corridor is the perfect preparation for Njegoš.

At the top you'll see the mausoleum on the skyline. Inside steep walls a couple of latter day caryatids 6m high hold up a portico, behind which a pair of huge doors mark the entrance. On either side of this two corridors lead to iron grilles, behind which there's nothing but sky stabbing in. Inside there are marble walls and a gold ceiling and nothing else except Meštrović's giant statue carved from a single block of black marble.

Underneath (and the entrance is deliberately not immediately obvious) there's a crypt. This is cold, still, dark and silent, lit only by a dozen unwavering candles. The noise of rustling clothes and even breathing is unnaturally loud. At one end there's a plain stone sarcophagus, almost unadorned save for the word Njegoš in formal Cyrillic, the dates 1813-1851 and a cross. There is no other decoration here at all. It's probably the most hallowed place I've ever visited.

Outside, a small path leads to the viewpoint, from which more often than not you can see the clouds swirling above the bay of Kotor. On your way back look out for one of the friendly guardians of the mausoleum called Zoran Stanojević. He's a young poet who's already published a couple of books of very short, almost structuralist poems. He speaks some French and a little English and is usually keen to talk.

LAKE SKADAR

Skadarsko Jezero, famous in English history books as Lake Scutari, is the largest lake in the Balkans, being nearly 50km long and 15km wide. It is one of the strangest places in the country, full of strange, hallucinatory effects and colours, but is now increasingly well known as a nature reserve.

Most of the Lake Skadar belongs to Yugoslavia, but the southern end is in Albania, so maps are not available, although there is nonetheless some excellent walking in the area. In 1983 part of the lake was declared a national park, which has the odd distinction of having a fluctuating surface area – at low water 367 hectares, at high water 510 hectares.

The area has an abundance of wildfowl, unusual vegetation and numerous species of fish, but what people come here for, ultimately, is the lake. Steep grey mountains shimmer in the distance, while the colours of the mud and the water reflect the sky. The special effects are easily enough explained – the lake is shallow and still, and the mud has an oily, jelly-like consistency to it – but this doesn't reduce their charm.

The lake has no big towns nearby, and its population is now reduced to a few small fishing hamlets in the coves of the northern end. A series of tiny islands contain ruined and deserted monasteries and villages, and the population is very poor and still in decline. Current plans to reclaim the floodlands and cultivate them with fruit and vines may change all this.

As far as tourism goes there isn't much at the moment, and there's no official accommodation or campsite. The nearest place you can find rooms or pitch a tent legally is 27km away at the resort of Petrovac, over the hills and up the coast. Another coastal option is to take the train just one stop along the line to Sutomore – it tunnels through the ridge and is much quicker than the road. Most people opt to stay in Titograd (see below), which is a short 30km ride away by bus or train, but has few merits of its own. It's cheaper and less crowded than Sutomore or Petrovac, but hasn't got the advantages of the sea.

Lake Skadar is large at all times (370 sq.km of it) but after the snows melt it floods to an immense 550 sq.km, and rises three metres – a lot when the average depth is only 7m. The lake has the most fish in the Balkans, with 35 different species found here including carp, trout, eels and sardines. Many of these spawn in the Adriatic, using underground streams for the journey. Despite fishing of 1,000 tons annually from the lake there is no apparent decline in the fish population.

The bird life is also very varied, with the area being a favourite stopover for migratory geese and ducks, as well as home to many types of wildfowl. Both the great white heron and the pelican are found here, but to see them you'll have to go out at dawn on one of the flat bottomed boats used by the local fishermen.

The vegetation is equally fascinating, with the water being tinted green by many species of algae and marsh plants. In spring huge areas of water lilies appear, making views of the lake look even more like an inaccurate colour photograph than usual. In August the water sprouts large numbers of water chestnuts which are harvested rather picturesquely by old women in fishing boats – except in years of drought when the plants petulantly refuse to bear fruit despite plentiful water in the lake.

When you're in the area don't on any account go too close to the Albanian frontier – the border guards have a reputation for being understandably jumpy. On land there are large, clear warning signs that you are entering the border zone, but on the lake itself it's quite possible that you won't know where the border is – it isn't necessarily obvious. Make it your business not to stray too far south.

The only town near the lake is Virpazar, a tiny place with a railway station and a bus stop and not much else. It's famous for having been the starting point for Danilo's baptism or death campaign in 1702, after a monastery was sacked by the Turks.

From here a small road leads up to the village of Boljevići. Just before the village there's a road running to the left which goes to the villages of Krnjice, Šestani, Murići and Livari, all some way above the lake. These are good bases from which you can walk and you can be sure that you'll meet very few tourists here, which makes the local people especially friendly to those they do meet. Transport up here is non-existent, so you may have to walk – if you do, be warned that the road from Virpazar to Livari is all of 33km, whatever your map says.

Upriver of Lake Skadar is the small town of Rijeka Crnojevića. It was here, in the monastery of Obod, that the first book of the Balkans was printed in 1493 (the one now in the monastery in Cetinje); ten years later the lead had to be melted down for bullets, a fitting Montenegrin ending for it. Nowadays the village is a rather cutesy place with brightly coloured fishing boats and a couple of stone bridges.

TITOGRAD

Titograd is not a place where many people stay from choice. A bustling, modern city, it was rapidly rebuilt from the ruins of Podgorica after the last war as a gesture of defiance by Tito's newly united Yugoslavia. Podgorica had been the German and Italian headquarters of Montenegro during the war, so the Allies bombed it flat, leaving less than 10% of the buildings standing. Another blow was delivered by the earthquake of 1979, which damaged or destroyed many of the remaining old buildings.

But Titograd is an important transport centre, and is a logical starting point for explorations of inland Montenegro and, in particular, Lake Skadar – you may well pass through, even if you don't stop for long. The bus and train stations are right next to each other, a couple of kilometres from the centre of town.

The train station is one of Europe's more flyblown, and possesses a remarkably seedy bar. In summer the crowds fighting to get to Sutomore and Bar on the coast are quite awesome, and Belgrade-bound expresses are crowded too, but the railway journey up the Morača gorge is almost spectacular enough to make you forget that you're standing in the corridor. Local trains, by comparison, seem to be almost empty.

The bus station is quite wholesome, having been recently rebuilt, and has a fine terrace café upstairs from which you can look at the queues at the ticket windows of the train station, and have a beer and a *burek* from one of the kiosks downstairs. The bus station also has a small seven day supermarket where you can stock up with picnic provisions for the next journey.

Apparently Podgorica wasn't that interesting even before being destroyed, but if you should be staying here then there are nonetheless things to do. The city's main attraction is probably its *corso*, the spontaneous early evening parade common to all Mediterranean countries. It takes place here in Ulica Slobode, a main street which is closed to traffic from 5pm. Titograd becomes suddenly younger during the *corso*, and it's pleasant to absorb some of the life of the place.

What old buildings are left are mostly remnants of a Turkish style of which you can see better examples almost anywhere else, but if you have time make the 4km journey north to Vranićke Njive. Near here, where the rivers Morača and Zeta meet, are the ruins of Diaclea, once an important Roman town. There are still obvious remains of baths, the forum, a couple of early churches and an old bridge, and there are a number of monumental sarcophagi.

Titograd has a thoroughly inadequate supply of private rooms and a very secretive campsite, so you may end up staying in a hotel. Fortunately there are three which are all relatively affordable – The Podgorica, right on the river, is your first choice, with double rooms at £16. For the same price you could stay in the Ljubović, also a B category hotel, while the Zlatica is for some reason slightly cheaper at about £13.

BIOGRADSKA GORA

For a combination of walking and natural history there are few places in Europe which can match the attractions of Biogradska Gora. The national park is made up of virgin forest, mountain pasture and glacial lakes, and although there is no really difficult walking, the range is excellent, with trails from 850m to over 2100m. The park is quite old, having been a declared a protected area by Nikola I after it was liberated from the Turks in 1878. One of his better decisions.

The park is of European importance because there are now only three small areas of genuine primeval forest left – Bjeloveški Pušč in Poland, Perućica in Bosnia-Hercegovinia and Biogradska Gora, which

Biogradska Jezero, the lake in the virgin forest at Biogradska Gora.

is arguably the best of the three: it's the most accessible and well-documented, and it has the widest variety of flora and fauna. The park itself is quite small, but is surrounded by a protective zone three times its size, in which you'll find several hamlets, shepherds minding their flocks and woodmen making the traditional rafts out of whole trees.

Practical Information

Biogradska Gora is almost on the main road from Titograd to Belgrade (the same road comes through Rijeka, Split and Dubrovnik), and the Belgrade-Bar railway runs along the park's edge. The road leading to the park is just over 13km north of Kolašin and just under 7km south of Mojkovac, lying between the kilometre markers 1060 and 1061 on the main road. Turn east across the Tara river and follow the road 3.85km to Biogradska Jezero, the heart of the park at 1094m.

There's a campsite here (about £3), as well as log bungalows for those who'd rather be indoors (£8 for two). A very reasonable restaurant and a small park office complete the 'facilities' and the whole thing is still reassuringly low key – though I heard that there are plans for development afoot...

Hotel accommodation is available in Kolašin and Mojkovac, which means that if you have your own transport you can see the park and still live in comfort. Kolašin is a fairly ordinary town whose Bjelasica Hotel is reasonable. The only real advantage of staying here is that it's nearer to the Morača monastery (see below). The official park office is in Kolašin, but you shouldn't need to use it as everything's also available in the park itself.

You're more likely to end up in Mojkovac, even if you don't stay here, as it's the principal (and often only) way up to the Durmitor National Park, as well as being the nearest town to Biogradska Gora.

To arrive in Mojkovac now you wouldn't guess that it had ever been famous enough to warrant an allusion by Dante. But in the Middle Ages it was an important mining town, and by the 13th century the Brstvo mine was the largest in the Balkans, providing work for over 40,000. A coin was minted here which was like a Venetian one, only lighter: Dante refers to 'those who counterfeited the coin of Venice' in his *Divine Comedy*.

Mojkovac is still very obviously an industrial town, with the traditional emphasis on mining, although its population is now less than a tenth of its 13th century workforce. If you're arriving by train make sure you do get off here – the town doesn't look significant enough to be a proper stop. From the station it's a ten minute walk to the main road: turn right for the town centre and the bus station, left for the park and the Mojkovac Hotel, a distinctive triangular building, five or six storeys high.

If you come by bus from Belgrade or Titograd then you can be dropped off at the park entrance (just say Biogradska) without needing to see Mojkovac at all. But there are no exchange facilities or shops in Biogradska Gora, and Mojkovac has a bank and a couple of supermarkets, so you might want to stop here anyway to stock up on provisions. Moderately regular services head down to Kolašin if you're changing buses.

Someone at the information desk at the bus station lied confidently to us about bus departure times, but we easily discovered the correct ones from local people hanging around. Fortunately there's a superb café here. This allowed us to while away five hours on a rainy afternoon waiting for the next bus to Žabljak (heart of the Durmitor National Park) by talking to some Canadians who were waiting only four hours for their bus to Titograd. Try the interesting chilled red wine, served by the litre, and the excellent cheese omelettes.

The Hotel Mojkovac is a strange place, built relatively recently with a steep sided triangle for template, and already falling apart. Windows have swollen so that they're permanently shut, table lamps flicker, doors have to be kicked open, and it varies from being virtually deserted to alarmingly crowded. This only happens at about 1.30pm when coachloads of stunned looking Montenegro-in-one-day tourists are disgorged into the dining room for the break between Durmitor and the Tara Canyon in the morning, and Biogradska and the Morača monastery in the afternoon. I admire their stamina.

The hotel has double rooms with damp bathrooms and a better than average breakfast for about £15. Use the plentiful hot water supply and the hint of drains will soon go away. On Friday nights (and possibly at other times too) the hotel has a band of Montenegrins who perform folk music of sorts which is greatly appreciated by the locals who come and carouse here, drinking heavily and cheering wildly. The music's not really traditional, but is genuine folk music in the sense that it's what the country people here want to listen to. Watch out for the star turn, an adroit waiter who twirls his tray alarmingly, and serves even beer with panache.

From Mojkovac you ought to be able to catch a bus at least as far as the turning for the park, but even if you can't (or if you don't fancy the wait) it's not critical – it's only just over 6km to the junction, and there's a Partisan cemetery and a café to divert you on the way. Unfortunately there's also a fair amount of traffic on the road, so be careful, and don't expect trucks or buses to move over for you. It takes an hour or so if you don't stop, after which you cross the Tara and follow the metalled road up to the lake (Biogradska Jezero) – it's clearly indicated.

The 4km stretch from the main road to the lake is very pleasant, rising first of all above the river, then the railway bridge above it (don't photograph this, it's a strategic point for the military; there's a sign down below telling you not to), before straightening out and drifting up through the forest. Altogether you climb from 850m up to nearly 1100m, but the gradient is gentle and the forest is beautiful; huge trees blocking out the light far away, with the road making an incision along the side of the valley.

At the head of the lake you'll find the campsite and a small wooden kiosk. You can buy an excellent 1:30,000 scale map here, complete with 25m contours, marked footpaths and viewpoints. They also sell natty biros and tacky postcards. Along the northern edge of the lake are several unobtrusive bungalows and just beyond these is the restaurant – try not to catch this as one of the excursions arrives: it will suddenly fill to bursting with familiar accents (Worcester, when I was last there) who stay for an hour, look out across the lake and then head off to the next stop on the itinerary.

The Virgin Forest

Biogradska Gora is carefully controlled by law to ensure that the primeval forest can develop in peace. Although the rules are strict, they are only enforced in practice by the care and attention of those who visit it, so don't do anything disruptive to the ecology. Even people who live here can't cut wood or hunt in the reserve itself, so there's no reason why outsiders should do so. Because of this you may find the paths difficult to follow at times, but with the aid of the map and a compass you shouldn't get too lost – the park isn't very big, and once you climb a little you come out onto mountain pastures, from which you can usually see where you are.

Scientifically the virgin forest is incredibly rich, containing 86 species of trees and 25 plant communities, along with no less than 220 species of plant which are only found in this reserve. The woods are also very dense, attaining figures as high as 1300 cubic metres per hectare.

Naturally a forest as varied as this provides a habitat for many rare mammals and birds, and although you probably won't see them (most are nocturnal, and shy) brown bears, and both golden and white martens live here, as well as many less rare animals such as foxes and deer. Eagles, owls, grouse and wild ducks are all fairly common, and in winter wolves and wild boar venture into the park for shelter. But it isn't the statistics that impress so much as the dreamy feel to something so primitive and ancient. Deep in the forest the smells of damp wood and heavy resins are almost intoxicating, while huge trees form an umbrella overhead. The silence is wonderful too, broken only by the movement of an animal or bird in flight, or a stream tumbling across clean rocks and fallen trees.

Take one of the rowing boats out onto the lake when there's no one around, row up to the far end, and head round the corner, out of sight of civilisation. Dead white trees stand in the shallows, reeds turn the end of the lake into marsh and the complimentary senses of decay and life are quite eerie. Under a small bridge at the lake's southernmost point is a small subsidiary (you'll have to pole the boat over the shallows). This is surrounded by immense trees and fresh large-leafed plants. Trout flicker in the clear water and old tree trunks gradually founder in the mud.

Boats are hired out by the hour from the kiosk and cost around £1.

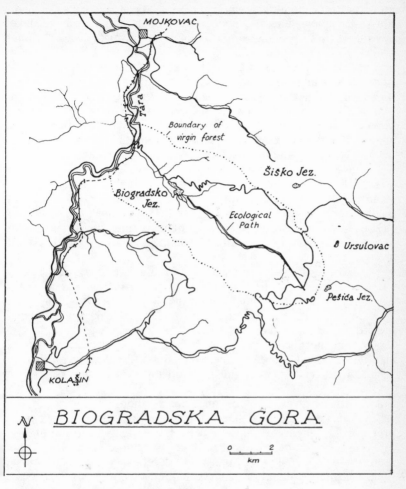

Walking in Biogradska Gora

The most popular walk in Biogradska Gora only takes an hour or so –
it consists of a simple tour of the lake, and is best done in a clockwise
direction. The walk may be short, but it gives a fine impression of the
forest and catches the reflections on the lake from every possible
angle.

Next most popular is the walk up to the source of Biogradska Rijeka
(the river Biograd). This walk takes about four hours, though you
should add time for observing the superb flora along the way. Start by
walking along the north side of the lake, and at its end curve round to
the left and then follow the trail from where you meet the river.

The path is marked for the whole of its length, but is often
overgrown, and the markings aren't always visible. As long as you
continue southeast and keep near to the north bank of the river (left as
you go up) you should be able to find your way, coming across the

proper path in the most unlikely places. The source is at a little over 1700m, so allow time and energy for a 600m climb from the lake, though this is fairly shallow, and is spread out over the whole 8km or so.

From the source, or just above it, as you come out of the forest, you can see the main peaks of the Bjelasica range. The nearest to you (less than 2km) and not easily accessible from this point, is Zekova glava, at 2117m. To the east is the summit of Crna glava, at 2139m the highest in the area. On the other side of Zekova glava is Troglova (2072m), from which there is an excellent view down onto the forest.

Once on the mountain pastures you can often make your own way up to the various summits, which are almost all rounded peaks. Be warned that occasionally they drop away alarmingly on one side, which is only really a danger if you're walking in poor visibility. Look out for pockets of snow, which can be found in sheltered north facing hollows as late as the beginning of July. Also on the pastures you'll come across sheep grazing; these are kept for making *kajmak*, a pungent local cheese.

The pastures most easily reached are those to the east of the lake. The continuation of the road going up from the main road leads through the forest and comes out on the slopes above it, giving a fine view down onto the trees, many of which are over 60m tall. Beyond the ridge there are five small lakes, all lying between 1820m and 1900m. The most beautiful of these is Pešića, set in a wonderful natural amphitheatre, but you should also see Šiško, which is easily reached by a clear path leading from the road up onto the pastures.

Finally, it's worth pointing out that the weather in Biogradska Gora isn't all sunshine and clear skies. A forest of this nature has one main prerequisite – plenty of rain – and Biogradska gets it, to the tune of 2159mm annually (compared to 610mm in London). The least rainy months are June, July and August, but don't expect it to be dry even then. Despite the damp, autumn is the best time to be in Biogradska Gora – you may only get one chance to see a primeval forest changing colour, even if you do need a waterproof.

The Morača Monastery

At the head of the Morača river, and over the pass from Kolašin, 26km away, is the monastery of Morać, one of the great tourist attractions of the area. If you can catch this beautiful 13th century building between tour buses then you should do so – it's a good example of the Raška school. It's harmonious to the eye partly because it was built on a golden section principle: its length is defined by the sum of its height and width.

Most of the best frescoes were destroyed after the Turks took off the roof, but the ones that remain give a good idea of how it must have looked, and the 16th century restoration and frescoes are by no means ugly. The monastery is on the main road to Titograd and buses can usually be persuaded to stop here. Leaving isn't always so easy – you have to rely on a charitable driver stopping to pick you up. If in doubt wait until you can get to the more accessible Mileševa, in Serbia.

DURMITOR AND THE TARA CANYON

Durmitor is one of Yugoslavia's best national parks for walkers. There is a wide variety of trails, ranging from paths across mountain pastures to extensive possibilities for climbing and mountaineering, and the park includes the spectacular Tara Canyon, Europe's deepest. There are footpaths from 500m up to over 2500m, and the area boasts numerous glacial lakes, a mild summer climate and more than enough room for all the people who could possibly want to use it.

There are several means of access to Žabljak, the village at the entrance to the park. A small airport nearby apparently flies people in from Titograd and Dubrovnik in summer, but nobody in the area seemed to be aware of this. Unless you have your own transport you'll probably arrive on the bus. An irregular service runs up from Nikšić – a name you'll recognise from Yugoslavia's most popular beer bottles – in the few months when the road is clear and if the bus company thinks it's worthwhile. Although Nikšić is beautifully situated, it's a modern, industrial town, and when I was there (June) the bus to Žabljak wasn't running.

There are two more reliable routes, from Pljevlja in the north, and Mojkovac in the east. Mojkovac has the advantage of being on the main road from Belgrade to Titograd, and on the railway from Bar to Belgrade. This is lucky because it doesn't have many other advantages (see *Biogradska Gora*). Three buses a day run from each town, at suitably inconvenient intervals – 8am, 9am and 5pm from Mojkovac when I was there, and the 5pm bus left in a downpour at 6pm.

The road from both towns meets at Djurjevića Tara, the spectacular bridge across the gorge. If you've come up from Mojkovac then you will have seen the increasingly steep walls of the canyon, and from this point on there's no path alongside the river. If you're lucky the bus will stop at the café by the bridge, which crosses the gorge in uneven hops. The bridge is nearly 400m long, and from the middle it's 150m down to the water below – which may not sound much, but it's higher than the tallest cathedral.

At the southern end of the bridge there's a sad war memorial to Lazar Jauković, an engineer who helped build it in 1941. In 1942 he was with the Partisans, holding Durmitor against Italian and Četnik forces attacking from Pljevlja, so when the need came for the bridge to be blown up the job fell naturally to him. Jauković destroyed the main arch, and the enemy had to withdraw as there was no other way across the river. When he was subsequently captured the Italians thought it a fitting end to have him executed on the bridge that had played such a large part in his life.

Žabljak is situated on a wide mountain pasture at 1450m and is a fairly new village. The first houses weren't built until 1871, and the first people to winter here were the Partisans in 1941. Although Durmitor wasn't inhabited, it has always been a place of refuge, and by May 1941, only two months after Yugoslavia capitulated, there were already 680 members of the Resistance in the area.

They freed Durnmitor in the armed uprising of July 1941, and it became an important symbol for Yugoslavia as the first part of the country to be liberated. After heavy fighting the Italians took Durmitor again in August, but dozens of guerrilla groups made life so difficult for them that they were forced to withdraw, and through the winter of 1941 the Partisans used the area as their headquarters, with the Durmitor Hotel, built in 1934 for climbers, becoming a hospital. Tito lived in one of the huts nearby.

In 1942 the area fell again, only to be liberated a third time, then becoming the Partisans' supreme headquarters. After the retreat from Sutjeska, in 1943, the area fell again, for the last time. The Italians and Četniks started a series of terrible reprisals, in which almost the entire remaining population were taken out and shot, or locked inside their homes before being burned alive. In one instance 45 women and children were herded into a large hut which was then razed to the ground; in another, 500 people, mostly old men and young children, were executed in a single day.

In September 1943 Durmitor was liberated again, and stayed free for the duration of the war, but the area had lost over 1400 civilians, and more than another thousand had been killed in battle. A concrete memorial to them stands in Žabljak. Although marred by a bronze relief that owes too much to socialist realism, it's saved by the faces of one or two fiercely moustachioed Montenegrins and the immense lists of names, already faded.

Žabljak is now a small town, thriving on the cash injection of foreign tourism, and if it's a little grasping at times, it's probably a fair compensation for the poverty and troubles of the past. The groups of tourists here stay in one of the three new hotels and tend not to venture very far into the mountains.

Winter sports are just beginning to make familiar traces on the slopes nearest to the hotels, and there are a number of ugly ski lifts springing up. Fortunately this hasn't reached anything like the level of development found in the Alps, and most of the mountains here are too inconsistent to be developed further. Although advertised as being a ski resort it's worth pointing out that if you've ever skied before you'll find this pretty trivial.

Accommodation: There's no problem finding somewhere to stay in Žabljak – not only are there four hotels, but there are also private rooms, a campsite, and a number of mountain refuges.

The Jezero Hotel is the newest of the four, and seems to border on Class A – all rooms have bathrooms, and the price reflects this: around £30 a night. The Planinka Hotel nearly matches this standard, and the pair are used for the package tours, which means that they're either full or nearly empty. The Planinka changes money, but you may find the bank (just down the road) less fussy over grubby dollar bills. In the lobbies of both hotels you'll find papier maché relief maps of the area.

The Žabljak Hotel is small, central, and a step down from the two new ones. It has double rooms for around £18, complete with cracked plaster and dodgy electrics. The Hotel Durmitor still looks like a Partisan hospital, and was a poor deal at £17 when I was there. In the hallway a moth-eaten stuffed eagle set the tone, and the rooms were moderately awful, with peeling plaster, ill-fitting doors and a single bright light. In the morning we came down to breakfast in the vast dining room, alone at the corner table with the stained cloth (as near as we got to an egg). After an hour or so a recalcitrant waiter brought us some tired bread and a sweaty chunk of sheep's milk cheese. In place of coffee we had cups of tepid milk with lumps of old chocolate powder in it. (We did stay there by mistake, after arriving late on a rainy Sunday night, and had a private room for the rest of our stay.) The Hotel Durmitor may soon be upgraded, in which case ignore the above.

Finding a private room wasn't as easy as it ought to be. Montenegrotourist had (and presumably still has) a monopoly on all accommodation in Žabljak. The tourist information kiosk at the bus station quoted reasonable prices and said that we should arrange rooms at any of the four hotels. All but one of them referred us back to tourist information. The Hotel Žabljak, right across the road from the kiosk, turned out to be the key, but charged us a little over double the official rate, on a take-it-or-leave-it basis. And you won't be able to avoid the 30% surcharge if you stay less than four nights. I ended up paying just over £8 a night, for a prolonged stay in an excellent private home.

Camping in the area is a viable option, though the weather at this altitude is always unpredictable, so if you're under canvas make sure it's really waterproof. The campsite is just outside the town on the main road, and has only minimal facilities (water and field latrines).

There are also a few mountain accommodations in the area, and nobody seems to mind if you camp beside these. The largest is a hostel, at Škrčka Jezera (1723m), between the larger and smaller lakes. This is open from mid-June to the end of September and has a dormitory which sleeps 25 and a limited number of smaller rooms which sleep another 15 altogether. Basic foods are available.

There is also an Alpine hut at Velika Kalica (2020m), under the north face of Šljime, which can take a dozen people at a pinch, and this is equipped with cooking facilities. Collect the key from the Durmitor National Park office (see below). A shelter at Lokvice (1800m), behind Medjed, has kitchen equipment and a ten bed dormitory, and is suitable for camping. The small shelter at Valoviti Do (2170m), underneath Bobotov Kuk, is open all year round, but only has room for five people, and is more of an emergency refuge – there is a fire here.

Facilities: For a town so small Žabljak has almost everything you could need: a bank, two supermarkets, a pharmacy, a petrol station, a fruit and veg market, a cinema (original versions, 25p) and a post office, from which you can dial direct international calls and, on occasion, get through.

What the town doesn't possess is any kind of snack bar, *bife* or *rostilj*. Most of the tourists are staying in full pension hotels and eat there, which is not cheap if you have to pay the going rate. There's a cake shop which might satisfy a mid-afternoon pang, and a noisy bar on the way to the park, but apart from this the only carousing that goes on is in the Working Men's Club, just opposite the larger of the two supermarkets. Tourists get strange looks, but the beer's fine, the prices correct and the TV has nothing but old English and American serials subtitled into Serbo-Croat. For nourishment I survived quite happily on various picnics collated from the supermarkets, which were enhanced by the eggs I boiled on my host's cooker.

The national park office, just past the Durmitor Hotel, has a shop attached to it (the place you might mistake for a garage, on the left hand side). There you can buy a comprehensive guidebook to Durmitor and the Tara Canyon, in English, for about £5. This includes a 1:25,000 map, complete with 20m contours, marked and unmarked footpaths, locations of shelters and all the rest.

The guide was written by Branislav Cerović in 1986, who personally marked out some of the trails in the 1930's, and has climbed and walked over every part of the park in the intervening half century. (Incidentally, Stanfords in London stock it – about £8.) A larger map, of the same scale, is also available (don't worry about the small discrepancies between the two, since the guidebook has a 1986 map and the larger version dates from 1983). To get the most from the park you should invest in both. The shop also sells wonderful hand made woollen sweaters, for £10-15. I hesitated, and missed my chance.

Inside the office (which has very irregular opening times) you can negotiate for the key to the Velika Kalica Alpine hut, and obtain any supplementary information you need.

Note that although the park is maintained to a certain extent, there is no official mountain rescue, and calling an ambulance up here would probably take several hours. If you have mountaineering experience you will only need the map, a compass, and emergency equipment (an altimeter is also useful); in any other case you shouldn't leave the marked paths, and you should be particularly careful in the early summer (up to the third week of July), since there are still many patches of snow around. Some of the harder trails require an ice-axe and/or ropes at this time of year, and you should be especially careful anywhere of frolicking on steep snow if you haven't already learned how to do so safely – a friend of mine slid down across only 15m of compacted snow here, and tumbled over the scree at the bottom. He wasn't seriously hurt, but he was shaken.

Durmitor National Park

Because it lies in a historically troubled area the Durmitor mountain range and the Tara Canyon weren't explored scientifically until relatively recently. Several reports were published at end of the 19th century, but the first mountaineers didn't come to the region until 1926. By 1935 the main paths were marked and the area attracted an increasing amount of attention, although it wasn't declared a national park until 1978.

The area was shaped, as can be seen clearly, by violent tectonic movements, followed by river and glacial erosion. This has left a good variety of mountains, ranging from sharp peaks to vertically cut summits and rounded saddles. The area is also rich in lakes, some of which are perfectly situated, surrounded by deep forests or stark cliffs. Altogether there are over twenty, with Crno Jezero (literally, the Black Lake) being the most famous: it's a large pair of joined lakes, surrounded by rich forest and overshadowed by the looming bulk of Medjed rising 750m above it.

The Tara cuts into this landscape, which ranges from 1300m up to just over 2500m, in a unique gorge which is up to 1200m deep in places, and has cliffs up to 1000m tall, making the canyon the biggest in Europe. It claims to be second only in the world to the Grand Canyon. There are easy trails leading to the upper edge of this, with quite stunning views. Rafting trips are also organised along the river gorge (see below).

The area has an interesting pattern of trees and other flora. In the canyon there are deciduous trees up to 850m; up to 1300m it is then predominantly beech woods. Between 1300m and 1600m there are conifers, and above this, because of a minor temperature inversion, more beech, up to 1800m. Above 1800m there is mountain pine. The meadows and mountain pastures are rich in wild flowers, and herbs are common higher up; you'll smell them as you crush them underfoot.

The larger wildlife is fairly rare, being limited to a few chamois, some deer, and in spring and autumn a few bears – the guidebook points out reassuringly that these are 'strictly herbivorous'. Apparently there used to many wolves in the region; they're now increasingly rare. Look out instead for two sorts of eagles – the grey and imperial species both live here.

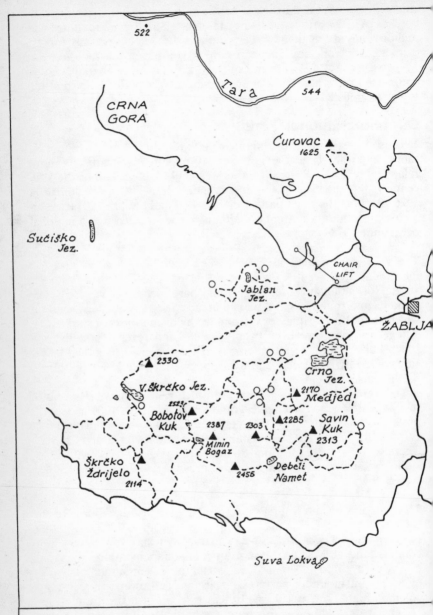

522

Tara

544

CRNA
GORA

Ćurovac ▲
1625

Sučiško
Jez.

CHAIR
LIFT

Jablan
Jez.

ŽABLJA

2330

Crno
Jez.

V.Škrčko Jez.

2170
Medjed

2525
Bobotov
Kuk

2387

2303

2285

Savin
Kuk
2313

Minin
Bogaz

Škrčko
Ždrijelo
2114

2455

Debeli
Namet

Suva Lokva

N

DURMITOR/TARA

0   1   2   3
k m

- - - TRAIL
O   CABIN
    (Landma

Žabljak's climate is typical for a village in the mountains 1400m above sea level – which is to say that it's cooler than most parts of the country, has fairly high precipitation and the weather is highly unpredictable.

The area is covered by snow for over 120 days a year, and the annual average temperature in the village is only 5°C. Even in August the average is only 14°C, and the January average is below -5°C. In the mountains the annual average is closer to zero, with a July high of 8°C. Even if it's hot enough for shorts when you start out you should always have long trousers, a sweater, a waterproof and emergency supplies with you. Temperatures below freezing are not unheard of in August, and hypothermia is a very real danger here.

The annual precipitation is about 1500mm (20% higher on the mountains), of which a good proportion falls as snow. The area is much drier than Biogradska Gora, but you can still be drenched at any time by sudden showers while out walking. Clouds can also form and descend onto the mountain peaks very quickly, so you should always try and be sure of your position, on the assumption that you could soon be enveloped in fog. This can clear as fast as it arrives, and it can be quite alarming when you're plodding up a steep path in the fog to find that there's an unexpected and precipitous drop to one side.

Although Žabljak is actually within the limits of the national park, most of the walking starts from Crno Jezero, 3km from the village. A metalled road runs as far as the lake, passing the Jezero and Durmitor hotels, and the national park office on the way. A barrier keeps the last 800m or so traffic free, though traffic isn't one of Žabljak's most serious problems.

You can reach the top of the Tara Canyon via footpaths and country roads, directly from the village – see the walks detailed below. Getting to the bottom of the gorge is less easy. There's one country road which does descend into the canyon, but most people reach the central stretches by raft (again, see below). Access in this case is from the bridge at Djurdjevića Tara.

TRAILS IN THE NATIONAL PARK

Most of the trails in the Durmitor National Park are suitable for single day walks, taking anything from two to twelve hours. Longer walks, lasting two days or more, can easily be planned, with stopovers at the hostel or refuges, but don't be caught out at night without proper equipment. I heard a worrying story from someone who had been obliged to bivouac here in May, and had slept in a plastic survival bag. He was warm enough when he went to sleep – too warm if anything – but on waking he found that his breath had condensed onto the inside of the bag and then frozen, leaving him sheathed in ice. Don't let it happen to you.

If you have transport then you can sometimes avoid the access routes mentioned here – in particular the 40 minute walk from the village to the lake – but if you haven't then you can invariably return by different paths each day, as the area immediately surrounding Žabljak is mostly open pasture which can be crossed anywhere.

Crno Jezero

The shortest, and most popular, walk in the area is the circuit of Crno Jezero (the Black Lake). It takes a couple of hours if you dawdle, and could almost have been made for the package tour brochures. Although you're more likely to see other people here than anywhere else in Durmitor that's not to say that it's crowded, and it makes a pleasant warming up exercise or recuperative afternoon walk.

From Žabljak town centre it's an easy 40 minute walk to the lake, and there's no way of getting lost. Although there's a short cut across the meadows from the Jezero Hotel to the Durmitor there's also a stream here (until July) which is more difficult to cross than you'd expect – the stepping stones are slightly too far apart and aren't secure.

Follow the metalled road through the woods, and at its conclusion you'll find the lake, with a chalet beside it which looks as if it ought to furnish refreshments but wasn't open in June. Directly in front of you is the solid block of Medjed, with its vertical face hanging over the lake. From here the footpath is clearly marked either way round the lake, and is 3.5km long. The clockwise direction is marginally better.

Crno Jezero is the second largest lake in Montenegro, and is situated at 1416m, just below the level of Žabljak. It has two basins, separated by a shallow bank, and this causes the lake to divide in two by late summer. It is supplied for the most part by springs inside Medjed, and drains out through sink holes, except for the small stream flowing towards the town.

The water that goes into the sink holes stays underground for all of eight days, emerging over 700m down and 20km away from the lake. The stream also disappears, just before Žabljak, and takes nine days to reappear, 10km away and over 800m down. If the area were made of less porous rock it's sure that there would be plentiful rivers and streams; as it is the only apparent water is restricted to springs, short streams and the lakes – and even these are often seasonal.

As you walk round the lake you'll come to a place marked on the map as Titova Peć – Tito's Cave. This is really little more than a sloping part of the rock, but Tito used this as a hideout on a couple of occasions and the place is now one of the many memorials in the area. The plastic flowers are rather pathetic, but the hundreds of old one and two dinar coins hammered into the dead trees nearby are suitably emotive.

At various points towards the end of the smaller lake there are dried up or feeble waterfalls; in May and early June these carry the water from the thaw into the lake, flooding the paths and filling the lake to its limit. Further round are a couple of other memorials, for which you'll need your best Cyrillic – it's not uncommon to see foreign visitors standing in front of them mouthing out the letters one by one in an effort at transliteration.

Savin Kuk

This walk is one of the most satisfying in the whole of the Durmitor range. It's fairly long (around nine hours in all) but never dangerous, and takes you to the summit of one of the higher peaks, Savin Kuk, at 2313m. The peaks higher than this all require some mountaineering skills, or take longer – and the highest, Bobotov Kuk, is only 200m higher and doesn't even have such good views. There are several ways of reaching the foot of the mountain from Žabljak, but if you don't know the area it's best to take the classic route up and extemporise on the way down.

Start by going to Crno Jezero, and take the path to the left of it, following the shore until you reach an obvious junction – one path continues on the flat, around the lake; the other leads up into the mountains, and is signed as such. This path is quite wide, and easy to follow, and every so often there are markings to guide you. At 1510m there's a small spring and a water trough – just over half an hour from the lake – after which the path levels out a bit and the woods open up.

Soon after this you'll come to a shepherd's cabin on the left of the path, after which there are large pastures broken by ruined dry stone walls to the left, and more open karst on the right. If you're feeling foolhardy then this karst is the most direct route to the summit; the marked path is both easier and quicker. Just past the second hut the path splits, with one branch going straight on. The marked path to the right leads to Savin Kuk. It was here that a little girl came out and rather coyly offered us fresh milk in exchange for chocolate.

At the base of the mountain, from this side, you can clearly see the steep ridge of Šljime (2445m) to the left, and the bulk of Savin Kuk to the right. From Žabljak to this point takes a little under two hours. The path goes up the gap between the two mountains, only appearing on Savin Kuk itself after the lower of the two summits (2143m).

On the day I was here there was fog down to 1800m, and I only discovered the rather daunting views on the way back down. Going up in the fog in June you catch tantalising glimpses of fairly large patches of snow, and can usually just see the red markers ahead one at a time. In normal visibility the path is very clear, being more or less straight up to 1850m and then zigzagging fairly steeply until you reach some scree.

The trail crosses this and then curves round to the right, coming out on a saddle between the two summits, slightly above the lower of the two. From here it's only a short walk to a spring with a small trough. The delicious cold water here provides a welcome break at 2180m, before the last stretch. Just after the spring there's a T-junction at the edge of a cliff over 200m tall. Look straight down and you can just see the Alpine refuge to the left, at the base of the cliff.

Take the right hand path here, and it's only twenty minutes to the summit. You'll find a rubber stamp there, and wonderful views across the Durmitor range and the huge pastures round Žabljak. I arrived in thick fog, which cleared slowly, delivering this view bit by bit. There is a tricky, unmarked, path which goes from here down the gully beyond the summit and traverses across and down to the refuge. Don't attempt this unless you're a good mountaineer (you'll need an ice-axe until the end of July, and should take it carefully, whatever your experience – there's a 350m drop from the top if you slip).

I went back to the junction on the cliff, and had intended to cross from here up onto the ridge of Šljime – this involves a traverse across snow followed by a steep, assisted passage across rock leading up to the 2400m ridge. The fog was still swirling heavily on this side, and with an inexperienced companion and no ice-axe I wasn't prepared to do it. A German mountain guide I spoke to said that the traverse is difficult to descend, but fine to climb – in good weather and with some experience. There's a clear way down from this ridge to the pasture at 1600m, and an alternative is to climb up this instead of Savin Kuk. I've been informed that it's very steep, but not technically difficult. Be aware of the cliff on the right hand side, especially in poor visibility.

On the way down from Savin Kuk, past the spring, you can stop off at the lower summit, which gives another fine view across the area, though the main peak obscures the rest of the mountain range. At the base of the mountain you can now choose one of several ways home to Žabljak. From above you will have seen the various routes quite clearly, and it makes a pleasant change to cut across the pastures and approach the town from the other side. This also has the advantage of giving you a very satisfying view of the peak you've just climbed.

The whole trail could be done in about seven hours; nine leaves a comfortable margin for a picnic, time to explore, and occasional breaks.

Medjed

The views from the top of Medjed are excellent, looking straight down from the ridge onto the lake 700m below. However the mountain is not suitable for ordinary walking, and none of the three routes are marked as being less than 'moderately hard' (Savin Kuk gets a 'moderately difficult'). I didn't climb Medjed, partly because of the weather conditions, but have heard that the view is worth the rather exposed ascents. See the guidebook for detailed descriptions of the ways up.

Bobotov Kuk

Although not as famous as Medjed and Savin Kuk (the most obvious peaks), Bobotov Kuk is nonetheless the highest (2523m) and most climbed peak in Durmitor. From Žabljak it's not easily distinguishable, being hidden amongst the further peaks, but it is possible to climb the mountain in a day (10-12 hours). It's more mountaineering than walking, as can be seen from the guidebook's 'very hard climb', 'recommended to use ice-axes', and 'a real test of daring'. This is the mountain I would most like to go back and climb; in June I had neither the equipment nor the company necessary.

The several routes and approaches are well covered in the guidebook, but you shouldn't attempt it unless you've had some mountaineering experience, including climbing, crossing snow, and using an ice-axe. Don't let this put you off – it's said to be worth every effort.

Ćurovac (Tara Canyon)

Back from the giddy heights, this is an easy trail which leads up to the edge of the Tara Canyon, giving views down nearly 1100m for the price of a 200m ascent. The walk is a little over 12km, and took me six hours, including a two hour break for rock climbing. It can be done in under three hours if you're in that much of a rush.

The trail starts on the road branching off from the main road by the Planinka Hotel, in Žabljak. The way is clearly marked on the map, though you'll note that much more of the road has been asphalted since the 1983 map was published (another 2km or so). On a corner, about 5km from Žabljak, and quite clearly marked, there's a trail leading off the dirt road. This winds up through the karst and leads to the summit of Ćurovac (1625m).

This is on the edge of the canyon, and gives a superb view down to the blue ribbon of the Tara below as it passes the community of Tepca. Even this far away you can hear the river as it passes some rapids just beyond Tepca, and the scene is often complemented here by eagles gliding across the gorge and over towards the mountains of Durmitor. Look out for swallowtail butterflies, which might just divert your attention from some enthusiastic horseflies and mosquitoes.

At and near the top there is some excellent and fairly easy climbing and clambering on firm rock, with some supplementary vertiginous views for the clear headed. I clambered down about 100m and found a superb spike 15m high to climb.

From the summit the path continues in an arc, going down a steeper slope than the ascent, towards a large *polje* (a meadow formed by a collapsing underground cave) which from above looks as neatly mown as a football pitch. It's an illusion – and the field actually contains wonderful grasses, flowers and herbs, and makes a fine picnic spot. The path across this isn't obvious, but if you head towards the telegraph poles at the end you'll find that they cross the road eventually.

If you continue along the forest road instead of returning to Žabljak then you'll find that it soon comes out into the canyon itself, and descends in a zigzag to the river, passing through the community of Tepca on the way. A clear donkey trail cuts the corners of the dirt road and descends quickly to about 1000m, after which the slope is more shallow to the Tara, but by no means as flat as it looks from the top. Be warned that it's a very long climb back up to Žabljak if you come down as far as the river – allow at least five hours for the return trip.

The route to Crna Gora (Tara Canyon)

An even higher view of the Tara can be had from the road leading to the remote village of Crna Gora (not to be confused with the republic of the same name – Montenegro), about 15km from Žabljak. The village lies on the narrow plateau above the place where the Sušica and Tara canyons meet, and is one of the most inaccessible in Yugoslavia.

The gravel road leading to it skirts around several rounded summits and attains an altitude of 1900m before dropping back down to about 1450m. It takes around two and a half hours from Žabljak to the stretch of road which looks down on the Tara, and nearer five to reach Crna Gora. Double these times for the return trip.

Although you can take the road all the way from Žabljak there are a number of shortcuts which save time and are better than walking too much on metalled roads. You can actually start anywhere in Žabljak between the Planinka and Durmitor Hotels and walk due north across the pasture up to the ridge, all of 500m away.

From here, or from the bottom of the woods, if you've walked into them, you should be able to see the metalled road in front of you, running along parallel to the ridge. Turn left onto this road and follow it until you reach the bottom of a chair lift, on your right. The road you want to join runs along the top of this, and there are several ways of joining it, simplest (and steepest) of which is to walk up under the chairs, crossing the road on a zigzag as you go. Before the top you'll reach the road again, and you can either turn onto it here, or go on up to the top, where you can have a break at the restaurant, in the unlikely event of it being open.

A less man-made route is to start by walking up the path to the left of the pylons and then cut left, passing through the small settlement of Bosača. At the last hut turn right and head straight up across a steep green pasture. This leads to a steep track, which you follow until the ground levels out. Leave the track here as it drifts left, and turn half right – you should join the road in 200m or less. You will have bypassed the restaurant by this point, so you'll have to backtrack 500m or so if you want a break.

From here you stay on the gravel road – the land falls away rapidly to the left at first (there's a path across this, which leads to Crna Gora by a quicker route, but carefully avoids any of the views of the Tara) and then rises up as the road takes a hairpin bend (you can cut across this). Soon afterwards the road reaches a crest and on the other side of this is the Tara, at first seen only in the far distance. From here onwards there are increasingly good views of the gorge, until you reach a long curving piece of road under Velika Štuoc (2104m).

There's a new gravel road leading up to the top (large amounts of

snow, even in late June), which isn't marked on the map, but this leads
to a military installation of some kind. Don't venture too high up here,
and in any case don't cross the fence at about 2050m. The view from
the road is only slightly inferior.

Other trails

The area has an almost unlimited amount of walking and
mountaineering, including some excellent trails to the less visited
glacial lakes, long paths across pastureland, and easy climbs up to
mountain summits between 1700m and 2000m.

Particularly recommended is a visit to the Mala and Velika Škrčka
lakes. These are quite a distance from Žabljak (six to seven hours) but
the hostel is situated between them and will find a place for you, even
when full, so you can make it a two day excursion. The lakes are
situated at 1700m, but most routes there go up to at least 2000m.

Many more walking possibilities and the mountaineering
approaches to all the peaks in Durmitor are detailed in the guidebook.

Rafting on the Tara

The best way of seeing the Tara Canyon is from inside it, and the only
practical way of doing this is on a raft – the gorge is often too narrow
for roads or footpaths, and the routes which go round the cliff faces
can easily be over 30km long.

Most rafting trips leave from Djudjevića Tara and finish where the
Tara and Piva join to form the Drina, at Šćepan Polje. The 88km trip
lasts from 3-5 days, with the nights being spent under canvas. Some of
the longer trips run along the Drina too, passing through Foča and
fetching up at Višegrad – though it should be pointed out that the
Drina is considerably tamer than the Tara.

The rafts are the real thing – simply logs strapped together – and
carry ten passengers and a crew of two. These men are extraordinarily
adept at their job, which is a good thing considering the state of the
canyon. Most trips are organised by Unis Tours, and cost upwards of
£100 a head. Very often you'll have to make your own group of ten to
book, or put up with one of the shorter tours. Unis Tours can be
contacted at Tršćanska 7, 71000, Sarajevo, and will be happy to supply
a brochure in English with all the facts.

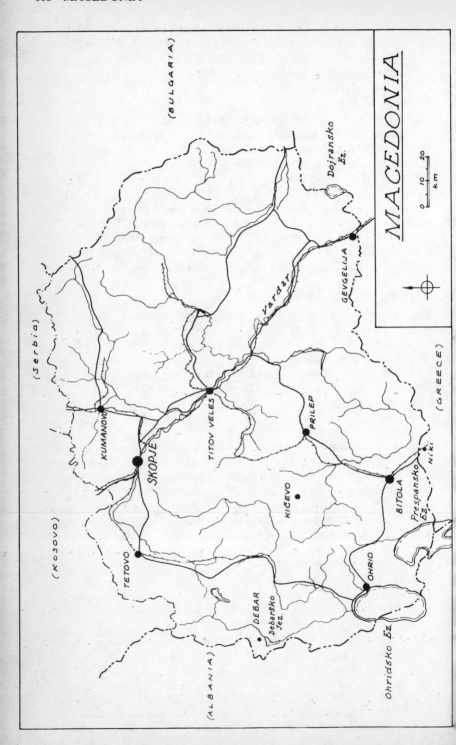

Macedonia

The ancient Greeks considered the Macedonians a race of ignorant peasants, but under the tutelage of Philip, and his son Alexander (356-323 BC), it became one of the most powerful and influential states in the world.

Alexander came to the throne at 20, and as soon as all of Greece was his, he set off towards India, travelling over 30,000km and winning every battle he fought. He was only forced to turn back by his homesick troops, many of whom hadn't seen home in ten years, and he died aged only 33, head of an empire that was bigger than the USA. After his death the empire fragmented rapidly under the control of his generals (Ptolemy amongst them) and Macedonia never really recovered.

The expansion of the Byzantine empire led to the incorporation of Macedonia, and for most of the period from the 6th century until the Ottoman Turks arrived in the 14th, it was under their control. Tsar Samuel, based in Ohrid, looked for a time as if he could create a state outside Byzantium, but his troops lost a crucial battle in 1014, and all 14,000 of them had their eyes put out for their trouble – except one in a hundred, who only had one eye blinded so that they could lead the rest home.

The Turks held Macedonia for longer than any other part of the Balkans, and despite continuous uprisings and revolts, led by the Hajduks (local freedom fighters), the turn of the century saw the decaying Ottoman Empire still in control – this was largely because Russia and Austria both wanted it and couldn't come to a sensible agreement. In a unique attempt at co-operation, Serbia, Greece and Bulgaria finally managed to fight on the same side in the first Balkan War in 1912, and succeeded in ejecting the Turks. No sooner were the Turks evicted than the Bulgarians staked their claim on the whole country, immediately provoking the second Balkan War (1913) which eventually spilled into the First World War. Only after this, in 1919, was Macedonia divided into its present state, with part of it going to Greece and part to Bulgaria. Most of the country was absorbed by Serbia and became part of the new Kingdom of the South Slavs.

Macedonia's history for the fifty years from 1893 has a lot to do with the Internal Macedonian Liberation Organisation (IMRO), which originally started with the simple ideal of a free, independent, Macedonia. Factions within IMRO soon declared different local aims, and for the majority of outsiders it became impossible to judge the situation. In the first decade of the century there were numerous uprisings, including one in the small town of Kruševo, in the heart of Macedonia, and for over three months the rebellion had all the airs of open warfare, before being violently suppressed.

After the First World War, IMRO quite rightly saw Yugoslavia as its main oppressor, and pro-Bulgarian factions encouraged terrorism and an increasingly high profile, including assassinations abroad and the regular bombing of the Athens Express. This didn't endear foreign opinion to IMRO, nor did associations with Bulgaria and fascist Italy help their cause.

Serbia over-reacted to the uprisings, and outlawed not only the Macedonian language but even the name Macedonia, provoking intense local feeling against Belgrade which was prevalent until after the last war. Some idea of the level of local frustration can be appreciated from the fact that until the first schools opened in 1945 there had been no formal education in Macedonia for over 500 years – and under the Serbian dictatorship it was illegal.

By 1941 some of the most vociferous fragments of IMRO had gone to the Bulgarian side, allying themselves with the fascist axis, and when Macedonia was handed to Bulgaria in the same year, it became a puppet state under German control. Fortunately the majority joined the Partisans, and the restoration of the borders to their 1919 state (in 1945) has given most of Macedonia a fair deal. But in the south you'll hear the Yugoslavian part of the country referred to as 'Free Macedonia', and there are still sensitive borders on all sides of the republic.

Since 1945 Macedonia has undoubtedly been better off, though it remains one of the country's most backward and impoverished regions – not surprising, given the amount of catching up it has had to do.

Macedonians are proud of their language, which although similar to Serbo-Croat in many ways, is much closer to Bulgarian. The alphabet is almost exclusively Cyrillic here, and not knowing it can be a disadvantage. Equally, you can make yourself popular very easily by knowing even a few words of Macedonian – 'thank you' is *fala*, as opposed to *hvala*, and 'cheers!' is *nazdravje* instead of *živili*.

Perhaps as a result of the centuries of oppression, Macedonian culture is now flourishing prominently, and I met more artists here than anywhere else in Yugoslavia. Almost everyone seems to be a poet, a singer or a musician, and they all have the cheerful air of educated rebels. I was once passing a mildly drunk afternoon conversing with a boatman in bad French when I realised that he had quoted Rousseau and Goethe in consecutive sentences. I can't imagine the same thing happening at home.

However, by the standards of the West, Macedonia is still underdeveloped. In remote Moslem areas you'll still find women almost completely covered up, and in the south fields are even now ploughed with oxen. Horses and carts are as common as cars on provincial roads, and most of the back-breaking work in the fields is still done by stooping old women who work incredibly long hours. Times are changing, however, and the first indication of this is in the widespread adoption of jeans and other western clothes.

Most people travelling across Macedonia are speeding through on their way to Greece, and the majority don't know what they're missing. Macedonia has a fine combination of culture and scenery, with monasteries, icons and frescoes which are among the best in the world, and unique lakes and mountains. As yet it is virtually untouristed, but this situation can't last for long.

SKOPJE

The capital of Macedonia is now a thriving, modern and industrial city; something of a contrast to how it must have looked on the morning of 26th July 1963, just after an earthquake had left 1,000 dead, 3,000 injured and over 100,000 homeless. More than 80% of the city was in ruins and Tito championed the disaster as a cause for international co-operation – he got it: aid came from all over the world, and most notably from *both* the USA and the USSR.

Today's Skopje is modern and functional, housing nearly half a million in buildings that have been designed to withstand earthquakes up to force 10 on the Richter scale. After all it's not the first time that Skopje's been affected by earthquakes – the city was totally destroyed in 518, and has had tremors ever since.

The city was important to the Turks from the end of the 14th century until the first Balkan war, and even now has more of a Turkish feel to it than anywhere else I've been in Europe.

Initially, Skopje can be a disconcerting place – especially if you arrive without any Cyrillic at 6am on the all-night bus from Dubrovnik. With a different alphabet you suddenly feel illiterate, and the early morning crowds, the different faces, the smells of grilling meat, and the drunks asleep on tables in the bus station cafés make it something of an adventure – particularly after tourist-conscious Dubrovnik.

The bus station is the best place to arrive, being situated right next to the Čaršija, the old Turkish bazaar. The main sights are all here, dotted amongst the ramshackle houses which collapse gently around the cracked streets. Early in the morning the only people here are barrow boys pushing trolleys, men in skullcaps standing in doorways and women wearing baggy Moslem trousers. The oriental atmosphere is even stronger here than in Sarajevo, one of Yugolsavia's most obviously eastern cities – perhaps because unlike Sarajevo, Skopje never had any Austrian influence to moderate either the architecture or the way of life.

On Saturdays there's an excellent open air market here. This is one of the largest and most colourful in Yugoslavia, with country people coming in from miles around to sell what little they have. As always in such places you ask yourself how people can possibly make a living with only a dozen cabbages to sell.

In the middle of the bazaar there's a small church called Sveti Spas (the Church of our Saviour). This was built in the 17th century and is for the most part underground – the Turks let the church be built, but only on condition that it didn't overshadow any of the city's mosques. The church wouldn't be of note were it not for its exceptional walnut iconostasis, which took nearly 12 years to carve, and was finished in 1824. This is so detailed that the church seems even smaller than it really is, and when you look at it closely you can see that finishing it in under 12 years was pretty sharp work. It was carved by two brothers, Marka and Petar Filopivski, who went on to carve two more altar screens, even more detailed and skilful than this one. One of these was unfortunately destroyed in the Kruševo uprising, but the other survives, in the monastary of Sveti Jovan Bigorski, near Mavrovo (see *Western Macedonia*). After seeing this one you should try and see the other. A charming feature of both screens is that the brothers appear in their own work – you can see them here chipping away with an apprentice in the far right panel.

In the courtyard of Sv. Spas there's a solid looking stone sarcophagus containing Goce Delčev, the man who gave his name to a boulevard or avenue in just about every town in Macedonia. He was one of the earliest leaders in IMRO, and was apparently a fine strategist and fighter, perfecting ideas about guerilla warfare in the mountains which were later used by the Partisans. He was killed in 1903, and even now his picture hangs with Tito's all over the republic.

There are several mosques in the Čaršija, though they all seem to be falling into disrepair and it's difficult to believe that there is much of a religious community left. The most impressive of the mosques is Mustafa Pasha's, complete with beautiful carpets, calligraphy and fine abstract tracery near the ceiling. If it's closed (and it often is) you can get good views of the interior by pressing your face up against the windows giving onto the tatty garden behind. Make sure the mosque is actually closed before you do this.

Near here there is the National Museum of Macedonia, which contains the surviving fragments of several of the museums that were destroyed during the earthquake, including a fairly good archaeological collection. The museum is housed in the recently restored Kuršumli Han, a building which gives a very good idea of the typical *han* design. *Hans* were fortified night stops on the Ottoman trade routes, and Skopje was one of the more important staging posts. There are another couple of *hans* here, but none show the style better than Kuršumli.

Above the bazaar is the Museum of Contemporary Art, a building that looks just like a museum of contemporary art, right down to the gaudy sculptures outside that ought to be in a psychedelic playground. In 1963 the curator appealed to artists worldwide to donate a picture to the gallery, and judging by the results they're a tight-fisted lot – though Picasso's contribution is good by default; he didn't produce much that wasn't of value. A couple of very simple paintings stand out, including a Czech seascape and a French abstract, but the collection is, on the whole, disappointing.

Better art can often be found in the gallery at the bottom of the bazaar, by the river. This has temporary exhibitions of modern work, and has the advantage of being in a beautiful building – the Daut Pasha Hammam. Originally a Turkish bath, the building is now cool and spacious, and even if the current exhibition is no good the building alone is worth the paltry entrance fee.

Practical Information: There's a tourist information office just up from the bus station (away from the river) and they handle the only private rooms in town. They'll furnish you with a map (as will the travel agent on the corner of the bus station) which shows you the rough layout of the city, including locations of everything you could possibly need.

Cross the river on the old stone bridge and you'll find yourself in the heart of the busy new town. Cheap cafés are abundant round here, as are *rostilj* and bars in the Čaršija. Be warned however that they all close up by 11pm.

Accommodation isn't as easy as you'd expect – the city isn't really geared to independent tourism. There are few private rooms (looking obvious at the bus station may get you one), and the hotels aren't particularly cheap, with nothing under £17 for a double. There is, however, a campsite not too far out of town. I took the option of arriving at 6am and leaving mid-afternoon.

SOUTHERN MACEDONIA

Bordering on Albania and Greece, the lakes of Ohrid and Prespa are one of Yugoslavia's greatest attractions. Mt. Galičica (2275m) stands between the two lakes, while Pelister, one of the highest mountains in the country (2601m) lies just to the east, and each peak forms the basis of an interesting national park. The area is also an important cultural centre, with a mass of well preserved Orthodox monasteries, as well as the extensive Roman ruins of Heraclea.

Ohrid

After Sv. Kliment (one of the most influential of Cyril and Methodius's disciples) showed up here in 886, Ohrid became one of the most important cultural centres of Europe. Sv. Naum joined him in 900, and together they developed the Cyrillic alphabet, encouraged the building of churches and monasteries, and established an important school of icon painting.

Ohrid is now an increasingly busy town with a rapidly expanding tourist industry. And it has everything that even the most demanding visitor could want – monasteries, museums, beaches, mountains, a pleasant climate and, as yet, not too many people.

The town is situated in the southwestern corner of Macedonia, at the

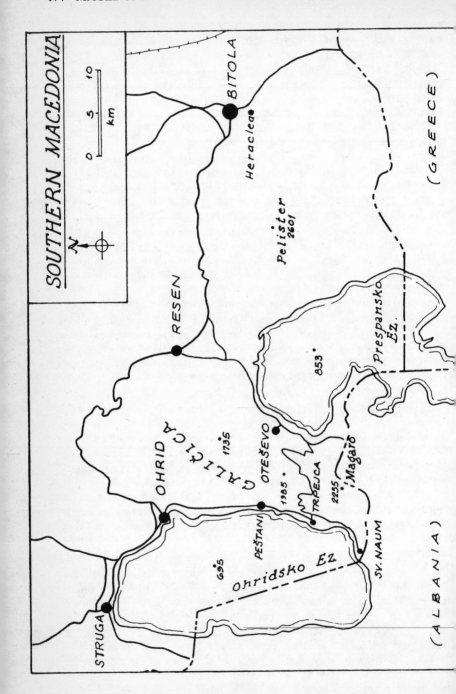

head of its eponymous lake, about four hours from Skopje by bus (two and a half if you believe the brochure or drive like an Italian). The route bypasses the Mavrovo National Park (see *Western Macedonia*) and crosses some wonderful scenery before reaching the plain at 700m. There's a small airport nearby, and flying either to or from Ohrid makes a lot of sense – I took the bus down from Dubrovnik (21 hours), and flew back (40 minutes).

Practical Information: Accommodation is no problem here – there are around 5000 private rooms in the area. These are handled by travel agencies and the tourist office – which is otherwise not much use, though they will sell you a map of the town and they have stocks of the Galičica National Park brochure. The chances are that you'll be accosted at the bus station anyway, and here you shouldn't have to pay more than £8, though you may need to bargain strenuously. The official rate is £8-12. The Palace Hotel, just down from the bus station, is overpriced and tends to be package territory. Camping is possible at several sites along the shores of the lake (see *Galičica*).

Eating is also hassle free. The fish restaurant (Riben Restoran) by the port is excellent, both in quality and price (full meals with wine at around £8 for two). The *belvica* (see *Lake Ohrid*, below) is particularly good. Picnics can be made up from the numerous supermarkets and the daily fresh market, and the bakeries provide not just bread but also delicious *gevreks*, Macedonian rolls baked with sesame seeds.

The travel agencies opposite the bus station are useful, with services including exchange, local information, travel bookings, and excursions to places that are otherwise hard to reach (notably Sv. Jovan Bigorski and Debar in Western Macedonia, about £13 all in). Generalturist is the best of the bunch. Look out here for Vejsel Rašit, the young Turk who drives the Generalturist minibus. In his English homework I discovered the phrase 'Driving fast is my hoby' – and I can personally vouch for this.

Ohrid's sights are all neatly tucked into the old town, a maze of distinctive narrow streets leading up to the ruined castle of Tsar Samuel at the top of the hill. The houses have horizontal wooden beams amongst the stonework, and their upper storeys project above the lower. This design is apparently earthquake resistant, with the secondary advantage of being good looking. The castle has a fine situation and offers superb views across the lake to Albania on the southern and western shores. If you climb the ramparts, do so carefully – they aren't all as secure as they look.

On the way down from here towards the lake you'll come across the sandy ground plan of a completely levelled early Christian basilica. Brush the sand away gently and you'll find some exceptionally well preserved mosaics dating from the 4th or 5th century. Cover it up again before you go – the sand's there to protect them.

Below this, on the footpath along the lake shore, you'll find the beautiful monastery of Sv. Jovan Kaneo perched harmoniously on a small cliff promontory. The building is tiny and has very little inside it, but its position is impeccable (it's on the cover of this book).

Ohrid has a number of other churches, which are more famous for their interiors, of which the best are Sv. Kliment and Sv. Sofia. Sv. Kliment is an architectural mess, with the original shape quite lost amongst the later additions. But inside it has some of the most beautifully restored 14th and 15th century frescoes I've ever seen. On mentioning that I was from the press the guardian gave me a detailed tour, convinced I was a priest, unlikely as it must have seemed with my Nikon and boating shoes.

Next door to Sv. Kliment there's an Icon Gallery, one of the top four collections in the world. Some of these are breathtaking, including a positively renaissance St. Matthew, a cheery looking Sv. Kliment and a sage Sv. Naum.

Sv. Sofia stands at the bottom of the old town and is one of Ohrid's oldest churches. It was almost demolished by the Turks in the 19th century, but has been painstakingly restored and contains some tremendous 11th and 12th century frescoes. In the apse there's an unusually well preserved Virgin and Child. This was actually the artist's first attempt; unsatisfied, he covered it with a second version. The restorers discovered this and took off the top one – it now stands to one side against the wall, for comparison.

If it's open, the church of Sv. Bogorodica nearby also has some lovely detailed 14th century frescoes in its tiny inner church. You should also try and make time to visit at least one of the three Orthodox churches still in use. These contain icons whose age can only be judged by their condition, so little did the style change over a 500 year period. One of them houses a casket containing some of the bones of Sv. Kliment – in a rather touching allegory of Macedonia itself, the rest of the saint's bones are divided between Greece and Bulgaria.

If you haven't tired of culture by this time then the National Museum has an interesting collection ranging from Roman artefacts to natural history. It's housed in a particularly well restored example of Ohrid's indigenous architecture.

The new town hasn't many attractions, but one you won't miss is an enormous old plane tree (*Golem Činar Platan*), at least 500 years old and probably nearer 1000. Its fractured trunk comes out of the ground in three parts, and apparently used to house a café. Now it provides a meeting place for the old men of the town, who congregate here in their fezes while the town's youth drift along the lakefront in the summer *corso*.

Ohrid is a place of inspiration not just to the casual visitor but to the Macedonian people, and it provides a focus for much of the new creativity of the area. One of the better known residents is the self-taught painter Vangel Naumovski, who has had exhibitions around the world. His early pictures owe something to Chagall and Fauvism, but his later work is almost entirely abstract, influenced more by nature than anything man-made. A gallery, Ohridska Porta, showing his latest work, is attached to his house.

arthquake resistant houses in Ohrid's old town.

Lake Ohrid

Ohrid lies at the head of one of Yugoslavia's largest and most beautiful lakes. At four million years it's only equalled in age by two others in the world – Lake Tanganyika, and Lake Baikal in the Soviet Union. The lake is situated 695m above sea level and is one of Europe's deepest and clearest, with a depth of 289m and 22m visibility. Nearly a third of the lake and half of its shore lie in Albania. Lake Ohrid's age and isolation make for varieties of fish that are elsewhere found only as fossils, and the lake is particularly famous for its trout and eels.

The trout, *pastrmka letnica*, distinctive because of its black spotted sides and red underside, is common here and one of the tastiest dishes I've ever eaten. If you don't try it in Ohrid you'll have to catch the Trans-Siberian Railway all the way to Baikal to get some. It's usually served Ohrid style, with a tomato, paprika and onion sauce, but this kills some of the flavour and it's better simply grilled. A more delicate version of the same is the younger, smaller, trout, *belvica*.

Ohrid's eels are also a unique breed, but they may be dying out. They live in the gloomy depths of the lake for 25 years or so, attaining a fearsome length, and then swim over 5000km to the Sargasso sea to spawn. The young eels then come back to Ohrid to complete the cycle. Since the Crni Drim (the only exit from the lake) has been dammed, the elvers can no longer travel back to Ohrid, and although efforts have been made to ferry them upstream of the dams in trucks, it's not yet certain if the experiment is working. It appears on menus as *jagula* on the rare occasions it's caught. Bear in mind before you try it that it's an endangered species.

(For details of attractions along the shore of the lake see the section on *Galičica*, below.)

Struga

Just 14km west of Ohrid, and also on the lake, is the small town of Struga, which, as the little brochure points out, is rapidly becoming a tourist resort. Catch it before it does.

Although so close to Ohrid, Struga is a complete contrast, and it even has a different climate, being near Continental to Ohrid's mild Mediterranean. The Crni Drim river starts here, and cuts through the mountains and hills that protect its neighbour, so that while Ohrid hardly ever has temperatures below zero, they're relatively common in Struga.

The town is also much more obviously Moslem, Albanian, and poor, though new hotels and tourist complexes are springing up like weeds. The Albanians are easily recognised by their white fezes, and there is still a significant part of the population that wears traditional costume, which is almost unseen in Ohrid. Struga's big attraction, apart from its obvious situation on the lake, is its Saturday market. This is rapidly becoming adapted to the wishes of the package tourist, but remains a lively touch of the old style amongst the modern hotels. Struga also has a couple of splendidly unkempt Moslem cemeteries.

Galičica

The Galičica National Park, covering the mountains between lakes Ohrid and Prespa, is one of the most frustrating in the country. It has exceptional walking possibilities, ranging from Lake Ohrid (695m) up to Magaro (2255m), near the Albanian border, and down to Lake Prespa (853m). But because of its sensitive military position (one of the limits of the park is the border zone) the best map of the area is a hopelessly inaccurate sketch in the small brochure on the park, at roughly 1:125,000. On the tourist office's map of Ohrid there's a rather fanciful aerial view of the lake and the park, and although this is also inaccurate it does give some idea of what the park is like. Obviously none of the official information is effective for walking on unknown terrain at over 2000m.

After a day of fruitless questions, pointless interviews and increasing frustration I discovered that there is actually a Galičica Mountain Association, and this is situated on the lakefront, about 250m from the port. It's a voluntary organisation, run by the very wonderful Vladimir Tuntev, who works in the National Museum but is also the area's official mountain guide. He speaks an interesting mixture of French, Italian, English, Macedonian, German and Serbo-Croat, and can be contacted in advance by writing to him at Planinarsko Društvo 'Galičica', 96000, Ohrid.

Practical Information: There are numerous walks in the area that take from five to ten hours, and a couple more that extend over a period of two or three days. There's a refuge in the middle of the park, and the key is held by the Mountain Association in Ohrid. There are also several campsites along the shores of Lake Ohrid, and a couple more on Lake Prespa. The best are Elšani and Gradište, north and south of the village of Peštani, on Lake Ohrid. The campsites tend to be populated by families on holiday, but they rarely get beyond the beaches. If you're not camping then a private room in Ohrid itself is probably your best option.

Buses run regularly along the eastern shore of Lake Ohrid – hourly from Ohrid to Peštani, and thrice daily (at odd times) from Ohrid to Sv. Naum. There's no obvious transport between the two lakes – the best way is to catch a bus from Ohrid to Resen, and then another from there to Oteševo. These buses are irregular, and decentralisation has meant that it's impossible to find out from Ohrid, for example, what time the buses leave from Resen for Oteševo. The mountain pass between Trpejca and Oteševo is a good 30km road, rising to about 1600m. It doesn't carry public transport.

While walking in the park you should carry plenty of water (two litres per day per person is recommended) – there is only one water source in the whole area, at 1300m. Also bring adequate protective clothing – the weather can change very quickly.

Don't go into the border zone in any circumstances – you stand a genuine risk of being shot. To be safe (unless you're with a guide) you shouldn't walk in any of the area south of the pass between the lakes, or to the east of Sv. Naum. – although the border is very clear in the trees (a huge swathe has been cut out of them), it isn't marked above the tree line, and there's technically nothing to stop you straying into Albania. The border zone stretches some way into both countries.

I went (with Vladimir as guide) on a fairly steep ten hour walk up to the highest point in the park, Magaro. If you can get him to lead you, you won't regret it – he's the perfect guide, pointing out flowers, birds, healing plants, rock formations, ancient and modern history and anything else that crosses his mind. He's an expert mountaineer, having climbed summits as far apart as Mt. Blanc and every major peak in Bulgaria. His fixed rate is ridiculously low; he only asked two of us for £3 for the whole day's work (6am to 10pm), and seemed to consider generous our offer of double that, with several beers thrown in.

The walk to Magaro starts early, with the departure of the morning bus (6.15am) to Sv. Naum. Ask the driver to let you off at the junction for the pass over the mountains to Lake Prespa – this is situated between the kilometres marked 20 and 21. From here you walk straight towards the mountain face, staying on the metalled road, which drifts left as it approaches the cliff.

An almost invisible turnoff to the right leads up a steep gully. The path starts about 15 minutes from the road junction, and is marked by the road being on a bridge of sorts – but even Vladimir crashed about in the undergrowth before finding it. This isn't a proper path, and is probably used by less than twenty people a year. It follows the course of one of the steep rocky streams caused by the melting snow, and is called Zlidol, the Devil's Well.

On the way up here there are poisonous leaves that cure warts in two days – and the heavy white sap that comes out of the stems looks suitably evil. We stopped for a *pausa* after we'd been climbing for nearly an hour, and looked down through the leaves to the lake, now 550m below us. Half an hour after this the gully widens and becomes more shallow, though still leafy and rocky.

A path joining the route from the right near here is the Via Egnatia, one of the most important Roman roads. This led from the Adriatic sea to Constantinople, and although it has now been disused for centuries the track is still quite clear. This leads to the top of the cutting, and comes out near the road across the pass – though the gully saves something like 10km of road.

The pass, at 1550m, is an extraordinarily beautiful mountain cutting, with old deciduous trees, lush grazing and a whole mass of plants and herbs which aren't found anywhere else in the world. It was here that we were shown how to collect handfuls of Galičica Tea, a delicious, healthy infusion unique to this mountain. From the pass you can see the main massif of Magaro to the south, a giant sized slope that's too steep to take direct.

Instead, the route takes a long traverse through two small woods and across the bottom of the slope, and leads to the edge of the ridge, at 1725m, suddenly giving a view of the whole of Lake Ohrid. It takes just over three hours to reach this point. The 27km road between Ohrid and Sv. Naum is clearly visible, and across the lake you can see the Albanian mountains plunging into the water. The scars there are from nickel and chromium mines. To the south, beyond the cut in the forest marking the border, you can see Albanian rice paddies and terraced fields – these were built with the aid of the Chinese before Albania cut itself off from the rest of the world.

The next part of the walk is the hardest, and involves an infinitely slow ascent up the long steep slope. It's a good idea to have a stick here, as you can't afford to slip. The route is made lighter by the sudden appearance of gentians, and yellow violets. After an hour and a half or so you arrive at what ought to be the summit but is actually false. Nonetheless, at 2140m the steep part of the walk is done. From here onwards you're well into the border zone, and the frontier isn't marked this high up.

The terrain up here is still scarred by shallow trenches and fortifications. these date from two terrible summers during the First World War, when the area was viciously fought over. Magaro was in French hands and other summits were in the control of the Germans, Bulgarians and English. The dead had to be buried in 20cm graves, and the stench must have been appalling. We came across a rusty French billycan and a tin from 1916, and these brought the events home more than any historical facts.

Five and a half hours after leaving the bus we arrived at the summit, a windy, romantic place, marked by a triangulation pillar. In the distance there's an Albanian lookout post, while on either side the two lakes spread away into the haze. Eagles cry and slide past on the wind, and in mid June there was still enough snow to make a marked contrast with the bare hillsides.

The route we took down from the summit was fairly tricky, and you wouldn't find it without a good map or a guide. At first it led along parallel to the border, and then came out at the top of a spiky cliff. The path down from here to the flat base of the bowl at 1900m was slippery and very steep, and the stick was a great help. This crater is like a moonscape, with stark cliffs on three sides and an emptiness I didn't find anywhere else in Yugoslavia. (In fact we didn't see anyone at all on this walk until we returned below 800m and approached the village of Peštani.) We stopped here for a picnic of hard boiled eggs, country ham, heavy bread, home grown tomatoes, spring onions (which turned out to be whole cloves of young garlic) and a flask of *rakjia*.

From here there was a fairly clear path which led down to the road on the pass in an hour, and we walked along this to the corner where the road starts to go down towards Lake Ohrid. Soon afterwards a steeper path dips to the left and this points directly towards Peštani. It was used as the supply trail for the troops during the First World War, and is wide enough for mules. It takes under an hour to reach Korita, the water source at 1300m, and just over another one to reach the network of paths near the shore at 800m. Another hour sees the shore road and the village of Peštani, by which time you ought to be ready for a beer or two.

When you're in the Ohrid area one of the essential sights is the monastery of Sveti Naum, right down on the Albanian border. There are six buses a day from Ohrid to Sv. Naum in July and August, but only three outside these months, and no bus between 6am and early afternoon. In high season there are also four boats a day to the monastery, and although this is a very agreeable way to arrive, it does mean seeing the monastery in a limited, crowded fashion. A better option, and one that's cheaper than you might expect, is to hire a boat, complete with boatman. A number of these ply the obvious spots looking for custom, and one can be hired for about £8 or so. Look out for boat number 501, whose skipper, Imedi Biba, is also the local Primary School teacher. He speaks remarkably good French (and some English), and is a mine of interesting information on his never visited homeland of Albania.

We decided to see Sv. Naum by taking the early bus, which arrives a clear hour before the monastery is open, and then walk back the 16km or so to Peštani – since buses return from there to Ohrid every hour. This was perfect: we were at the monastery when it opened, and there well before anyone else arrived. We saw it alone, with only the mating calls of the frogs and the occasional cry of a peacock to disturb the silence.

Until recently Sv. Naum was a mental asylum – Naum is the patron saint of the mentally ill, and his tomb is in a tiny side chapel here. These days a tourist hotel has replaced the inmates' lodgings, and once everyone's woken up and the kiosks are open, it loses its charm fast. Although the monastery was founded by its patron in the tenth century, the present buildings aren't older than the 17th and 19th centuries – this doesn't detract from either the place or it's incredibly beautiful surroundings.

The walk to Peštani has only two disadvantages – it's metalled road all the way, and you'll probably see around 15 or 20 tourist buses on their way to the monastery. Otherwise the walk is a pleasant one, with the route running along cliffs above the lake for a large portion of the journey. Kilometre posts give you a clear idea of your progress (start before 27, end after 11), and on the way you can stop at a small cave church, right by the lake. The church is accessed by cutting through the Gradište camp site (Kilometre 13) and heading north along the beach. Walk round the promontory and Sv. Bogorodica Peštani is tucked away behind it. It's a strange place, almost invisible if you haven't brought a torch, and the frescoes are virtually translucent with the

The monastery of Sveti Naum on the shores of Lake Ohrid.

spreading damp. A solid altar carved from the rock is still used, and is the repository for small notes, tatty postcards and other votive offerings. For a long time it was inhabited by a hermit monk, and it makes you wonder what passed through his mind in the gloom of the winter months.

You can get back onto the road to Peštani by climbing up above the church and making your way onto a moderately unsafe cliff path. You have to negotiate the chicken-wire fence somehow, but if you follow it to the corner you'll find a suitably person-sized hole in it. From here it's only twenty minutes or so to Peštani.

Peštani is famous for a pair of local winds. The pleasanter of the two is the Štremec, which breezes in off the lake and cools down the towns and villages on the shore in the early evening. More violent, and fortunately much rarer (it blows every fifteen years or so) is the Elžik. This occurs when hot and cold air meets on Galičica and forms a local tornado which comes spinning through Peštani. When it comes, it lifts up boats, cars and whole buildings, and dumps them 20 or 30 metres out in the lake.

In just a few hours from Ohrid you can reach several remote villages in the mountains. Konjsko is just over two hours away, while Velestovo or Ramne can be accessed in little more than an hour. These villages mark the beginning of paths into the mountains, and are full of people ready to exchange a cheery 'dobar dan!' at a moment's notice.

Lake Prespa

The frontier point between Albania, Greece and Yugoslavia lies in Lake Prespa, at 853m. Most of the lake is Yugoslavian, and it's a quiet place, with few of the obvious cultural attractions of Ohrid. Although it attracts fewer foreign visitors, the lake is popular with locals, and on summer weekends the small resorts become positively crowded.

The lake is accessed from the unprepossessing town of Resen, on the main road from Ohrid to Bitola. Nine buses a day go through Resen; considerably less than that head down the 21km road to Oteševo, the principal lakeside resort. Boats leave from here on tours of the lake, and these stop off at the island of Golem Grad, with its poignant ruins of the monastery of Sv. Petar. The boat then goes on to Senje, a village right on the Albanian border and inside the border zone – this is the only way you'll see it.

The lake is something of a bird sanctuary, providing a home for wildfowl, marsh birds and breeding pelicans. In the mountains of Galičica beside it there are bears and the now rare lynx, and the combination of altitude and remoteness provides an ideal home for several varieties of eagle. The lake itself is interesting too: although it has no outflowing river, the level stays almost constant. A network of underground streams run underneath Galičica to Ohrid, the most obvious of these being the one that appears picturesquely at Sv. Naum.

Be careful, particularly on the lake itself, of the Albanian and Greek borders – although highly sensitive they're not marked. Don't try to cross into Greece in this area – the border's closed. The nearest crossing is at Niki, just south of Bitola.

On the eastern shore of the lake there are a number of other resorts, smaller than Oteševo. The first one you come to, 14km from Resen, is the fairly uninspiring town of Asmati. Your reason for stopping here is the church of Sv. Djordje in the village of Kurbinovo a couple of kilometres away. Its frescoes, dating from 1191, are both interesting and in an exceptional state of preservation. Just down the shore from Asmati is Pretor, generally considered to have the best beaches.

Pelister

The Pelister National Park, situated between Lake Prespa and Bitola, is famous for its rare pines and crocuses, and lately for the moderate skiing possibilities on Pelister itself (2601m). But it suffers from the same dearth of publicly available information as Galičica – detailed maps are out of the question, and I didn't even see a sketch map. What I did find was a brochure in Macedonian, and later I saw the guidebook to the mountains and refuges of Macedonia (also in Macedonian, but only in Cyrillic). Vladimir Tuntev kindly translated some of this, while I took notes – spellings may be incorrect for this reason.

The edge of the park is about 15km from Bitola, itself reached by buses nine times a day from Ohrid. There's also a less regular service from Skopje. The best place to stay is at the Kopanki Dom refuge. This is a large chalet at 1600m, and it's open all year round. To reach it take a bus from Bitola to Begova Češma, 18km away. From here there is a marked path to the refuge, about 40 minutes away. The route to the top of Pelister takes a little over three hours, and though a guide is not essential, Vladimir recommends it.

Another trail, taking nearly five hours, leads from Kopanki Dom to Golimo Jezero, a beautiful glacial lake at 2420m. There is a refuge (Dom) here which is open at weekends (Friday to Sunday night). Golimo Jezero can also be reached directly from Bitola – go to Trnovo and then ask the way to the village of Nizepole. From here there is a marked trail. The route takes about six hours.

There is a direct route from Golimo Jezero to the summit of Pelister which takes about two hours. A third refuge, Neolica Dom (1440m), is four hours from the lake, and has the same opening times. This can be reached from Bitola on foot. Walk to Lavče (about two hours), and from here it's about three hours on a marked path.

Bitola and Heraclea

Bitola, Macedonia's second city, isn't a place to linger in, but it does have enough attractions to merit a long day trip from Ohrid (a much shorter one if you have your own transport), or even a night stopover if you're on your way into Pelister. Nearby are the ruins and superb moisaics of the important Hellenic and Roman town of Heraclea, and the town has a lively market on Tuesdays, part of which is still housed in the original *bezistan*, a Turkish covered bazaar.

To reach Heraclea, follow the road leading south towards the Greek border for about 3km – it's well signposted, and is less than an hour on foot from the town centre. Heraclea was founded by Alexander the Great's father, Philip, and later became an important stop for the Romans on the Via Egnatia. The ruins are not only beautiful, but perfectly situated, and the mosaics are of special note.

Bitola looks as if it offers an easy access to the Belgrade-Athens railway. Unfortunately only the slowest trains stop here, and those irregularly. If you want to take the train to Greece it's best to do so from Titov Veles, last stop in Yugoslavia for the expresses.

Prilep

Dry and dusty and surrounded by tobacco fields, Prilep is an unlikely place to want to stop. But it was once a vital town, the second base of the unfortunate Tsar Samuel of Ohrid, and subsequently home to the ambiguous character Prince Marko. Marko is the subject of many heroic songs and poems, and is the centre of two entirely different stories – in one he is the mythical Turk-killing hero who lives to 300 and has a magic horse that speaks and drinks his wine; in the other he capitulates, fights for the Turks, and only keeps his Princedom as a servant of the Sultan. The ruined castle on the hill above the town is the main attraction, though there are also a number of churches and mosques worth visiting.

WESTERN MACEDONIA

Tucked between the Albanian border and the main road from Skopje to Ohrid is a region full of mountains, monasteries and Albanians. Public transport is a problem though, as is finding out information on site. The Mavrovo National Park is Macedonia's largest, and is highly popular with weekenders from Skopje, but I couldn't find a map of it anywhere. Equally, there is excellent climbing and walking just west of Tetovo, centred on Popova Šapka, but beyond a wonderfully amateur picture brochure there seems to be no information on this area either. Foreigners are few and far between, and tend to appear briefly in tourist buses and then drive off after half an hour.

Mavrovo National Park

The road from Debar to Gostivar follows the Radika Gorge as it cuts through the Mavrovo National Park, and as you go along it becomes obvious that there must be some exceptional walking here, from 400m up to summits over 2100m. At the head of the gorge is Lake Mavrovo, artificially created by a dam and centre of the park. There are a several accommodations on the lake, including the overpriced Hotel Radika, in the village of Levnovo (Tel 094 89063), which has the air of a place built for far more guests than it would ever accommodate. It may be more cheery in winter, but in summer it was dismal and neglected.

Mavrovo is on the road from Skopje to Debar, which is serviced by a fairly irregular bus – get off at Mavrovo Anovi. Information on the park is either very well hidden or non-existent, but Mavrovo is busy at weekends and in summer, and is a moderately fashionable skiing resort in winter. Both the scenery and the atmosphere seem to be more interesting to the west of the lake, near the village of Volkovija, and were there only facilities such as cheap accommodation or a campsite I'm sure the area would be perfect for walking.

Freelancing is difficult here, particularly because without any kind of map the park can be dangerous. The mountains are quite fractured below the Alpine pastures, with scree slopes ending in vertical drops, and forests running out at the edge of sixty degree slabs of broken rock. Above the tree line the steep pastures look quite tenable, and if pointers exist to paths leading uphill there must be ample opportunities for superb high hill-walking.

Debar

Hard on the Albanian border, Debar is a sleepy place full of old men in white skullcaps and cheeky faced children who offered me crisps and cherries. Situated where it is it's hardly surprising that the first language here is Albanian. Once upon a time Debar's craftsmen were famous throughout the Balkans for their metalworking skills, but the town seems to have been in steady decline for centuries, and the 1967 earthquake destroyed most of the old buildings. What's left is a rebuilt town with the occasional remains of dilapidated mosques. There's not much to see, but the chances are that you'll have plenty of time to see it in, as buses are few and far between.

The real reason for a trip to Debar is that however you arrive the journey will be spectacular. The road from Skopje runs past Mavrovo and then down the Radika Gorge, while the road from Ohrid follows the Crni Drim on its descent towards the Adriatic. Both rivers join just before Debar to form the Drim, which promptly turns towards the sea and runs out through Albania.

When I was here in June there was only one bus a day from Ohrid to Debar, and the service from Skopje wasn't much more frequent. The Crni Drim (the Black Devil) is the outflow from Lake Ohrid, and starts in Struga. The banks of the river are so steep that the road has been cut into them, and at times seems to hang above the river. Until the mid seventies this was the main road from Skopje to Ohrid. Originally the Crni Drim was a fast flowing torrent, but it's been tamed substantially by a series of dams essential to Western Macedonia's electricity supply. Now it's a mysterious river, varying between still lakes and a fast flowing stream. In the lakes half submerged trees stand dead or dying patiently, and the sky seems to fall inwards towards the valley. As the countryside opens up, the rolling hills become populated with tiny villages, each with a spiky white minaret, its metal top askew.

Before each dam there's a 'no photography' sign, and these should be respected. Finally, just before Debar, the road runs across the top of a dam, and there's a heavy military presence. One side of the dam is Yugoslavia, while on the other lies Albania. Look out for the distinctive villages and terraced fields there – it's probably as close as you'll ever get.

Sv. Jovan Bigorski

Overlooking the Radika Gorge, 20km from Debar, you should try and visit the monastery of Sv. Jovan Bigorski, home to the best remaining work of the wonderful Filopivski brothers. The monastery stands high up on a hillside, and faces beautiful pastures across the valley, with patches of snow catching the light even in late June.

Reaching the monastery is a problem if you don't have your own transport. Buses are irregular, and even if you get one to drop you off there's no guarantee that the next one will pick you up on its way past – and this is no place to be stranded. I cheated in the end and went on a Generalturist excursion from Ohrid.

The monastery was founded in the 13th century, but all of the buildings you see today date from the 18th and 19th centuries – the church was completed in the 1820s. At one time the monastery was home to nearly 200 monks, but now there's a solitary guardian who shows the groups round almost mechanically.

Sv. Jovan Bigorski's main attraction is its walnut iconostasis, which was carved by Marko and Petar Filopivski from 1830 to 1838 with the aid of ten assistants. If you've seen the iconostasis in Skopje's Sv. Spas then you'll immediately notice the maturity of this work, where the figures are finer and the decoration less clumsy. Scenes from the Bible make up the main part of the iconostasis, but underneath each icon there's a carved version of the same, copied into three dimensions. The brothers have put themselves and a couple of apprentices into the left hand end, and very charming they look too.

After completing this iconostasis the brothers went on to carve an even better one for a church in Kruševo. Apparently this was their finest work, but it was destroyed by fire when the 1903 uprising was quashed by the Turks.

One of the disadvantages of seeing the iconostasis with an excursion is that most people don't even give it five minutes, drifting back to the bus as soon as the guide stops talking. Remember that it took eight years to carve – ten minutes of your time doesn't do it justice.

The church has several other points of interest, including the oldest icon in Macedonia, a darkened Christ surrounded by ancient silver dating from 1020. Outside there are some rather gaudy 19th century frescoes depicting classic Biblical scenes. Look out for a very naughty looking devil stealing somebody's soul, and a pacific God receiving the souls of the saved. A couple of the frescoes were damaged by the 1967 earthquake, but fortunately the iconostasis survived the shock.

The rest of the monastery is also interesting, with a large upstairs refectory having seating for nearly 300, and a small pulpit for the monk who would sing during the meal. The heads of the monastery sat at a raised, curved table at one end, with the rest of the room containing three long tables with benches. The ceiling and walls are beautifully decorated, and studded with paintings of previous occupants. The grapes in the decoration are not simply an appreciation of the good things in life, but represent an important symbol of Macedonia. On the 10th and 11th of September each year a special Mass is held here, and free food is provided for all comers.

EASTERN MACEDONIA

This is certainly the least visited part of Macedonia, and probably of the whole of Yugoslavia. There is no tourism industry as such, partly because there are so few obvious attractions that are marketable. As a result public transport is extremely sketchy, accommodation is largely non-existent, and there are only two campsites in the whole region (near the Greek border). Walking opportunities are minimal, and especially so in summer, when temperatures are extreme.

If you come here you can be sure to find villages where national costumes and ancient customs are the norm, but you really need your own transport, and at least a smattering of Macedonian – Serbo-Croat is very much a second language.

Titov Veles is an easily accessible town on a very old site, though there is little to see now. Its main attraction is the railway station, last stop before Greece for the expresses. Just south of here, and still on the main road (and therefore accessible), is Gradsko, in itself a forgettable little town.

People come here to see the ruins of **Stobi**, a town even older than Heraclea. These were only discovered in the 1860s, and excavations didn't start until after the First World War. Even now only a fraction of the site has been exposed. To get the most from it you really need a guide, which would be fine if you could find one.

The southeastern corner, like that in the southwest, is marked by a tectonic lake on the border. Greece and Yugoslavia share Lake Dojran, which is attractive enough, but hardly worth the fuss made of it. Its fame rests on the cormorants that until recently were used to herd fish into pens. The fisherman now practise a more prosaic lifestyle, and stun the fish with electric shocks.

WALKING THROUGH YUGOSLAVIA

by Simon Palmour

In May and June 1984 Simon Palmour and his friend Marie walked from south to north through Yugoslavia as part of 200 day hike across Europe. They planned their route from large scale war maps obtained from the Royal Geographical Society in London, and found that a fairly direct route across the major mountain areas was possible. Starting at Lake Prespa they crossed Macedonia and went over the Šar Planina range into Kosovo. They traversed Montenegro via the Durmitor range, and then walked through Bosnia and Croatia before crossing Slovenia and the Julian Alps.

We tried wherever possible to use footpaths and tracks – fortunately when roads, inevitably, had to be used there was seldom heavy traffic. We carried a tent and cooker, and camped wild (save for a weekly visit to a hotel for a wash and comfort) and stayed in peoples homes when invited. Never once did we have problems with our camping, and we never used a campsite.

Starting at Nakolec we follow a sandy track the length of the greater Prespa lake, with peasants busy on our right and the blue lake and snow-capped mountains crystal clear to our left. We camp in a marshland at the northern end of the lake, toads croaking us to sleep. On our way to Evla at the foot of the Galičica mountains people talk of the wolves we will meet: 'Why not take the Resen road? It is much safer and there is a bus'. We manage to find a path into the mountains though, and a shepherd dozing in the shade awakes to sketch in the sand the route we should take. His directions are fine and we emerge from the forest to find a gushing spring draining the snow-covered plateau. Camping alone up here with views back to Prespa, we are in total peace. A donkey track takes us steeply down to Ohrid, then a road along the lake to Struga.

We follow a track from Struga to Maroništa then take the quiet road north up the Crni Drim valley. At Gorenci we meet some young girls who tell us we can camp in their garden. As we get into our tent they bring us glasses of hot sweet milk. A footpath winds its way up the road to Galičnik where snow covers the way to Mavrovo. On the plateau there is not a soul about; no one will be up here until the snow has gone. Near Rezčane we are surrounded by a pack of wild dogs which thankfully disperses when I nervously pick up a rock to throw at them. At Vrutok some more people let us sleep in their garden. We skirt Gostivar and take a back road through Vrapčista and Dobri Do, meeting people all the way who offer advice and good company. At Negotino there is consternation that we want to cross the Šar Planina: 'Wolves to eat you, wind to blow you away, snow too deep and Albanian border guards to shoot you!' Eventually three boys take us up to their village with their donkeys carrying our rucksacks. Revived by their mother's yoghurt and bread we go to Lomnice where the whole village greets us. Another horseride for our packs as we are shown a pasture to camp on, high above the village. Crossing the Šar Planina, next day, is a magnificent experience, snow and rock and isolation.

Brod is another village where we are surrounded by curious and friendly faces. Next day at Dragaš a Belgrade man buys us lunch and a huge crowd of children bring us cheer after the police have questioned us for a while. A quiet road leads us to the hills overlooking Zur, where we take a path to Našec, meeting a schoolteacher who invites us to his school, centrally located between six villages, and serving them all. Our path across the Kosovo plain is hot and full of contact with countless people. We stay with Ibrahim and his family, ethnic Albanian Moslems, and everywhere are amazed at the welcome the Albanian people give us. We follow the road, or tracks where we can, through Dakovica and Dečani to Peć.

A magnificent mountain traverse across Montenegro follows. First the Rugovo Gorge where the limestone cliffs loom sheer to the deep blue sky, then a path through the Alpine pastures of Boge over the mountains to descend to Kaludra. Forestry workers give us lunch and call out 'Welcome to Montenegro!' as we carry on our way. A boy guides us through Ivangrad then we head up to Lubnice and our next range. A family, just up with their sheep for three days on the summer pasture, lets us stay with them, father prowls with a gun for wolves. There is more snow to negotiate before we plunge down to the army town of Kolašin. Through Blatina the next range is a plateau, with farmers setting up for the summer on the pastures that the melting snow is just revealing. Many a glass of brandy is drunk in celebration. At Krnja Jela one family invites us to spend the afternoon with them, another puts us up for the night. We follow the road to Žabljak but turn off at Pašina Voda to head across the Durmitor mountain plateau. Oxon are being used to tow sledges across the snow up to the pasture, the mountains tower behind us. We descend to Plužine and a group of schoolchildren guide us through a string of villages to Orah, where a man playing a *gulze* entertains us. We find our way across another plateau to descend into Bosnia at Avtovac.

We follow the road as far as Rilja where a track takes us across a *polje* to Nevesinje via an old Turkish bridge. Vultures soar above the Mostar road, unfortunately so do warplanes. The army are so sensitive about this that they arrest us for the afternoon just to check us out. It is inconvenient and unpleasant – not the end of the world but the mosques of Mostar lose their charm after this experience. From Mostar to Livno we follow roads and paths across limestone karst, dry and barren with occasional open wells for relief, through villages of friendly people and around the windswept Buško lake.

Livno to Titov Drvar via Glamoč is good walking over lonely bleak hills with isolated villages, lines of mountains around us and a pocked limestone plateau. The policeman who checked our passports last night as we camped by a church is the first to buy us a drink this morning in the bar. Later on as we take a back path to Martin Brod a woman gives us lunch in her spick and span living room, before going out to work the land. We enter Croatia and the bleak south is giving way to the westernised north. At Dnopolje a family back from Germany give us milk and bread then point the way to the path that tracks through the forest past the Ozeblin peak and down to Korenica, awash with tourists.

Through Vrelo and Babin Potok we skirt the crowds at the Plitvice Lakes and head instead into the woods to follow a railway line to Javornik where men give us water from their well. After discreetly avoiding another army base we follow a stony track to Lipice where a man nearly shoots us in our tent as he hunts rabbits in the dusk and then invites us to spend the night with him and his wife. There is brandy for breakfast. The tarmac road to Jasenak is uneventful but from there to Mrkopalj the track takes us to a magnificent forest where limestone citadels burst through the trees and forestry workers use horses to drag the timber to their carts. Ljubomir, an ex-Partisan, invites us to stay at his summer house in the forest and sample some Croatian hospitality.

Trails take us through more delightful woodland north to Osilnica, rivers emerging free from their limestone confinement. The way to Studenec via Cabar and Travnik is mainly on quiet roads but we find a track from there to Cerknica that takes us deep into the country. To Idrija then Cerkno by road, but what a pleasant road it is with the river for company and the thought of the mountains to come. We stay with a couple of Slovenians and clearly sense that we are nearing Italy and Austria. At Cerkno the marked mountain trails of the Julian Alps begin, the snow is still prevalent, and the huts not yet open, making the walking all the more exciting. We meet occasional farmers, but no other walkers as we climb Porezen then Kobla before descending to Bohinj. From Savica at the head of the lake we climb past the Komni and Bogatinom huts up to the Vratca col, with Triglav impressive to the north and the Adriatic to the south. We plunge off a hanging valley to the Lepena hut then make our way via Klancem and Gor Log to the Italian border at Predil.

INDEX OF PLACE NAMES
(For other subjects see *Contents* page.)

NOTES

NOTES

NOTES

NOTES